TO BUCKTAIL AND BACK...

A Million Miles of Memories

A Collection of Stories From ...

TOM ALLAN

Omaha World-Herald
Nebraska Byways Columnist

Cover Photo: Fall trees reflected in a mill pond at Champion, Neb.

Published by The
Omaha World-Herald Co.
1334 Dodge St.
Omaha, NE 68102
Edited by Nancy Evans
and Paul Hammel

CONTENTS

BUCKTAIL?

It's the name of one of the now long-gone ranch house post offices once scattered throughout the colorful Nebraska Sand Hills.

It symbolizes my advice to visitors to the state – as well as to many residents who don't know what they're missing – "Get Lost!" by leaving Interstate 80 to discover the real beauty of Nebraska, the warm friendliness of its people and its genuine Western heritage.

I had the best job in the world as a roving reporter-photographer for 43 of the 54 years I worked for the Omaha World-Herald. I deem it the best because most of my World-Herald career editors gave me a free hand to fulfill the innate desire to discover what's over the next hill and who's around the next bend of the road. Mine was a most rewarding job, not only to find the Bucktails, but also to feel the pulse and relate the heartbeat of the Midlands.

I also served as the newspaper's Ambassador of Goodwill, speaking at countless civic clubs and other public gatherings.

I used to cause dismay for the paper's executive editor, the late Frederick Ware, when he would ask whither I was headed. I would reply, "Getting lost at either Bucktail, Wet Otter Tail or Kennedy, or somewhere in between."

While receiving many tips for stories by letters or phone calls, I found the best stories by just stopping and chatting for a while at a local cafe or bar. I often flipped a coin backing out of my driveway to decide which way to head.

Often I'd baffle Ware and the late State Editor Irving Baker by saving a story I had discovered at Henry in the farthest northwest corner of the state and turn it in simultaneously with one I'd found at Rulo, the most southeastern village.

"I must have gotten lost," I explained.

But I always found the real Nebraska along its Byways.

During my years with the World-Herald, I covered many of Nebraska's natural tragedies such as tornadoes, blizzards, forest fires and floods. I covered many of its biggest murders, including Charlie Stark-weather's killing spree in 1958.

Big stories included interviewing three presidents, foreign dignitaries, senators and congressmen, governors, and sports and movie stars. On assignment, I strayed from the Byways to the "Green Hell" of the Amazon jungle, the Alcan Highway, Mexico, Finland, Germany, France, Canada and Switzerland, plus several trips to my native land, bonnie Scotland.

But I discovered it was the little stories that brought a smile or tears to eyes that brought the most response from readers. It convinced me that in our hectic world people are crying out for simple stories that touch the heart.

It's why I always tell young journalists to seek the human equation while aspiring for earthshaking Pulitzer Prize-winning stories. I urge them along the way to "stoop and pick the little daisies."

I was startled during my induction into the Omaha Press Club's "Face On the Barroom Floor" society at an October 2001 roast when one of the roasters, my son Tam Allan, told of my long-standing "love affairs with two mistresses."

He told the audience that they had caused the family stress and anxiety due to my often long absences resulting in too many missed birthdays and anniversaries. I relaxed only when he explained he was talking about my love affairs with the state of Nebraska and The World-Herald.

I confess I am hopelessly in love with Nebraska despite her being a most exacting and cantankerous mistress. Too often when I was lulled by the tranquillity and beauty of her Big Sky sunrises and sunsets, she'd belt me with the savagery of storms. I've had to outrun a tornado and often felt the icy sting of her blizzards, been singed in a forest fire, survived her floods and been bashed by her hailstorms.

The late Gregg McBride, the longtime pundit of Nebraska athletics and founder of the Top 10 ratings for high school teams who became known as "Mr. Sports of Nebraska," once told me: "To be a good journalist there is no such thing as a time clock or 40-hour week. You must be willing to devote as much time and effort as it takes to get a complete story."

And then the jolly old Scot, who had an understanding wife in Evelyn but no children except every athlete in Nebraska, surprised me by adding, "Because of the total dedication good reporting requires, it's best not to have a wife or kids because the sacrifices they have to make are so unfair to them."

In retrospect, I agree and humbly apologize to my family. I know my dedication to the job was a factor in a divorce from my first wife, the former late Jeanne Abels of Topeka, Kan. She was a sweetheart, a coed at Ottawa

University when we became engaged. My abrupt entry into the Army the day after the Pearl Harbor attack put our marriage on hold until she remembered the legacy of her grandmother, Hattie Wade, a cook at an Indian mission in Kansas.

Hattie had accepted a marriage proposal from a young Indian Wars Army trooper named "Wild Bill" Harrington of Harrington Hollow, Pa. In his joy at receiving an honorable discharge, "Wild Bill" skedaddled for home without her. Undaunted, Hattie packed a suitcase, showed up at Harrington Hollow and reportedly greeted "Wild Bill" with: "OK, handsome, I'm here to make you an honorable man. Marry me as you promised!" He did, they moved back to Kansas, and lived a long, happy life.

Jeanne, upon learning a colonel's wife had joined him and was living in a tent behind our headquarters at Dawson Creek, British Columbia, somehow hopped a train full of Army replacements and construction workers, and arrived to give me the same "Wild Bill" ultimatum.

The British Columbia Constabulary arranged our wedding at nearby Grand Prairie in July 1942. Jeanne became the "den mother" for my buddies in our one-room apartment over a hardware store in Dawson Creek. The honeymoon ended three months later when the Japanese attacked Dutch Harbor and the island of Attu in Northern Alaska. Our headquarters was moved north to Fort St. John and Jeanne and other wives were ordered home.

I almost beat her back to the States. Being a technical sergeant, I was ordered to proceed "by any available means as fast as possible" to Officer Candidate School at Camp Lee, Va., three days after her departure. Sgt. Harry Blum of New Jersey and I busted a gut using every means of transportation, from rides on a dog sled to a cargo plane carrying coffins of civilian construction worker casualties back to the United States and then assorted trains to get to the school. Unforgettable was our greeting when we arrived in parkas and mucklucks.

"You are the dumbest GIs in Army history," growled a grizzled 30-year career master sergeant. "In all my Army career I've dreamed of getting a set of orders you have. No date or time was given for your arrival. They gave you permission to draw rations and supplies anywhere and use any means of transportation. You could have spent a lifetime traveling the world as a guest of Uncle Sam."

Our eager offer to obey orders, celebrate and come back later ended with a snarling: "Stand at attention! You are now the dumbest cadets of OCS Class No. 13."

After graduation in January 1943, a mistake on a teletype sent 250 new 2nd lieutenants to the headquarters of the Third Air Force of the Army

Air Corps at Fort Worth, Texas. Astonished at the flood of shavetails, the brass quickly scattered us to numerous bases throughout the South. I ended up at Army Air Corps Base in Charleston, S.C.

After mundane tasks, I was assigned to command an African American transportation unit and train them for European service. I got into trouble when, unknown to me, my troop unanimously signed a petition (a no-no in the Army) asking that I be allowed to command them in Europe.

Their request was summarily denied. So were my desperate requests for transfer to any overseas assignment with a curt, "You are already a returnee from overseas service." That qualification was later forgotten in the pressing need for officers in the South Pacific, and I was sent to the 13th Air Force where I ended my World War II active duty career with the 7th Airdrome Squadron in the Philippines.

Jeanne had joined me at Charleston with our infant daughter, Susan, but left for home when I was ordered overseas.

Susan attended Wayne State College where she met and married James McGrath of New York who became the longtime wrestling coach and business teacher at Ralston High School. She died too young on March 3, 1973, within 24 hours of being infected by a mysterious virus while co-sponsoring a Colorado ski trip with her husband.

Susie left us two great grandkids – Chris, now the wife of Dave Martin of Omaha, and Kelley McGrath, a University of Nebraska-Omaha graduate who is a pharmaceutical representative in southeast Nebraska. Chris and Dave provided me with two of the liveliest of great-grandchildren, Tyler David and Ellie Sue.

Jeanne also bore me another great daughter, Mary Wade, a University of Kansas cheerleader and graduate, who married Steve Miller, an arch-rival University of Missouri graduate and basketball player. Now living in Littleton, Colo., they have a beautiful and brainy daughter, Laurel Ann, an honor graduate of Vanderbilt University.

Jeanne and I had a son, Tamas Robert Allan, a graduate of both the University of Nebraska and its College of Law, who after passing the Nebraska bar forsook a law career, using his expertise instead as a Lincoln developer. He and his wife, the former Kathleen Nolan of Kansas City, provided me with another brainy granddaughter, Kristin, now a student at Southeast High School.

After our divorce in 1968, Jeanne moved back to Topeka and remarried. She died of cancer a few years later.

I was more than blessed by 31 years of marriage (until her death in July 1999) to Marilyn J. Stroman, a sterling girl from Sterling, Neb. "Maidie" was a "Rosie the Riveter," building bombers at the Martin Bomber

Plant at Omaha's old Fort Crook during World War II. She then taught herself law and became a clerk in the Nebraska Supreme Court before becoming secretary to the late Supreme Court Justice Paul E. Boslaugh. She later worked in Washington D.C., for Rep. Phil Weaver before becoming the 35-year matriarch of Nebraska Capitol lobbyists.

When we married in 1968 we became an unusual team, with an understanding that she would never lobby me about stories I was working on and I would never question her lobbying activities.

With no children of her own, she lovingly "adopted" my grown-up brood and grandkids. Without the duties of raising kids with a husband often in absentia, she didn't fight my duties. She joined me in them. She saved the day many times by driving my photo film to Omaha to make a deadline. She became a "mother hen" for the crew when I covered Husker football.

She didn't see the Huskers win their first national championship against Louisiana State in the 1971 Orange Bowl. She had volunteered to be a messenger for our photo crew, making frequent trips driving their film alone through Miami's notorious "Little Havana" to their dispatch headquarters at the downtown Associated Press office. Late in the fourth quarter while en route back to the game, she was stopped by a Miami police officer who exclaimed: "Lady! Are you trying to get mugged? Do you know where in the hell you are? I'm going to escort you back to the game and baby-sit you until it's over."

Once she conned a telephone installer out of his needle-nose pliers and mended a broken fax machine at a Husker-Oklahoma State game at Stillwater so we could transmit our stories before deadline. And when she retired from lobbying in 1992, she became my "co-pilot," driving me along the Byways while I composed stories on my laptop computer.

Thus, this is an apology to all of my family for putting up with me and my job over the years. All of them, as well as many readers, insisted I write these memoirs.

They include my best-remembered stories. I've added notes on how I found them, plus personal comments about them and all the wonderful characters I have known.

I dedicate it to them and my family.

The proceeds from this book will go to the Tom Allan Scholarship Fund for students at the University of Nebraska College of Journalism who are interested in small-town journalism careers.

Allan on deadline at The World-Herald *in 1951.*

CHAPTER ONE

BEGINNINGS

An ill-advised prank with a test tube cleaning brush that resembled a spider launched my 61-year journalism career. Playfully running the brush up the arm of my pretty chemistry lab partner at Kansas' Ottawa University in 1936 caused her to go into screaming hysterics. I didn't know she had a phobia about spiders.

My expulsion from chemistry ended my hopes of becoming the doctor who would discover the cure for cancer or the common cold.

Instead, I remembered the teaching of the late H. Arthur Lee, a suave, life-long bachelor who gave up his job at The Kansas City Star to become press agent for his boyhood pal, screen star Buddy Rogers and his wife, Mary Pickford. But after two years of Hollywood's glitter, he was satisfied to live out his life as the journalism teacher at Council Bluffs' Abraham Lincoln High School, from which I graduated in 1936.

Hoping to become as glamorous as Lee, I whetted my newfound appetite for journalism working on the campus newspaper and yearbook.

At the end of my sophomore year I wrote to William Allen White, publisher of The Emporia Gazette who gained national fame as the "Sage of Emporia," asking his advice on leaving a small, four-year liberal arts college for one of the prestigious journalism schools at Columbia, Northwestern or Kansas universities.

I had become acquainted with White, for whom the University of Kansas later named its journalism college, when I sought acceptance in his personal journalism school. Students were exposed to the sagacity of the sage while working at the Gazette without pay during the summer.

Both his school and my hopes of enrollment ended when President Franklin Roosevelt's Depression-beating youth programs required payment of a minimum salary.

White's response to my letter surprised me. It began with the word "WHY?" and then continued with, "Why would you want to go to a major "J" school where you will be just a number among many? My advice to you, young man, is to spend your final two years at your liberal arts college cramming as many electives in as many different fields as you can.

"Then after you graduate, go to work for a small-town daily or weekly newspaper where you will be required to do everything from reporting and writing to helping with the newspaper carriers and even janitorial work." White ended with, "I guarantee you will learn more practical journalism in six months than you possibly can at a major "J" school."

I took his advice and, after graduation, he helped me land my first job as a do-it-all cub reporter on the combination Wellington Daily News and its Sumner County weekly located in Kansas near the Oklahoma border. White even assured the Wellington publisher, H.L. Woods, a longtime friend, that I had the "possible makings of a journalist."

Woods, a stately, elderly gentleman, hired me for $10 a week. Every Saturday morning he approached employees with his glasses perched on the end of his nose and his business ledger in his hands.

"I owe you $10," he would say before counting out 10 $1 bills and handing them to me. Then he extended his palm and said, "In exact change, please give me what you owe Uncle Sam and the state of Kansas in income taxes, and I'll see that they get it."

Despite my meager net pay, I thought I was the richest man in the world. Ten bucks less taxes was a fortune in the midst of the Dust Bowl and Great Depression years, particularly when lovable "Ma Dowd" charged only $4 a week for room and board. I got richer being part of a football officiating crew that netted me $5 for an afternoon six-man game and another $8 for an evening 11-man game.

I also had the fringe benefit of a free breakfast after an early morning chore chauffeuring Woods around Wellington, the place he affectionately called "My Town."

Woods was the best of journalism professors. Once I wrote a scathing story debunking a "miracle" performed by Aimee Semple McPherson, a flamboyant, nationally known evangelist whose Wellington appearance brought visitors by the busloads from throughout Kansas and beyond. Many in the overflow crowd swooned, not only from the stifling heat in the non-air-conditioned building, but also when McPherson bade a lovable deaf mute town character to speak, and then dramatically announced when he gave one of his usually unintelligible grunts, "He said God! A miracle has come to pass." I reported that many in the crowd went wild with joy, but the town's lovable character still couldn't talk in a post-miracle interview.

After reading my story, Woods walked over to my desk, put his arm around my shoulder and quietly said, "Son, always remember you can catch more flies and gain more readers with honey than you can with vinegar."

He was a father figure and treated me like a son. He expressed both shock and pride when, on the day after the attack on Pearl Harbor, I volunteered for induction into the Army. He didn't hide his tears when he gave me a bear hug and wished me Godspeed as I boarded a bus for Fort Leavenworth. He also wrote me frequently during my five-year World War II service on the Alcan Highway and the South Pacific, saying my old job was waiting for me at a bigger salary.

I know I broke his heart when I didn't return to Wellington, and I have often wondered what would have happened if I hadn't gotten big-time aspirations and accepted a job at The Topeka Daily Capital.

Sen. Capper, Here I Come

The Topeka Daily Capital was the biggest newspaper in Kansas and the flagship of several newspapers, including the national Capper's Weekly as well as agriculture-oriented magazines. All were owned by Arthur Capper, who after a term as Kansas governor, served 30 years in the U.S. Senate.

As he aged, the senator seldom campaigned for re-election. His raspy-voiced Sunday broadcasts by his Topeka radio station, WIBW, and his annual free birthday party, to which all Kansans were invited, were more than enough to ensure election night victory.

During my stint as city editor, front page headlines and stories ran for days before the free picnic reading, "The Senator Is Coming!" then "Pressing Washington Duties Force Cancellation" before suspense was ended with the triumphant banner: "Senator Capper Will Be Here!"

I always felt we staffers sold our journalistic souls by the "yes-he-will-no-he-can't" suspense stories and in the exhaustive coverage given the birthday party picnic.

In addition to dominating the front page, the sports page gave full coverage to the softball games, tug-of-wars and horseshoe pitching tourney. Capitol beat reporters went all out covering the senator's speech and getting responses from VIP and political attendees. The Society page usually featured the important ladies in attendance and their fashionable attire.

Bobby Fisher, the chief photographer assigned to take the mandatory front page photo, always told the VIP presenting the heavy appreciation plaque to the feeble senator, "Be sure to hold on to it so the senator won't drop it when my flash gun goes off!"

Since the Capital was a morning paper, I served as night stringer for The Associated Press. For some reason, the Russian newspaper Pravda thought Alf Landon, Kansas' defeated presidential candidate in 1936, was still a major national Republican Party spokesman. Several times the AP relayed Pravda's request for Landon's comment on the issue of the day.

Veteran wire editor Mark Dunlap and I always knew the odds were good we could find Landon at the country club when he wasn't out of town celebrating another of his oil and gas wells "coming in."

"Not again," Landon would chuckle when we reached him by phone before always adding, "You and Mark figure out a good statement for me to make. Then call me back and read it to me." When we did, his usual answer was: "You guys are getting better. That's a good one. Send it."

Dunlap's colorful language always got better as the night wore on. After a diligent search, we learned his fluency was enhanced by frequent round-about trips through several offices to the teetotalling senator's office, where he had stashed a bottle of booze.

Several times I had to drive Dunlap home as he signaled his last piece of editing about 1 a.m. by sticking his head into the top of a large wastebasket by his desk and hollering at the top of his lungs, "Powder River!"

How Dry Was Dry Kansas?

In his final years Sen. Capper seldom made it back to Topeka except for election nights, his birthday party and the annual gathering of all his editors.

His editors knew the senator's feeling about the evils of booze in dry Kansas where pundits used to say, "Kansans will vote dry as long as they can stagger to the polls."

The late Jack Jarrell, The World-Herald's longtime Washington bureau chief and a Kansas native, often recalled the story of a Senate agricultural committee hearing over which Sen. Capper presided.

"As he often did in his final years, the aging senator fell asleep after his usual afternoon glass of milk during a hearing in which attorneys were testifying about the alternative fuels benefits of alcohol made from corn," Jarrell recalled. "Senator Capper woke up with a start, his face aghast, and then, pointing a gnarled finger at a young testifier, roared, 'Young man, do you mean to tell me this wonderful government of ours is involved in the vile and evil booze business?' The hearing was summarily ended."

My days at the Capital became numbered when I gave photographer Fisher time off to help a Life magazine photographer do a photo essay on

"How Dry Is Dry Kansas?" I agreed to it, provided the Capital got some of Life's photos and could break the story on the morning of the magazine's publication.

The two photographers rented a canvas-topped truck and snapped photos through peepholes of booze imbibers leaving "dust-quenching" establishments. Included were imbibers with booze-filled coffee cups staggering from a watering hole across the street from the newspaper, a block from the state Capitol.

The photographers also climbed a tree to take photos of some of Topeka's most influential citizens, including the Capital's editor, Milt Tabor, imbibing at a country club bar.

Tabor was infuriated when he saw the first editions of the "Dry Kansas" front-page spread. "You have ruined me!" he ranted. "Tear out the front page story. I'm writing a front page editorial to replace it.

In it he berated the "inaccurate" Life magazine article and its cowardly staffers for taking pictures of honest, law-abiding citizens sipping soft drinks and then daring to claim they were imbibing alcohol-laced cocktails.

I'm not sure Tabor ever knew Fisher was involved. But Bobby soon headed for St. Paul, Neb., where he published the weekly Phonographic before heading for other publishing ventures in Arkansas.

And I jumped at the chance when the late World-Herald editor, Fred Ware, called saying, "Gabe Parks and Paul Williams, former Topeka Capital city editors who are now on our staff, tell me you might be interested in a job. If you are, drive up for an interview."

I did – fast.

Allan and chief photographer Lawrence "Robbie" Robinson covering the capture of Blaine Ellis in 1952.

CHAPTER TWO

WORLD-HERALD DEBUT

Leaving Topeka for The World-Herald and Nebraska in November 1947 actually was a homecoming.

I had migrated in 1929 at age 9 from my native Scotland to Oxford, the town I call my Nebraska hometown. I later moved with my American Baptist pastor father, the Rev. William Allan, to Trinity Baptist in South Omaha, graduated from the now-gone Garfield Grade School and attended my first two years of high school at South High before moving to Council Bluffs, Iowa, where my father was pastor of the First Baptist Church.

I already was a two-year veteran of service to The World-Herald, having been a carrier of Route 2 in South Omaha in 1931 and '32. I worked harder and sweated more lugging papers than I ever did as a reporter.

In my first Army physical, the doctor immediately knew I had lugged a heavy newspaper bag over my left shoulder during my formative years. "You must have carried papers as a young boy," the medic diagnosed. "Your left shoulder is an inch behind your right."

Fred Ware, then the World-Herald's executive editor, neither gave me a physical nor a mental-proficiency exam when I arrived for a job interview.

Ware, who had served as one of the paper's most colorful sports editors, immediately spotted a gold track shoe on my tie chain that I won as a member of Ottawa University's consecutive conference championship track teams. His hero was Henry F. "Pa" Schulte, the 1919-'20 University of Nebraska football coach who gained legendary status as NU's longtime track coach. Ware was instrumental in getting the field house on the north end of Memorial Stadium named for Schulte.

After a half-hour of talking track, Ware said, "So when do you want to start working for the Herald?" It was as simple as that, and I was hired on Nov. 7, 1947 – literally on the run.

Ware told me I would do nothing the first few days but study The World-Herald's writing stylebook, which he wrote, as well as several survey books on the paper written by contracted experts.

I had hardly finished the first chapter of Ware's book when Hugh Fogarty, then the city editor, assigned me to cover an auto accident along with Earle "Buddy" Bunker, the paper's Pulitzer Prize-winning photographer. I finished the task, but not the book's next chapter when he assigned me to cover a major fire that had destroyed the downtown LaFlange building the night before.

So began my action-packed World-Herald career to Bucktail and back. During my tenure I logged well over a million miles "getting lost" in Nebraska as well as detours to neighboring states and around the world.

Included were jaunts to Washington, D.C., and finding a Nebraska doctor 500 miles deep in the Amazon jungle who was paying a "debt of gratitude" to former head-hunting Indians for saving his life after an airplane crash.

There also were treks to Helsinki, Finland, to cover the "folksy, down home" role in the Cold War SALT talks of U.S. Ambassador Val Peterson, one of Nebraska's most colorful former governors.

I trained for a week to become a member of a Strategic Command B-47 crew to fly from Lincoln to Upper Heyford, England, on an assignment covering SAC's "Ever Ready" missions during the Cold War. There was a jaunt to France on the anniversary of the World War II liberation of St. Lo by Nebraska's famed 134th Infantry, a trip to Mexico covering Nebraskans participating in President Eisenhower's People-to-People program and a trek back up the Alcan Highway as well as seven trips "back hame" to Scotland.

Across Nebraska I wore out 20 company cars – all "No. 18" – and was working hard at wearing out the last of a string of illustrious, but long-suffering editors when I retired in January 2002.

Council Bluffs' 'Home Field' Advantage

My first few weeks as a general assignment reporter ended when I was assigned to the Council Bluffs bureau, which again was a homecoming. I lived in Council Bluffs, had graduated from its Abraham Lincoln High School and was well acquainted with the late Frank Lane, an AL classmate who was the ace reporter and later editor of the Council Bluffs Nonpareil.

Frank never forgave me for my first major "scoop," the Dec. 4, 1949, story of Mrs. Marie Turnquist, 65, of "pleasingly plump" girth who had become trapped for 60 hours in a midget-sized bathtub while she was baby-sitting a home. The tub was built to the tiny specifications of a Little People widow, who with her late husband had been a circus performer.

I was aided in the scoop by knowing Mrs. Turnquist well. Known to friends as "Aunt Marie," she had been a member of my father's parish. Also a plus was that Martha Allan, longtime nurse for Dr. Earl Ballenger, was my stepmother.

When Mrs. Turnquist failed to keep a doctor appointment and did not answer the telephone, "Mother Hen" Martha investigated. There was no answer at the front door. Walking around the house Martha heard a muffled cry as she passed the bathroom window. She broke into the house with the aid of a neighbor and together they pulled Mrs. Turnquist from her three-day prison and took her to the hospital.

Mrs. Turnquist, except for raw and blistered hands she suffered in frantic efforts to escape before she became so weak she "could only pray," was in surprisingly good shape.

"I didn't sleep," she related in my exclusive interview while she laughed heartily at her predicament. "I never got hungry, but I wanted water so bad. I could see the bed I had turned down so nice. Oh, it looked wonderful."

Martha had alerted me to the story and arranged for the bedside interview, and I beat the deadline for the Saturday evening paper.

But I became nervous, sure my news scoop was in danger when James Keogh, then city editor who later became a Time magazine senior editor, told me, "This is too good a story. Can we hold it somehow until the Sunday paper where we can give it the space it deserves?"

I talked Keogh into saving the story for the Sunday city edition, printed early Sunday morning, because I knew Max Namen, the Nonpareil's police reporter visited The World-Herald's loading dock Saturday evenings to pick up a copy of the early edition to prevent being scooped.

We were successful in holding the story, thanks to Martha agreeing to delay telling police and fire rescue men. And Dr. Ballenger helped by posting an "Absolutely No Visitors" sign on Mrs. Turnquist's hospital room door.

The Nonpareil, an evening paper, couldn't recoup on the story until its Monday evening edition. For some reason, my old classmate Lane was furious and refused to talk to me – for at least a week – before we became good friends again.

A First Little Daisy

The Council Bluffs beat provided me with my first little "daisy," a tear-jerking heartwarmer, on Oct. 25, 1950. It began with a preface: This is the story of the human factor often overlooked in the traffic death of a child. It could happen to one of your children. You could be the driver. The bereaved parents hope all motorists read it. If it makes you think and drive more carefully, they feel their son did not die in vain.

The story began:

Death and small boys are strangers.

They meet but seldom and then usually by chance. When they do it's usually suddenly.

Their introduction can be accompanied by such sounds as a little boy's happy laugh, the patter of feet on the street, a truck's roar, screeching brakes and tires, a thud, an anguished scream, curt orders of a rescue squad working in vain – then silence.

Little brown-eyed Denny Jones, 18 months, met death that way just 13 days ago.

And the silence still hangs heavy over the home of his parents, Mr. and Mrs. Bill Jones, 1714 Avenue G.

These warm fall evenings they sit quietly in the back yard remembering. Or they try to hide their sorrow in work on a new family home where little Dennis might have lived.

Big brothers, David, 3, and Robert, 8, and sisters Patricia, 10, and Glenda, 5, are quieter now.

It's strange without Dennis. The scars may never heal.

The silence is not broken by his excited, little squeals of laughter. No one has to run to keep him out of mischief.

Still standing untouched in the yard is the little red wagon and his favorite – an overturned toy wheelbarrow.

Denny was playing with the wheelbarrow just before it happened. He had begged to play outside just a little while longer while his mother hung out some clothes.

Then Denny, as children often do, scampered toward the street. Patricia started to run to his side.

"I had just called to see if he was all right," Mrs. Jones recalled sadly. "Then I heard Patricia shout, 'Denny, Denny!' There was a scream and then a thud. He was just lying there. I picked him up and brought him to the house. The rescue squad was called. I guess it was too late then."

Sitting in the yard cuddling "lonesome" David, she said with a smile though tear-brimmed eyes: "He was the busiest little guy you ever saw. He loved to climb things. I must have pulled him down from my kitchen cabinet a dozen times that morning. He banged up all my kitchen pans, playing. Until those pans wear out, I'll always remember."

Mr. Jones, an Illinois Central car man, who was at work when it happened, added: "I guess we will never know why these things have to happen. We have consolation in our other children. We've got to live for them."

The sad-eyed parents said they gained solace and comfort in the words of the Rev. Robert Howard, who spoke just before Denny was buried in a little grave at Walnut Hill Cemetery.

There is a look of hope in their eyes when they repeat their pastor's words, "If this boy's death in any way contributes to making the streets safer for other children, then he accomplished his deed on earth."

Mr. and Mrs. Bill Jones prayerfully hope their son will not have died in vain.

CHAPTER THREE

HIPPODROME OF TEARS AND LAUGHTER

After the stint at the Council Bluffs bureau, I came back across the Missouri River to become a police reporter for seven years in the 1950s, headquartered at the long-gone Central Police Station at 11th and Dodge streets.

It was my "graduate school" of journalism and human relations. With a daily parade of law violators, from drunks and vagrants to murderers, I called it a hippodrome of tears and laughter studded with gems of human decency.

Those were the days when police reporters were issued badges differing only from the regular police badge by the word "press" which was easily covered by your thumb while tagging along on gambling and prostitution raids as well as major investigations.

We were allowed to sit in on questioning of suspects by detectives. While covering the daily parade of violators, we even sat at a desk at the end of the judge's bench.

The days were often spiked by humorous frivolity from a cast of colorful characters as good or better than those in Broadway plays. Once reporters even matched the scene from the Broadway play, "Front Page," by removing a prisoner from a holding pen in the detectives' room and taking him to the press room for our own questioning.

Among the well-remembered characters was Henry "Michelangelo" Greenhagen, a drunken painter who was conveniently arrested every time a room at the station needed painting.

He turned up missing for a couple of months from his lower Douglas Street haunts despite an all-points search. I was startled one day when a stone sober and healthy-looking Henry tapped me on the shoulder in a store and said: "It finally dawned on me I could make a living painting. So I locked myself in my hotel room and quit drinking cold turkey and I've been sober ever since. Tell the guys at the station hello for me and that I ain't coming back."

Other memorable characters:

Phil Abboud, a Creighton University Law College honor graduate, was the busiest of attorneys. He was part of the "Unholy Trio" which included Bob Cornett, a well-known bondsman, and George Vanous, Cornett's assistant, who made sure bailees made court on time. They averaged as many as 30 cases a day.

Abboud was a tiny, dapper man who wore immaculately tailored suits and smoked long, black cigars. When his next case was called, he carefully placed his unfinished stogie on the marble wall outside the courtroom.

Once when I asked him why he was wasting his talent on minor law violators, he replied: "I average 25 cases a day. The going fee for legal representation in this court averages $25 to $30 and I always demand cash up front. That's more than enough for a good living. Besides, court is usually over in time for the horse-race betting at Ak-Sar-Ben. I sometimes take a case that interests me on up through District Court, but this way I can relax without having to burn the midnight oil in legal research."

Abboud never figured out who replaced his cigars on the ledge with soggy ones fished from a nearby spittoon. The culprit was Detective Inspector Ernie Brown, a character in his own right, who often coaxed a confession out of a suspect by giving him what he called his "double-whammy lie detector test."

Using a paperweight magnifying glass he would announce, "I'm looking deep into your soul," while peering into the suspect's eyes. Then between questions he'd hum gospel tunes while placing a finger on the suspect's pulse and drawing a straight line on a legal pad.

"Oh-oh!" Ernie would roar. "You are telling a lie and you ain't gonna be counted up yonder!" when a false answer caused him to veer his pencil across the pad. It was amazing how many times the suspect confessed his sins.

Once while testifying before the judge, Brown gasped and shouted: "There's a crisis occurring. Duty calls. Excuse me your honor," as he left the courtroom on the run.

I caught up with him in time to see him catch some of his detectives, led by Chester C. "Green Hornet" Dudley, red-handed in an act of what Brown labeled "grand larceny."

Through the window behind the judge Ernie had spotted the hooked end of a long pole the detectives were using to dislodge from the third floor ledge a nest of three baby pigeons that Brown had been carefully baby-sitting for an intended succulent squab dinner.

I considered it a privilege to be a rookie police beat reporter when Eugene T. Mahoney was a rookie cop.

I always told Mahoney I knew he would go far and be a success in any endeavor. He proved it by becoming a state senator, director of the Game and Parks Commission and head fund-raiser for both the Game and Parks and Henry Doorly Zoo foundations.

Mahoney first proved it by convincing then Police Chief Fritz Franks that Omaha's cops were getting too fat and needed a gym to get in shape. The chief agreed and had a fully equipped gym installed in the basement. The only cops I ever saw use it were Mahoney and other officers who moonlighted as "World Champions" in surrounding small town "rasslin" matches.

Mahoney later became the crusading head of what was known as the Morals Squad, and gained fame for a raid on a burlesque show at the old Town theater featuring "Evelyn West and Her $50,000 Treasure Chest."

He'd tipped the press that Evelyn was baring too much of her assets and he and his squad would be raiding the matinee performance. The front rows were packed with members of the Omaha media, but Mahoney jumped the gun.

Evelyn had barely dipped one shoulder strap when Mahoney bellowed: "Police! Stop the show – you are under arrest!" as he and his squad thundered down the aisle. They were closely followed by Floyd Kalber, a TV personality who later went to national network fame, and me, both shouting, "Mahoney, she hasn't done anything yet!"

Mahoney had to eat crow when in a post-raid interview Evelyn derided him and his squad while praising the press as "you dear, sweet boys who really know true art."

The late Ed Zorinsky, who Mahoney later helped get elected U.S. senator, was intrigued by Mahoney and police work in his younger days. He'd often leave his father's wholesale tobacco company to accompany Mahoney on Morals Squad raids.

As political newcomers, they first erred in running the campaign of a candidate who was running for police commissioner – against Mahoney's own chief of police, Henry "Heinie" Boesen.

Early election night when he already was a shoo-in, Heinie appeared in the press room with fire in his eyes looking for the "(bleep bleeps)" Mahoney and Zorinsky.

I greeted Heinie with: "I really hate to tell you this, Chief. But as you know both Gene and Ed hold second lieutenant commissions in the Army reserve. They had orders to attend a military police school. By now they are well on their way to Camp Gordon, Georgia."

By the time MP school was over, Heinie was ensconced at City Hall and had forgotten their transgressions – and Mahoney provided further proof of his promotional mastery.

He suggested to new Police Chief Harry Green that Omaha should have an Honor Squad made up of at least 6-foot, 200-pound officers complete with special shoulder patches to greet visiting VIPs.

The next day Green called a news conference to announce the formation of the new Honor Squad – with Mahoney as its leader.

One of the favorites of Omaha's "finest" was Sgt. Bea Dinzole. The personable Bea was the force's only female officer besides Capt. Agnes Savage, who headed the administrative office. Bea was matron of the women's jail and also worked with the Morals Squad.

Bea, a widow, often asked me to help her find a good-looking and preferably rich Sand Hills rancher to get her out of the police station doldrums.

Presto! With the help of Detective Inspector Ernie Brown, I found her dream come true during the questioning of a suave, elegantly dressed con artist who had been arrested for fleecing elderly women out of down payments on non-existent ocean cruises.

He agreed to go along with our ruse, posing as an agent seeking a policewoman to act as a hostess and security guard for the college-age sons of leading U.S. businessmen on a six-month cruise.

I raised Bea's hopes by telling her I'd overheard a man asking at the police commissioner's office whether the Omaha police force had a likely candidate. She was an excited, nervous wreck when I later called and told her the agent was in Brown's office and wanted to interview her.

The con man outdid himself. When Bea floated into the office, he rose, bowed and kissed her hand before turning to chastise Brown and me with, "How could you tell me this woman was middle aged?" Then he held Bea's hand and announced: "You are young and beautiful and, from checking your record, a most proficient officer. I need look no further. You are hired!"

Brown and I began sweating about how we were going to break the news to Bea after the con man offered her $1,000 a week and an unlimited expense account to purchase cocktail dresses and gowns to host the cruise dinner parties.

Shortly after she left with a promise of a champagne dinner that night to sign her new contract, she frantically summoned me to her office.

She was elated when she met me at the elevator in the hall leading to both the men's and women's jails. She wanted to talk about the offer and what she might be expected to do during the cruise.

But suddenly the lights went out! – mine.

With my back to the elevator, I didn't see Brown arrive with the con artist in tow or hear him holler to the men's jailer, "Throw this guy's fanny back in jail!"

But Bea did – and she KO'd me with a right cross to the chin before kicking Brown back into the elevator.

And, for some reason she refused to talk to either of us for at least two weeks.

One Christmas Eve day was indeed a jolly time in Central Police Court for the usual lineup of drunks I called "The All-America Platoon" – thanks to the late jovial municipal judge, Les Palmer.

Palmer arranged for portly Lt. Frank Buglewicz, a court officer who moonlighted as Santa Claus at Yuletide events, to don his Santa attire and bring to court a Christmas tree festooned with "case-dismissed" slips.

As each defendant was called to the bench, Palmer greeted him with: "Merry Christmas! Now walk over to Santa who has a gift for you." Buglewicz, echoing the Yuletide greeting with a "Ho! Ho! Ho!" plucked a dismissal slip from the tree and handed it to the surprised defendant.

Judge Palmer, composer of several published songs, then led the whiskey tenor-dominated platoon in the Christmas carol, "Silent Night," before announcing he was picking up the tab for lunch at a nearby cafe. But before the platoon was allowed to leave the courtroom, Palmer announced he had arranged for a "prominent Omaha businessman" to give them an anti-booze pep talk.

Buglewicz and I almost fell out of our seats when the "prominent businessman" turned out to be the owner of a lower Douglas Street bar who ended his talk with, "Now let's all raise our right hands and swear we won't touch another drink until New Year's Eve – AT MY PLACE."

I always considered Sandra, a two-dollar prostitute and often-arrested patsy for the Morals Squad, a lady.

She told me she had once been a dancer in New York City's Follies, but the years and her profession had made her a blighted, tainted rose.

But Sandra's heart still beat pure. Many times she'd spot a young, fresh-from-the-country girl who had come to the city and gotten in trouble with the law. Sandra would con the jailers to make the wayward girl her cell mate.

Sandra explained: "I can do more than any social worker or preacher by scaring the hell out of her. I tell her, 'Look at me. I am Exhibit A of what you are going to become unless you shape up.' "

I know several times Sandra talked officers into taking a young woman to the bus station and purchase her a ticket home with funds Sandra had authorized for the purpose.

When she died, hundreds of Omahans who knew Sandra and her gentle heart overflowed the funeral chapel to pay final respects to a real lady.

CHAPTER FOUR

BAD GUYS, GOOD STORIES

Sad to say, the fun and games on the police beat too often was interrupted by bad guy indiscretions from bribery to gruesome slayings.

Still unsolved is the slaying of well-known gambler Eddie McDermott, 54, on April 28, 1953. He was shot gangland-style through the head with a .45-caliber pistol by a suspected member of the Kansas City mob as he parked his car in a garage next to the Bell Hotel on Dodge Street, a known house of ill-repute operated by his girlfriend.

Conveniently, most Omaha bookies and suspects were vacationing at an Iowa lakes resort when it happened.

Better Than 10,000 Words

Getting a confession from a deaf mute accused of strangling his wife was easy. He even agreed to allow me to take a series of photos spelling out "I killed my wife" in sign language. Before printing the photos, leery News Editor Hugh Fogarty had me get assurance from an expert that the sign language was correct and that the killer hadn't told me to "Go to hell."

Charlie's Girlfriend Guilty?

I covered Charlie Starkweather's 1958 killing spree that claimed 13 victims. It was a case that paralyzed the Lincoln area with fear.

Much has been written about the gruesome spree of Charlie, who was accompanied by his girlfriend, Caril Fugate. Charlie was electrocuted for his crimes. Caril served time at the Women's Detention Center at York before being paroled after years of claiming she was innocent and had been held captive by Starkweather.

I often have been asked if I think she was guilty. My reply has always been the same as veteran Lincoln detectives and Nebraska State Patrol criminal investigators, "Sadly, yes, and without a doubt."

I do not begrudge her release and move to Michigan. She was a model prisoner, became a Christian and dutifully served her time. But her claims of innocence have always bothered me.

I always thought it appeared she loved every minute of her capture and subsequent trial. She beamed at the approach of cameramen. Veteran detectives said they had never encountered anyone so calm and cool as when she met them at the door and claimed her family, who already had been killed and stuffed in an out-building, were in bed with the flu.

Questions lingering in my mind are:

Who held the gun while Starkweather committed atrocities on the Bennett teen-agers before shooting them in an abandoned farm storm cave?

Why was she so jovial, even flirting with ranch hands at the head-quarters of the old Spade Ranch at Ellsworth when she and Starkweather stopped for sandwiches and supplies? If she was a captive, as she claimed to be, all she had to say was, "Guess who is waiting in the car? The store had guns and ammunition, and the ranch hands all had rifles in their pickups.

Luck and Timing Beats a Deadline

On March 26, 1952, the late chief photographer Lawrence "Robbie" Robinson and I were sent to cover the chase of another killer, Blaine Ellis, somewhere south of Gordon.

Our coverage was the result of pure luck and perfect timing.

Ellis, a ranch hand with an anger whetted by too much to drink, killed George Mensinger, 28, a member of a prominent cattle-breeding family, his wife, Aleen, 24, and wounded two others at the Mensinger ranch eight miles south of Merriman. Before fleeing, he also killed a neighbor, Deo Gardner, who was driving to the ranch after being alerted by frantic rings of Mensinger's telephone.

No one knew where Ellis was heading in the vast stretches of the Sand Hills. But luck was on our side. In fact, we couldn't have written a better timetable or script.

We instructed Vic Kilts, the pilot of our chartered Beechcraft Bonanza, to head for Merriman where we hoped to land in a pasture, but it was too soggy from recent rains.

Instead we landed at Gordon in hopes of finding a car there. Just as we taxied to a stop the airport operator ran out and told us he'd received a telephone call that Ellis was holed up in a barn on the Andy Anderson

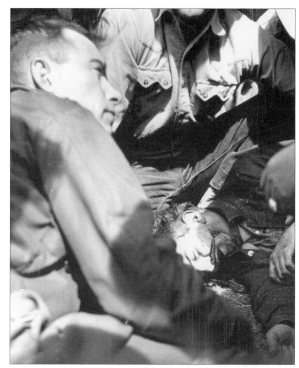

Allan (left) listens to Ellis' murder confession.

ranch, 28 miles southeast of Gordon. He drew us a map of the location.

As we approached we could see that a posse of ranchers had ringed the barn while waiting for lawmen to arrive. We thanked God that Kilts was a veteran Navy carrier flyer and was able to land in a pasture through a herd of cattle.

Again our timing was perfect. We landed next to the ranch owners, who had seen Ellis drive up and hide his car in their barn.

I had just finished interviewing them when someone shouted, "The (bleep, bleep) has set the barn on fire!"

The barn was engulfed in flames as was the get-away car which was just inside the door. A cowhand roped a rear bumper. As the car was pulled from the barn one of its doors flew open revealing a boot. Another cowhand grabbed it, but it was only an overshoe.

Kilts rescued a horse Ellis had saddled, apparently hoping to ride out the back door before discovering the posse had ringed his lair.

Again, perfect timing. Someone heard a noise in an adjoining small shed and everyone began shooting at it from all sides. Luckily, none of the posse was shot although wood splintered above our heads in another doorway in which Kilts was standing holding the spooked horse. He had placed his jacket over its head to calm it.

I was deafened when one of the posse fired an old blunderbuss over my shoulder. As I gasped, he shouted, "He's got a gun. I've got a gun. That makes us even!" before blasting away again.

When there was no sound from the shed, the posse rushed it. Flinging the door open, a rifle-totin' rancher recognized Ellis, who was severely wounded.

The rancher shouted, "You (bleep) of a (bleep), I'm gonna blow your head off!" and raised his rifle. Robbie and I threw ourselves at him shouting:

"Don't shoot! Let us get a picture first!" The rancher lowered his rifle. Robbie clicked his camera.

Just then we noticed the shed had caught fire from the barn and flames were licking up toward a 55-gallon drum of gasoline.

"Let's get the hell outta here!" Robbie shouted and we all grabbed Ellis. We had just carried him around another building when the gas barrel exploded and the shed disintegrated.

I lay on the ground beside the severely wounded Ellis and wiped blood from his mouth to get his confession. All he could say was: "I was a bad boy. I was a bad boy."

Just at that moment State Patrol Lt. Leo Knudson and Trooper Marvin Hansen – who'd be killed a year later at a roadblock – and Cherry County Attorney Bryan Quigley arrived and joined me on the ground beside Ellis.

After Ellis confessed to the killings, saying, "I don't know why, just the meanness in me," he was flown to the Valentine hospital but died en route.

And just then we hit it lucky again. A rural telephone company truck pulled up and the crew offered to patch into a phone line so I could call The World-Herald with the story.

Again, timing was perfect. We beat the deadline for the afternoon paper. And, thanks to the expertise of pilot Kilts, we got airborne after plunging down a ravine to gain air speed before soaring skyward. We got to Omaha in time to beat the deadline for all evening editions with a more detailed story plus a full page of Robbie's dramatic photos the next morning.

Editor Ware was ecstatic, but Robbie and I later agreed we may have made a tactical error. From then on Ware expected us, and all other reporters and photographers, to accomplish the nearly impossible by going long distances, getting the story and making it back before deadline.

The Town Hero Was a Killer

Rushville residents became apprehensive when 13-year-old Karen Talbot didn't return home from a movie the night of Aug. 20, 1953.

They recoiled in sorrow, shock and anger two months later when her body was found in a shallow grave at a ranch eight miles south of town.

Their feelings were compounded when handsome Duane McLain, 19, who had been one of Rushville High's most popular students and athletes, confessed to her killing because she had resisted his efforts to kiss her.

The day of the gruesome discovery, McLain, who had previously been cleared, was taken to O'Neill for a lie detector test. The case that had baffled law officers for months and had drawn nationwide attention was suddenly solved when State Patrol Sgt. Robert Nicholas asked McLain, "Don't you want to tell me the whole truth?"

His eyes brimming with tears, McLain replied, "Yes, give me a pencil and paper and I will write it all down."

In the four-page confession, he detailed how he had picked up Karen when she stopped for a drink of water at a flowing well while walking the short distance from the theater to her home. There he confessed he had hit the pretty high school freshman with his fist, knocking her out when she resisted his attempt to kiss her. Frightened, he put her in his car and drove to the ranch owned by his grandparents where he had been living alone.

When Karen recovered, McLain said she threatened to tell Sheridan County Sheriff Wendall Hills and her parents that he had hit her. McLain said he panicked, dragged her into the house and grabbed a hammer. When she broke free he chased and tackled her, and struck her several times with the hammer. Later he got a .22-caliber automatic rifle from the ranch house and "not bearing to look at her" shot her several times, removed her clothes and "buried her poor, limp body" in a nearby pasture.

McLain was returned to Rushville that night and after being promised by State Patrol Criminal Division Capt. Harold Smith and Lt. L.E. Knudson he wouldn't have to witness the exhumation, led them and Sheriff Hill to the grave at 3:30 a.m. After pleading guilty to a first-degree murder charge in a pre-dawn arraignment, McLain was taken to the Scottsbluff County Jail at Gering for safekeeping, lest there be demonstrations by angry Rushville citizens.

It was there that Capt. Smith, with whom I had worked on several cases, arranged for me to interview McLain in his cell.

McLain, who had been president of his senior class, an all-conference football player and editor of the high school newspaper and yearbook, calmly repeated his confession.

He wondered "what my fiancée, a 19-year-old Gordon girl, thinks of me now." Then with his head bowed and fighting back tears, he added: "I hope I am an example to other boys not to make a mistake in a moment of forgetfulness. I am sorry I let down the kids in Rushville as well as a couple of my football teammates, who were the best buddies a guy ever had."

We corresponded several times after McLain was found guilty and sentenced to life in the state penitentiary where he was described as a model prisoner.

Nearly 15 years later, on Dec. 16, 1968, he was pardoned by the State Parole Board despite protests from a visibly upset Rushville delegation.

McLain said he understood the protesters' feelings, adding: "I'd probably feel that way, too, if it had been a daughter of mine. But there is nothing I can do now to make it up to them."

Parole Board members said a factor in his pardon was McLain's excellent record working as a surgical technician on work release at Lincoln's Bryan Memorial Hospital.

Caught on Film and Tape

The late veteran photographer John Savage, who later became a state senator and founder of the Omaha Press Club, and I literally froze our fannies in February 1958 helping prove that even the best of good guys can go bad.

At first we were reluctant to believe an angry complaint by Larry Bowley, who farmed land he owned near the Missouri River as well as adjoining acres he leased at Eppley Airfield (then known as Omaha Municipal Airport).

Bowley accused airport manager Lee Huff Jr., of demanding payment of $1,000 in cash to get a lease to farm airport land.

We found it hard to believe because the suave, personable Huff was not only the best of airport managers, but one of the news media's best friends. He often tipped us on arrivals of VIPs and occasionally even delayed takeoffs so we could do interviews.

But Bowley was adamant, telling us: "If you don't believe me come on down to my feedlot early tomorrow morning where I have to make a $500 payment to Huff. He wants his cut in 10 unmarked $50 bills."

We decided to an on-the-spot investigation. Before the near-zero dawn the next morning, we met Bowley and attached a tape recorder to his chest before burrowing into a haystack to wait, with a camera ready, Huff's arrival. It was so cold we watched hot coffee we'd spilled from a thermos freeze on our parkas and wondered how long it would be for us to do likewise.

It seemed like hours, but in a few minutes Huff pulled up in his sports car and jovially greeted Bowley. He walked over to Bowley, who stood on the spot we had chosen for Savage's pictures.

Bowley wasn't so jovial, cussing Huff for his "illegal shakedown" and then deliberately counting out each $50 bill before placing it in Huff's outstretched hand.

After Huff drove off we went back to the office to thaw out, develop Savage's photos and play the tape for Editor Ware and News Editor Fogarty.

They decided we should go back and confront Huff with the charges and the photo evidence.

Huff greeted us warmly, but flatly denied Bowley's charges or that he was even at the feedlot that morning. Being friends, I told Huff, "Lee, John and I are going downstairs to have a cup of coffee so you can think about it. Then we are coming back to ask you again."

When we returned, Huff laughingly accused us of pulling a joke. Savage furiously slapped the 8-by-10 copies of the telltale photos on Huff's desk saying: "Lee, you damn dummy. This is no joke. What in hell do you have to say about these?"

Huff again flatly denied any wrongdoing, saying, "I just can't believe it."

And he did so again later at an emergency meeting in Mayor Johnny Rosenblatt's office. With his right arm upraised Huff declared: "On oath, so help me God, I never took any money. I lean over backwards because I know the responsibility of the situation."

Rosenblatt relieved him of his airport post pending "a fast and complete investigation."

Huff continued his denials of wrongdoing even when the floodgates opened on further accusations from airport employees, ranging from city-paid charter flights to his resort cabin and repairs to his sports car to his installing two city-owned window air conditioners in the Benson apartment of a friend.

But we all felt sorry for Huff, a veteran of both world wars and a longtime auto dealer before taking the airport post.

Even Mayor Rosenblatt said he "was completely surprised" by the allegations.

The next January the case against Huff came to a sudden end. Judge James M. Fitzgerald dismissed a grand larceny charge against Huff on a motion by Douglas County Attorney John J. Hanley.

Huff changed his plea from innocent to no contest on two counts of unlawful solicitation and was fined $522.75.

Trooper's Death Begins Long Saga

The saga of Loyd C. Grandsinger of Clearwater, S.D., began on April 9, 1954, when he was captured seven miles southeast of Sparks, Neb., by a 400-member posse of Cherry County ranchers, cowhands, sheriff deputies, newsmen and Nebraska State Patrol officers.

The 22-year-old Native American fugitive was bruised and exhausted

After a 16-hour chase, Loyd Grandsinger is brought to the courthouse.

from his cross-country flight when pulled from the Niobrara River, ending a dramatic 16-hour chase that began with the shooting death of State Trooper Marvin Hansen at a roadblock near Valentine about midnight. He was rushed to the Cherry County District Court at Valentine where he was charged with first-degree murder for the trooper's death.

Grandsinger and his brother, Leon, had been stopped at the road-block by Trooper Hansen and Cherry County Sheriff Bill Freeman following a burglary of the Wewela, S.D., post office. They were driving a reportedly stolen car. Leon immediately surrendered. Loyd engaged in a gunfight.

Patrol Lt. Leo Knudson said Grandsinger confessed to shooting the trooper with a .22-caliber pistol he'd stolen in Los Angeles. Hansen bled to death as he attempted to chase Grandsinger.

The day after Grandsinger's arraignment, when I was recruited by Patrol Col. C.J. Saunders and criminal division Capt. Harold Smith to take photos at the crime scene, Grandsinger told me he had fired at Hansen after the trooper fired at him. Escaping the scene using what he called an 'infantry crawl' he'd learned during Army service, he said he didn't know the trooper had been shot in the stomach. He told me he lost the pistol when he plunged into the river in an attempt to elude the posse.

Despite his attorney's claim of inadvertently enlarging the .22-caliber

To Bucktail and Back . . .

hole in Hansen's belt with a dowel during a court recess while pondering the next move in the defense, Grandsinger was quickly found guilty and sentenced to the electric chair by a Valentine jury. A ballistics expert testified that the bullet hole in the leather could only have come from a .22-caliber bullet.

But that was only a beginning chapter of the Grandsinger saga.

On appeal, Federal Judge John Delehant ruled Grandsinger was "without competent legal counsel" after the hole-enlarging incident and ordered a new trial.

Four years after the killing, Grandsinger was acquitted in a second trial. By then false rumors, later completely discounted, were rampant that Trooper Hansen actually had been shot in the gunfight by Sheriff Freeman.

The trial ended on the eve of Thanksgiving when winter storm warnings had been posted. It was later learned the jury, composed mostly of ranchers concerned about the storm, finally gave in to arguments of a lone jury member who'd had the lead in the play, "Twelfth Man Out," and held out for an acquittal.

Law enforcement and court officers, so sure of a guilty verdict, had not placed a hold on Grandsinger for the Wewela Post Office burglary and auto theft charges. I followed a joyous Grandsinger when he went to Pine Ridge, S.D., for an Ogalala Sioux "victory" celebration later that night.

There I turned down his request to help him write a book about his life.

On Jan. 29, 1958, another chapter in Grandsinger's saga unfolded.

State Trooper Bill Green, who was unaware of Grandsinger's identity, captured him after firing four warning shots over his head when Grandsinger attempted to flee through a cornfield after being pulled over near West Point, Neb., in a car reportedly stolen in Burke, S.D.

When I interviewed him at the Cuming County Jail, the bravado Grandsinger had displayed after his acquittal on the murder charge was gone. He had just signed a waiver agreeing to return to South Dakota to face a grand larceny charge for the Wewela Post Office burglary five years earlier.

"I just don't understand how I get into these things," Grandsinger lamented. "I guess it is just my fate."

Grandsinger said he hoped the 4-1/2 years he'd served in jail before the slaying acquittal would result in a light sentence or probation in the grand larceny charge. He denied stealing the car, claiming he'd paid the owner $10 to borrow it. Cuming County Sheriff Harold Welding said the owner denied Grandsinger's story, saying the car was stolen from his garage.

A Tense Night to Remember

One of my memorable experiences and resulting story occurred in St. Paul on the night of Oct. 6, 1953. I wrote:

St. Paul, Neb. – I talked the president of the No More War Association into giving up a dangerous armed siege at his home here early Wednesday.

Dr. Howard F. Eby, 41, a stocky dentist with cropped hair, did not give up easily.

But I had the road paved by Reid Zimmerman, World-Herald Public Pulse editor, and the clinching support of Capt. Harold Smith of Lincoln, head of the Nebraska State Patrol's criminal division.

Also add plenty of luck.

Capt. Smith, best known as "Smitty," and Howard County Sheriff Dan Schenk later informed me the standoff began when law officers went to Dr. Eby's office to serve papers on him for a psychiatric examination. Eby, they said, had drawn a gun on an Air Force enlisted man who came to the office to pick up his wife. He'd also blasted Legion members as "warmongers." When the officers arrived, Eby excused himself, returned with a gun and forced the officers to leave. The armed standoff ensued.

When I arrived at midnight I found Dr. Eby's neat, white home surrounded by an armed posse, in turn ringed by perhaps 100 bystanders.

The house stood quiet, ominous in the glare of fire truck and patrol car searchlights. Dr. Eby was armed and no one had ventured near the house since 5 p.m.

Sheriff Dan Schenk wisely stood his ground for fear of starting possible chaos and tragedy.

I knew Zimmerman had talked to the doctor by phone and gotten his promise to hold fire unless a rush was made on his home. I banked on that knowledge and the doctor's regard for Zimmerman, who had talked Dr. Eby into agreeing to speak to a reporter.

Capt. Smith agreed to let me try to talk to the doctor from the yard. There was no answer to my repeated calls and promises as I circled the house.

Knowing from the movement of curtains and blinds that Dr. Eby had watched me, I tried again, this time shouting: "Damn it, Doc. You told Editor Zimmerman you would talk to a reporter. Well, here I am and here's your chance. I'm going to telephone you in two minutes. You better answer or I'm leaving."

It worked. He answered his phone for the first time in hours and said I could come into the house if I was unarmed.

The handsome man met me at the door in his bathrobe. Although I had never met him, he greeted me like an old friend.

"Don't worry," he said. "They won't shoot you." Then he waved me into the bedroom at the front of the house. My heart turned a flip. In a neat row on the bed were a 12-gauge shotgun, .30-caliber rifle, .22-caliber automatic rifle, a butcher knife, hunting knife and an ax that had been sharpened to a razor's edge on the lathe in his home dental office. Piles of ammunition littered the dresser.

But my eyes were riveted on a human skull in the center of the arsenal. In its gaping mouth was a set of dentures. Pasted on the brow was a card that read "American Legion After Ebyizing."

Pretty good?" he asked. Then quickly, "Are you a Legionnaire?" I breathed thanks to Lady Luck that I could truthfully answer "no." My membership card had expired.

The doctor began a rapid-fire attack on the Legion and the Army.
I gulped.

I was an Army major and had hurriedly left for St. Paul from a Nebraska National Guard drill. I had shed my uniform jacket and GI pants,

Dr. Howard Eby, St. Paul dentist, sits on his bed with arsenal during standoff siege in his home.

but was still wearing an Army shirt bearing a Red Bull Division shoulder patch. I thought I was safe wearing a sports coat, having removed an Army ring from my finger, until Eby invited me to take off my coat.

I told him I was comfortable although I was sweating for reasons other than his having turned the heat in his house on high.

From then on we got along as old buddies.

Perhaps the turning point came when we talked about his three pretty daughters and my two. We joked that we were both going to run a sorority house and both confided we would sure like to have a son.

From then on it was Doc and Tom. He proudly showed me his dental office and lab, pictures of his parents and wife.

To me, it seemed like his bubbling enthusiasm changed to a touch of sadness when he pulled a framed political advertisement he had written from the wall and removed the back. Hidden underneath was his Army officer's commission as a first lieutenant.

"I am saving it to tear up at our political meeting," he said.

Then he began to tell me of his plans for the No More War

Association. I remained neutral on everything he said. It was no place to argue that no one hates war more than a soldier or a veteran.

He led me to the basement where he removed bricks from a wall and tenderly retrieved a huge scrapbook. It contained the names of 26 "complementary" members of his No More War Association and a form letter from U.S. Sen. Carl Curtis. He wept when he read the senator's message, "In reply to your question I, too, do not wish any more wars."

The clock ticked on.

Patiently, but desperately, I had been sweating an "in" to get him to agree to end his war.

Before I knew it I suggested he and his party needed a publicity agent and I was volunteering. He happily agreed. I told him he needed photos of himself being held at bay by the Legion. He first balked and then agreed when I told him I'd have to get my camera out of my car.

"Don't try anything funny and don't come back armed," he warned as I left.

While getting the camera I managed a whispered conversation with Capt. Smith, told him the situation and said I would try to get him inside the house.

After the pictures, I got my chance. Doc said I had to eat some "banana melon" and watermelon. I was mesmerized as he sliced the melon with the razor-sharp knife he always kept in his hand.

I told him it was too much melon for just two and asked him if my buddy "Smitty" could join us. He agreed after my assurance "Smitty" was not a Legionnaire.

I rushed out and grabbed the captain, telling him, "Please Smitty, leave your gun and don't mention war or Legion."

Doc balked when he saw Smitty's uniform, but relented when I explained: "It's a State Patrol outfit. He saves lives in traffic."

At the host's command, we ate the "banana melon" and watermelon although Smitty said he didn't like it. After the 3 a.m. repast I will never eat it again. Especially since I dumped a can of pepper on it to Doc's glee.

Our host kept up a rapid-fire conversation for 45 minutes, always making sure his arsenal was nearby. Smitty and I were like two bridge players scared of trumping the other's ace.

Then we threw him a curve.

I suggested, as publicity agent, the best stunt of all would be to sneak out of town and let the Legion-dominated posse be left holding the bag on the empty house.

But Doc said nothing doing. We had to sleep there.

Smitty then made probably the only tactical error in his long career.

He said he had a dental appointment at 10 a.m. in Lincoln. It took all of our wily imagination and persuasion to talk Doc out of immediate dental surgery.

Again we pressed our plan. This time it worked. The captain was allowed to get a patrol car backed up to the door. He tipped off Sheriff Schenk to our ruse.

Delighted, Doc pretended to be preparing for bed before turning out the lights in an upstairs bedroom.

We started to leave out the back door when Doc remembered to recover the association's files from the basement. Then he spotted his accordion and insisted on playing a tune. At about 4 a.m. his rendition of my suggested song, "Show Me the Way to Go Home," sounded awful.

At last we got him out. Smitty had me sit with Eby in the backseat while he covered him from the front. I had Doc crouch low to "fool" the Legion as we pulled out of the driveway.

On the way to Grand Island he expressed surprise at all the traffic so early in the morning – it was the fleet of patrol cars escorting us front and back.

When we pulled into the driveway of the Hall County Courthouse, Doc balked only momentarily at being taken to jail. He wished me good luck and called me his friend.

P.S. An aside to Doc – You said you were looking forward to this story. My only regret is having to use a ruse.

My only consolation is that it was best that way. You said you were "ready to blast them," remember. Someone in the crowd might have gotten an itchy finger. You might have. A tragedy might have been compounded.

Believe me, Doc, I did what I thought was best. I hope your swell family will approve. And here's hoping everything turns out for the best.

But everything didn't. After serving a short time at the Nebraska Psychiatric Center at Hastings, Dr. Eby practiced dentistry at Spalding. He ran unsuccessfully for the U.S. House of Representatives in 1956 and 1960. In early July 1960 he took his own life.

An Unwanted Award
The Dr. Eby standoff story won a Pall Mall Big Story Award and was broadcast on the cigarette company's national radio show.

The broadcast scared the hell out of me. Producers had Doc firing a gun at me. It and other Hollywood distortions of the story disgusted me. I told Pall Mall officials I did not wish the story to be used on television and made into a movie as they had suggested.

My wife used the $500 award check for a washer-dryer. The plaque is gathering dust in a closet. And I blame my lingering smoking habit on the carton of cigarettes the company sent me every month for a year.

CHAPTER FIVE

THE BEST OF DAISY PICKINGS

The best stories are the seemingly insignificant ones that happened because I paused to pick a "daisy" – a little story that brings a tear, tickles a funny bone, makes the pulse beat faster and warms the heart. Luck, timing and asking one more question are factors in finding them.

Among those I like best is one I wish I had a chance to re-write after the haste of making a deadline. It's the story of Miss Goetz, which I almost blew on March 12, 1957. I would have given it a new lead that would have told the story even more poignantly.

I should have begun simply with:

"A fond recall, hello, a song, a smile and then farewell to linger on in others' hearts."

Getting the story – and almost losing it – began late one afternoon when I returned to The World-Herald's city room after another long, sad day on the police beat. I was standing by the Society Department which has long since become the Living section in the paper. A phone was ringing incessantly and nary a staffer was in sight.

When I answered it, a man's voice asked, "Can you send someone to my house tonight to get a photo of a special dinner I'm hosting?" To keep the caller on the line until a staffer showed up, I asked a question: "What makes this dinner so special?"

The caller, after further questioning, told me he was Ernest Nordin Jr., former conductor of the Omaha Municipal Band, and he and his wife were hosting his former kindergarten and eighth-grade teachers for dinner.

After looking desperately in vain for a Society Department reporter, I asked one more question. "Your kindergarten and eighth-grade teachers! How old are you?" I became interested when he said he was 59. That meant his teachers must really be ancient.

Nordin added further intrigue by telling me he had been cleaning out a closet and had come across his old kindergarten workbook. It had reminded him of Miss Goetz, a beloved teacher at Bancroft School, who had taught not only him, but movie star Dorothy McGuire as well as other greats in kindergarten.

Nordin said he wondered if Miss Goetz was still living. She had never married, and he found her name in the phone book.

"I was amazed when she answered the phone and told me she remembered me," Nordin recalled. "When she told me my old eighth-grade teacher was a neighbor, I invited her too."

I told him I would stop by that evening and take a photo, but could not guarantee it would appear in The World-Herald. Little did I know that the photo and their story would be picked up by The Associated Press and make the front page of newspapers around the world, read by millions seeking a story that touches the heart.

In retrospect, I feel it would have been sacrilegious to attempt to write the story other than relate it chronologically. So I began with:

It was a happy occasion Tuesday evening at 4727 S. 13th St.

Mr. and Mrs. Ernest Nordin Jr., were entertaining Miss Laura Goetz and Miss Avis Roberts.

It was a long-awaited reunion for Nordin, Miss Goetz, who was his kindergarten teacher and who retired in 1942 after 40 years of teaching, mostly at Bancroft School, and Miss Roberts, who had retired after 35 years in the classroom and had taught him in the eighth-grade.

When this reporter arrived to chronicle the happy event, memories had rolled back to 1903.

A boy grown to manhood and his two teachers, mellowed by memories of thousands of happy faces, were singing "The Pussy Willow Song." It was a kindergarten favorite at old Bancroft School.

Held tenderly in Miss Goetz's hands was Nordin's kindergarten workbook. Between chuckles, the old lessons and names of hundreds of Johnnys, Susans and Richards flowed from her heart and lips.

To this reporter, indiscreet enough to ask her age, Miss Goetz, the personification of a traditional school marm, primly answered: "Young man! Didn't they teach you to never ask that of a lady? You may take our picture. I'll treasure it. You can write your story of everything else, but forget the age."

"Yes, Ma'am," I replied.

"Isn't this wonderful!" beamed Miss Roberts. "We've looked forward so much to this party."

"I love you both," said Nordin, his arms around their shoulders."

Still on my knees before them after taking their photo with an ancient and heavy Speed Graphic, I asked one more question, "What sort of a boy was this kid?"

"He was full of mischief," chuckled Miss Roberts. "We got very well-acquainted in the eighth-grade class because I usually had to keep him after school to clean the blackboards and pound the erasers. But, even so, he was kind of lovable."

Miss Goetz, her mind clicking crystal clear back over the years, added: "He was a nice little kid. I remember him as if it were yesterday singing at the Christmas programs and his father sitting there looking so proud."

She smiled wistfully, adding, "Of course, in kindergarten all my children were lovely and beautiful."

She bowed her head as if in benediction to a beautiful thought and a beautiful aura glowed on her face.

It was a benediction. For in the midst of that smile, Miss Goetz died.

Later Tuesday evening, Miss Roberts and Mr. and Mrs. Nordin went ahead with the dinner.

"It was her wish," Miss Roberts said.

Mr. Nordin added huskily, "She's still with us, in our hearts."

Beloved Bancroft school teachers Laura Goetz (left) and Avis Roberts with former student Ernest Nordin Jr., in 1957.

A stop on the Byways map…Venus, Neb.

CHAPTER SIX

BYWAYS, HERE I COME

In 1959 I was given the dream assignment of being The World-Herald's roving reporter-photographer with all of Nebraska except Omaha as my beat.

I was no stranger to Nebraska's wide-open spaces. I had discovered the place I love best, the Sand Hills, in the worst of times in 1936. At the height of the Depression and searing Dust Bowl years I became a member of a "gandy dancer" gang on the Chicago & Northwestern Railroad.

We replaced old tracks from Clearwater to Valentine to accommodate the long lines of cattle trains carrying drought-stricken livestock to greener pastures back East.

Gandy dancers got their name for the jiggling up-and-down dance they performed by balancing on one foot with the other on a shovel, tamping gravel under new rail bed ties.

I "danced" 10 hours a day, six days a week for 30 cents an hour in heat that averaged well over 100 degrees. Although the railroad retained $1.50 of our $3-a-day salary for meals and sleeping bunks in a boxcar, I ended the summer with a fortune in Depression-value dollars.

I was one of the few speaking English in the mostly Slavic-heritage crew out of Chicago. But I received more of an education in human relations than I ever did in college, in the Army or since. And when I left at summer's end, I was the toughest and most sun-blackened college freshman around.

Despite the almost unbearable heat, I fell in love with the tranquil beauty of the wide expanse of the Sand Hills. In wet years it became a "Sea of Grass," with the wind whipping wave-like through the range belly deep in grass.

I'll never forget the refreshing skinny dips in the nearby Niobrara River, the ice-cold creek at Long Pine or Valentine's Minnechaduza Lake.

In later years, I discovered the friendliness of "Greater Nebraska's" people on numerous assignments covering natural disasters and murder stories outside metropolitan Omaha and Lincoln during my police beat years.

My appetite for getting lost and finding stories in out-of-the way places was whetted by my roving assignment. It never waned in the next 43 years.

Yep, There Is a Bucktail

I got lost in October 1962 and found a long-gone ranch house post office down a Sand Hills trail in Sunnyside Valley several miles south of Highway 92 in Arthur County. I wrote:

Bucktail, Neb. – The postmaster here gets a chuckle when the mail arrives.

There are usually form letters for the police chief and superintendent of schools, and federal government urban renewal pamphlets and advertisements wanting to sell Bucktail new street cleaners.

Pardner, there ain't no police, school, blighted area or even streets in Bucktail.

It was on the map as the only town other than Arthur, the county seat, in Arthur County. Actually, it's only a ranch house rural mail station on the north end of the Paxton post office star rural route.

The postmaster is Mrs. Florence Cullinan. The mayor, police and fire chief, city manager and street commissioner is her husband, Harry Hubert Cullinan, 74.

Harry, a homesteading rancher, was postmaster for 37 years until he retired in 1958. The post office was dropped to a rural station status and his wife took over.

Harry, who reversed Horace Greeley's admonition to go west, was born in California. He came east to Sioux City and became a railroad telegrapher before heading west again in 1912 to a Kincaid Act homestead.

He originally settled four miles west of here, then later six miles south on Bucktail Lake. He finally brought the headquarters of his 9-Bar Ranch overlooking Sunnyside Valley in 1921. That was the year he started the post office in a soddy.

"There never was a store or anything else besides the ranch house," Harry said.

But Bucktail was the birthplace of a thriving business, a sideline to Harry's cattle raising. He introduced the use of potassium iodine to the range country to counter the iodine deficiency in soils and grasses. For nearly 30 years ranchers in 20 states sent orders to Bucktail for Harry's iodizing powder.

Despite the remote location, he's got proof of Bucktail's attraction.

To Bucktail and Back . . .

The names of visitors – hundreds of them – are all kept in a well-worn register.

Kennedy Got Busier

Another of my favorite out-of-the-way spots is Kennedy, the ranch house and now-gone post office of Jerry and Marianne Beel some 30 miles southwest of Valentine.

I discovered it accompanying Bureau of Reclamation engineers plotting the construction of the nearby Merritt Reservoir.

"We'll eat when we get to Kennedy," promised one engineer after we had driven cross country for miles. "It has a helluva cafe." When we got there he tossed me a candy bar and said, "Eat up."

Later, I had many more sumptuous meals cooked by Marianne, the postmaster who became an award-winning journalist for her photos and column, "Sand In My Shoes" in the North Platte Telegraph.

She recalled the avalanche of letters received after the slaying of President John F. Kennedy seeking a Kennedy postmark on commemorative envelopes.

To a philatelic company representative who brought boxes full of letters to be stamped, Marianne, who was used to stamping letters for her 35 postal customers while helping Jerry run the ranch, said, "Here's the stamp and stamp pad. Have at it, Buster!"

Fondly recalled is the story of a stuffy agent from an East Coast company who brought 10,000 letters to be stamped.

"First, he got lost and then high-centered and stuck on the trail. I had to get our tractor to pull him out and lead him to the ranch," she said. "Then, because of all the stamping I put him to, I had to feed him and put him up for the night.

"The next day when he left he had the nerve to ask me, 'How do you folks stand living way out here where there is nothing to see for miles?' "

Perky Marianne said she replied, "If it wasn't for dummies like you getting stuck on our trail, we could enjoy living out here in God's Country a helluva lot better."

More Important Than Venus de Milo

On April 11, 1971, I found Venus and put it on the Byways map with: Venus, Neb. – The Louvre in Paris has Venus de Milo. Nebraska has Venus de Bohemian Alps.

It's almost easier to get to Venus in France.

Venus, Neb., is one of those "towns" tucked 'mid the rolling hills of southwestern Knox County whose accessibility is best described by the natives: "Can take you right to it but can't tell you how. You best go a couple of miles and then ask."

Actually, Venus is nine miles north of Orchard and unlike its counterpart, Walnut, three miles to the northeast, is on the latest Nebraska road map. They are in the white space on the map west of Highway 14. It is an area the Germans settled in predominately Czech country.

Venus is the combination country store, gas station, cream and egg pick-up point and the visiting center of Mr. and Mrs. Arthur Von Seggern.

The Venus post office stopped service in 1959, but its sign is still in the window under the sloping porch roof. The lively dance hall and ball diamond across the road also are memories. As is the creamery station.

The "natives" are a little irked, and rightfully so, that Venus' most recent claim to fame was always listed on University of Nebraska basketball programs as from Orchard.

He is Dale Von Seggern, now of Columbus, who lettered three years for the Cornhuskers before his 1970 graduation. He went to Orchard High School, but his father is the mayor, police and fire chief, water and sewer commissioner and the entire city council of Venus.

Mom was the postmaster and now is co-operator of the country store.

Dad also is moderator of the perpetual world problem-solving forums around the old iron potbellied stove. On wintry days the ancient stove glows hot with corncob and wood-fed fires. So does the conversation fed by local, state, national and world problems of the day. Neighbors and strangers alike are welcomed – with one exception.

"We don't like politicians. They are all a bunch of liars," joshed Von Seggern.

Proudly he showed off the captain's chair, the conversation throne and subject since at least 1912. It has been used so much for sitting and gabbing around the old stove that its legs have worn off up to the first rung.

"Man, what stories it could tell, if it could only talk," Von Seggern said, plunking down in the chair and raising his feet to the base of the stove. "This is the way you sit in it."

How come the left legs are worn more than the right?

"Like I said, we don't allow politicians and we have no left-leaning politics here. Must just be that the wood was softer on the left legs," said the host.

No sooner had Mrs. Von Seggern mentioned how old-timers who come back for a visit like to sit in the chair once more than in walked Mr.

and Mrs. Leonard Davey of Bellevue. They'd left their nearby farm 17 years ago, but now are back "fixin' up the place" for a possible new tenant.

"I remember the old stove and chair when I was a kid of 5," said Davey, now 67. "Did that old stove ever feel good on cold mornings. I agree. It and the chair really could tell some stories."

The Von Seggerns took over the store – and Venus – in 1952. Here they completed raising their three sons and two daughters.

The old stove and country store tradition is being perpetuated by visits from their 14 grandchildren. Most of their names have been scribbled on the old stove's belly and they know the way to the big antique jar on the counter containing licorice twists.

In their minds, and in that of other area youngsters, Nebraska's Venus is the most important Venus of them all.

CHAPTER SEVEN

THE 'GREEN HELL' WAS PARADISE

In 1966 I was sent on a three-week assignment similar to the famed Stanley-Dr. Livingston quest in deepest Africa.

My quest was to find a Nebraska doctor and his wife who had crashed deep in the Amazon jungle in Brazil. They were repaying a debt of gratitude in medical service to former head-hunting Indians who had saved their lives.

Instead of the fabled "green hell" of the jungle, I found heaven, a personal Shangri-La that I described in a series of stories. This is the first published on July 31, 1966:

Mission Cururu, Brazil – A thousand trackless miles deep in the green hell of the Amazon jungle, Dr. and Mrs. James Maly of Fullerton, Neb., are fulfilling their destiny and repaying a debt of gratitude.

I found them here with Chicagoans Dr. and Mrs. Edward Stalzer and Bill Shields, 23, a University of Illinois medical student, providing medical care and establishing a jungle clinic for the Mundurucu Indians, once considered among the fiercest of the Amazon headhunters.

And here I also found a personal Shangri-La.

This is green oblivion, much of it unexplored frontier. The shortwave radio is broken again. The only links with civilization are the evening static-filled Voice of America and Armed Forces Radio broadcasts. There also is a once-a-month Brazilian Air Force C-47 or a tedious 10-day trip by jungle boat from Santarem on the Amazon River, 500 miles distant by air, down the winding Tapajos and Cururu rivers.

Ten days? It can take longer than that, because the bright blue Tapajos has murderous rapids at one point and is navigable but a few days each year. A boat, loaded with supplies for this remote Franciscan mission, sank in those rapids three months ago taking the life of a Humphrey, Neb., priest.

Currently, the only ties to civilization are the Cessna Centurian single-engine airplanes of Drs. Maly and Stalzer.

Mail takes months to arrive. It took three months for a cablegram telling of a serious illness in his family to reach a young Omaha priest at Almeirim, just 250 miles from Belem, the port city at the mouth of the Amazon.

But remoteness has its blessings. Here is a yet unspoiled Garden of Eden where breathtaking beauty and awesome brutality can be synonymous. A blizzard of pale green or blue or bright red butterflies hovers over a slinking jacari (alligator) and exquisite flowers – many yet unclassified – can hide the lurking coral or slithering giant anaconda snakes.

Only the so-called civilized people of the world pollute their rivers with sewage. I drank from the crystal clear Cururu without ill effect. Fresh water porpoises frolic in its waters 'mid cannibalistic piranha fish and the much more feared stingray.

Those head-hunting Mundurucu? Other tribes still tell with gusto how they once sliced the liver from a victim who brought them bad magic and ate it before the victim died.

But today these smiling, laughing Indians are killing us with the kindness of their welcome and hospitality.

They are illiterate, primitive and impoverished by civilized standards, and many are wracked by disease such as tuberculosis and smallpox – unknown before their contact with civilization.

Yet in their language there is no word for "please" or "thanks." For here there is no need to ask. Wants are willingly shared. Thanks is taken for granted and expressed by the eyes and a smile.

Drs. Maly and Stalzer with their registered nurse wives are expressing their thanks with their medical skills.

It all began a little more than a year ago. The Malys and the Stalzers, piloting similar airplanes, were completing a vacation in South America. They began a "shortcut" across the jungle from Brasilia. Everything went wrong from the start, from erroneous reports to inoperative radio beacons and an unceasing tropical rainstorm. Being similar aircraft, both began to run out of fuel at the same time.

"I sincerely believe it was all God-ordained," says Dr. Maly, a Creighton University Medical School graduate. "God knew those Franciscan missionary priests needed medical aid for those Indians. He looked down and saw two doctors and nurses flying over and said, 'Just a minute, folks.' Right then we ran out of gas after flying over miles of river that had flooded the jungle for miles on each side. As our engines began to sputter, my wife, Jan, screamed, 'There's a clearing ahead!' It was the only clearing we had seen in 800 miles of jungle and we decided to make crash landings."

Dr. Maly's legs were smashed when his airplane hit a half-sunken log.

Dr. Stalzer's arm was broken when he crashed following him in. Their wives suffered only bruises.

In a later story in the series I related how the crash, followed by silence, was recorded on Mrs. Maly's tape recorder that had accidentally been turned on just before the landing. Loud and clear it recorded Dr. Maly's groans and then Mrs. Maly's excited voice saying, "Somebody is coming!" and then followed by a pause and, "Oh, thank God! They're wearing clothes."

Mundurucu Indians, who had been cared for and modestly clothed at the Mission Cururu, rescued them and took them by dugout canoes to the mission. There they were cared for by Franciscan priests who arranged for the Brazilian Air Force to fly them to civilization.

While at the mission the Malys learned from Frei Placido, the Rev. Placidus Toelle, 84, of West Phalia, Germany, who had established the mission in 1920 and given a lifetime to serving the Indians, about the mission's lack of medical facilities and the Indians' desperate medical needs.

The need also was emphasized by the Rev. Marquard Paternik, 51, OFM, of Cleveland, Ohio, who had arrived at the mission 21 years earlier to aid the German Franciscans after all assistance was cut off by the Nazi regime. The need was echoed by the Rev. Edmundo Bonkosch, also of Germany, and Brother Dismas Dekin of St. Louis, Mo., as well as seven American and German missionary sisters.

"It became our obsession to return and provide that aid while repaying our debt of gratitude," Dr. Maly said.

Dr. Stalzer established the Cururu Mission Society. He enlisted the aid of Shields, the young medical student, for medical research. Funds and supplies were donated.

On June 25, Dr. Maly and his wife, a former Hebron girl he'd met during her nursing training, farmed out their six children to relatives, climbed into their new airplane and headed south "to begin sharing six to eight weeks of our lives with those in need."

I followed to find them. En route I also found:

▨ Dom Tiago (Bishop James Ryan of Chicago) and his handful of American Franciscan priests – seven of them from Nebraska – providing faith, hope, education, food, medical and economic aid by radio and outboard motor-powered canoes in a 200,000-square-mile jungle diocese.

▨ The Rev. Tom Krupski, Omaha-born and raised, who literally established faith, jobs, hope and democracy brick-by-brick in the Amazon

River port of Almeirim. As the first priest there in 100 years, he has built a school, launched a brick factory and has big plans for a co-op farm and hospital.

■ An unfriendly piranha that got too close to my nose for comfort, a giant anaconda boa constructor hanging over our canoe while fishing, a palm-sized tarantula that came to Mass and "half a million" piun (smaller than gnat-sized insects) that got under my skin.

■ The thousand and one delights of a three-day, 100-mile jungle boat trip to remote villages during which I became "associate doctor" and Cururu bogey man combined when I helped give vaccinations.

■ The establishment of the world's most remote Football Land U.S.A. Cornhusker Fan Club.

■ The inauguration of the Doc Maly Air Taxi Service specializing in mail, beer for thirsty priests and assorted hitch-hikers, including a planeload of emaciated lepers going to the national Lepersorium at Belem after they had been kicked off a riverboat as "untouchables."

In other stories in the series I recalled how the ancient Frei Placido had told me that as a young priest from Germany, he was eager to teach religion to the head-hunting savages.

"Then one day," he said, "a tribesman told me, 'My God brings the rains that put fruit on the trees. He guides my arrows on the hunt. He filled my wife's belly with fine sons and He makes me happy and warm inside.' Then he asked me, 'What does your God do?' I learned real fast to teach the Mundurucu 'Your god and my God are the same God.' "

The old priest also told me, "I did not have to teach them the Ten Commandments. Lying, cheating, stealing, coveting another man's wife and other sins mean banishment from the tribe. You are your brother's keeper because no man can live alone in the jungle."

Father Tom Krupski defied a couple of heart attacks and bouts with jungle fever to return to the jungle. He died there, but not before my wife, Marilyn, lobbied for the shipment of a truckload of donated medical supplies, and a sawmill and a portable charcoal factory had reached Almeirim to help him grow the economy. A young couple from Archer, Neb., a nurse and a University of Nebraska-Lincoln Ag College graduate, helped him establish a clinic and a communal farm.

He also became known to other priests as the best chef and bartender in the Amazon.

Dr. Maly had landed me amid a flock of chickens in the middle of Almeirim's main street with a curt, "There's a South Omaha kid here you ought to meet. I'll pick you up in a couple of days," before immediately taking off.

Father Tom, dressed in a white cassock had rushed down a hill from a funeral he had officiated and had eagerly descended on me like a giant white butterfly. I was the first American he had talked to in weeks.

While preparing a gourmet dinner, he asked if I would like a cocktail. I replied, "Sure, an ice cold Rob Roy, shaken not stirred," thinking I had asked the impossible in the jungle.

I gaped when I heard the tinkle of ice cubes and gasped when he handed me the chilled glass, causing me to exclaim, "Father, where in hell did you get the ice?"

He showed me his ancient kerosene-burning refrigerator and told me I had to drink sparingly because it could only make one tray of ice every 24 hours. He said captains of Brazilian Navy boats allowed him to take what he needed to stock his liquor cabinet from their ship's lockers after he took confessions from their crews.

Before I left Almeirim, Father Tom asked me to go easy mentioning booze in my story, explaining, "After I asked my mother, who lives in Grand Island, if she could stash a bottle of Scotch and bourbon into the bottom of one of the barrels of sample medical prescriptions from doctors and drugstores she sent me, she was sure I was becoming the drunken priest of the Amazon.

"She not only sent me WCTU literature, but sent me a letter telling me how she and my dad had driven to Columbus through a blizzard to meet my Bishop James Ryan, who was on a sabbatical in the States.

"My mother went into detail how they stood in line and listened as the Bishop met each of the parents of Nebraska priests, telling them what fine jobs their sons were doing in the work of the Lord.

"Mother ended her letter with, 'I was in utter shock when your Bishop greeted us with, 'Wow! You're Father Tom's parents? Your son makes the best martini I've tasted anywhere!' "

I kept it out of my original story, but it's too good not to be told. Jungle priest Father Tom always put a smile on my face and an extra warm feeling in my heart.

Helen Siefert (left) with lifelong teacher Margaret Hoshor.

To Bucktail and Back . . .

CHAPTER EIGHT

LOVE STORIES

Among the best of love stories was one I found at Bellwood in late January 1974 that was headlined, "The Love Is Unseen and Unheard." I describe it as:

A Magnificent Obsession

Bellwood, Neb. – There is beauty, warmth and serenity in a little white house on a corner in this Butler County community.

Visitors cannot help but be inspired, even awed, by the evident unselfish sacrifice, dedication, tenderness, togetherness and a sense of belonging there.

But it is understandable, for those are the ingredients of love, and a very special kind of love dwells there.

The home and the aura therein are all things beautiful which are felt, but have never been seen or heard by Helen Siefert, now 47. The bonds of an invisible prison have long been broken for Helen, who has been totally blind and deaf since infancy.

The house also is the retirement home of Margaret Hoshor, 67, the former Nebraska Panhandle country schoolteacher, who four decades ago sacrificed a promising career and chances for marriage and a family of her own, to dedicate her life to freeing Helen's vibrant, blithe spirit.

Now in the sunset years, they live in the glow of success – and love.

They are the Midland's counterpart to the story of the world-renown Helen Keller and her teacher, Anne Sullivan Macy. The comparison often has been made in national publications and by Edward Morrow, the now-retired World-Herald reporter and longtime editorial staff member who first chronicled the magnificent obsession in 1934, with poignant sequels throughout the years.

True, there were major differences as both Helens conquered the bonds of cruel handicaps.

There are those who know them both, including Miss Hoshor, who feel that Helen Siefert had greater potential than Miss Keller. But Miss Keller's parents were wealthy, while the parents of Miss Siefert, now living in Scottsbluff, were comparatively poor. Miss Keller's education included graduation from Radcliffe College and emphasized the literary, while Miss Siefert's training has been vocational.

Both conquered their handicaps to live life to the fullest.

Miss Keller was aided by affluence. Miss Siefert was assisted by the hearts of World-Herald readers and later by all Nebraskans.

Those readers, in answer to an eloquent plea by the late Henry Doorly, former publisher and president of The World-Herald, made an avalanche of contributions at the very depths of the Depression to send Helen, then 7, and Miss Hoshor to the Perkins Institution's blind-deaf department at Watertown, Mass.

Miss Hoshor gave up her teaching career in Morrill County to meet the institution's requirement that the child be accompanied by a teacher willing to devote at least eight years to her training. She did not know then that she was dedicating her life to Helen.

Their story, tugging at the hearts of Nebraska legislators, resulted in the establishment the next year of the first deaf-blind department at what is now the Nebraska School for the Visually Impaired at Nebraska City.

After a year at Perkins, Helen became the Nebraska school's first student. But a year later they moved to the New York Institute for the Blind's special blind-deaf department to take advantage of living and learning with other blind-deaf children. Until she was 21, Nebraska taxpayers paid for Helen's education and care there.

Both Helens, imbued with fiery spirits, fought, sometimes savagely, their teachers as they battled the initial restraints of discipline and training. Forgetting the scars, both teachers won with tender understanding and love.

Miss Siefert greeting me warmly last week, first caressing my face to imprint its image in her mind and then touched my lips with soft fingers to "listen" to my words.

She reads and writes Braille, and loves to read history and geography. She's a perfect typist. She cooks, bakes, cleans house, washes dishes and is the first up every morning to make coffee. She can assemble a 1,000-piece jigsaw in less time than the sighted. Her creative sewing and other craftsmanship is awesome.

Beaming and with amazing sure-footedness, she rushed from room to room, bringing dresses she had made for both herself and Margaret, knitted afghans and crocheted tablecloths and other gifts she had made for friends.

"Helen found one small disc of the crocheted tablecloth pattern in a box we bought at an estate sale and before I knew it had mastered the pattern and started the crocheted tablecloth," Margaret said.

"One night while I was baby-sitting across the street, she surprised me on my return with a beautiful cover she had made for a new toaster oven during my two- to three-hour absence."

The stories of Helen Keller and Helen Siefert have two parts. One cannot help but feel humble thinking of their teachers who devoted and dedicated so much. But here, too, are differences.

Anne Sullivan Macy's story was lauded on stage and screen. She was given national citations for her work and she married.

Only by prying and pressing for an answer does one glean from Miss Hoshor the ironical fact that for all her dedication and sacrifice she has received only one award – in the material sense.

It's a "distinguished service" medal made for her by some boys at the New York Institute where she served 16 years as principal and later as senior teacher until her retirement in 1972.

Twice she gave up offers of marriage to remain with Helen. Hers is a love shared only by scores of other blind-deaf children whose spirits she helped free during the years.

But there are no regrets. There is always a smile of serenity and beauty in her face from the inner warmth of having helped so many.

Morrow, who first saw the goodness in her, perhaps said it best in a recent note from his retirement home at Naples, Fla.

"Margaret Hoshor is, I think, one of the great women of all times. She has become a woman whose goodness and tremendous personality are apparent almost instantly. It would be easy for Margaret to be a shade self-consciously virtuous or even to regard herself as a martyr. Nothing of that sort ever touched Margaret. She was doing what she wanted to do – perhaps what a person of her singular character had to do – and I'm sure she never regretted not marrying or having a family of her own. Anyone seeing Helen could understand Margaret's evident joy at seeing a terrific job well done."

Miss Hoshor blushed when I read her Morrow's note.

"Oh, goodness," she said. "This has not been a magnificent obsession. It has been a satisfying life. Oh, no. I'm no martyr. I have had such a full life, a wonderful life in such a fascinating field. Helen wasn't my only child, you know, and it was a thrill to work with them even though their capabilities were so much less than Helen's."

There is one little touch of concern.

"I cannot help but feel tense thinking about the future," Margaret said. She has heart trouble and faces possible surgery for another ailment. She's aware of the difference in their ages and the strong possibility Helen will outlive her.

"I am sure my death will be a blow, but I am sure Helen could adjust and get along," Margaret said. "She has her family, and there is an aunt in California, but there would still be the need for trained guidance despite her ability to be independent. She can take care of herself. I'm probably being over-protective, but ... "

She quickly turned to happier thoughts.

When Helen brushed her lips to "hear" Margaret relay my praise for a knitted dress she'd brought in for me to see, Margaret clasped her hands.

"You mentioned rewards," she said. "This is mine."

Real Tears Were Fleeting

On a bitter cold November night at Battle Creek in 1964, I helped wipe away the tears and bring warmth and happiness to Nongart Niamsiri, 18, of Pitsanuloke, Thailand.

Nongart, more affectionately called Pia, pronounced "Pie" and meaning "little girl," was the first of several foreign exchange students hosted by Mr. and Mrs. F.H. Zimmerman of Battle Creek.

I had stopped along the Byways to get the story of her being away from her warm and sunny land for the first time. By coincidence, Lou Setti, 24, who had been Pia's teacher at a secondary school in Thailand while in the Peace Corps, had stopped the same day for a visit while on his way home to Boston.

Pia, with the Zimmerman's blessings, begged me to stay for dinner of a "genuine Thailand meal" she was cooking that night.

It was delicious but so spicy hot, tears began running down my cheeks as well as Lou's, the Zimmerman's, their daughters' Sharon, Vicki and Jane, and their sons' Francis and Bruce.

While wiping away our happy tears we noticed Pia's were continuing, accompanied by sobs.

"Pia is sad and homesick because this is the night of the Loy Krathong festival in her homeland," Lou explained, while comforting the "little girl."

"It is an ancient thanksgiving ceremony after the rice harvest is over in which her countrymen by the thousands kneel by riverbanks to launch little boats made of leaves containing bright flowers, a personal trinket and a lighted candle. When the rivers begin to gleam from the full moon and the candlelit voyages, signifying all your sins and cares are floating away, it is time for dancing, feasting and happiness."

At the Zimmermans, it was time for improvisation. It didn't matter

To Bucktail and Back . . .

we were 10,000 miles from Thailand or it was well below freezing and Battle Creek, from which the community got its name, was covered with ice.

While Mrs. Zimmerman and the girls created a little boat out of an aluminum pie tin and filled it with a candle and flowers from the dinner table bouquet, Mr. Zimmerman, his sons, and Lou and I chopped through the creek's ice, making a channel.

Then we all gathered on the creek bank as Lou helped Pia, shivering from the cold despite a heavy parka, light her candle. Then, beaming with delight at the tiny, flickering candle, Pia set her little boat afloat down by the railroad bridge on dark Battle Creek.

It was much more than perhaps the first-ever Loy Krathong celebration in Nebraska. The glow of love apparent between Pia and Lou intensified that night. They later married and had children, and live happily in Boston.

"Pia our 'little girl' still comes back to Battle Creek with Lou and their children to remember the night of one little candle. And she helps prepare Thailand dinners for our church suppers," Mrs. Zimmerman said.

The Good Samaritan

The Biblical admonition, "There is no greater love than that of a man willing to give his life for his fellow man" is best personified in a Sept. 7, 1964, story bearing the headline, "A Good Samaritan Is Lost":

Sometimes when an old name comes to mind a memory jumps up and hits you between the eyes.

Last May 5, I met truck driver Leonard Portis of Omaha at Shelby. The occasion was unforgettable. I had just barely outrun a tornado that cut a wide swath across the countryside.

I was a little shaky and had stopped to pick up a couple of truck drivers as I headed back to the path of destruction east of town. One was Leonard. He and his partner had seen the storm coming and stopped their truck. They piled in my car to see if we could help any victims.

The three of us were really shaken when we discovered trucks overturned and the farmhouse I had stopped at (to make a fast U-turn before gunning away from the funnel) had disappeared.

I remember Leonard saying, "Boy, you were lucky." I replied, "No, you guys were luckier besides being smarter. You saw it coming and stopped."

Big Leonard laughed.

The last time I saw him he and his buddy were helping extricate a trucker pinned in the cab of an overturned truck.

"Take it easy and stay lucky," he told me as I left to go in search of more victims. "Same to you, Lucky," I replied.

That was the name I remembered him by until a recent afternoon. A caller apologized for her interruption.

"My name," she said, "is Mrs. Leonard Portis. My husband often talked about you and the night of the tornado. He said you were the one who called him lucky."

The memory of big Leonard's laugh that night came back.

"Did you see the story about him?" she continued.

"I must have missed it," I said.

"They called him the Good Samaritan trucker," she said. "It happened last Saturday. He was driving on the freeway just outside Sacramento. He stopped for an accident up ahead. Then to be helpful, he started walking with a lighted flare to warn other motorists of the jam ahead.

"He was struck by a car driven by a drunken driver. Leonard lived but a few hours before he died. We buried him Wednesday at Nebraska City."

I felt numb.

"Could you help me?" Mrs. Portis asked. "The clipping of the wire service story from Sacramento listed his name as Norman Portis. I wouldn't mind too much but it is too ironic. They got it mixed up. Norman was the last name of the drunken driver who hit him. So could you tell the papers about the error?"

I promised I would and did.

I, too, was wrong. I'd called him Lucky Portis.

It was Leonard "Good Samaritan" Portis, a real right guy.

CHAPTER NINE

ONE NIGHT OF LOVE

In July 1997, my wife, Marilyn, and I ended a year's search in a military section of the cemetery at the village of Aix-Noulette among the poppy-bright fields of northern France.

Our goal was to provide a happier ending to the "one night of love" story of Robert "Robbie" Hunter, a young Scottish soldier, who was killed in World War I and buried in a foreign land far from the Ochil Hills of home, and his bride, Annie Allan (no relation to my family).

In several visits "hame" to Tillicoultry, Scotland, where Robbie, Annie and I were born, we had learned their poignant story. Residents seven decades later still recounted their love story in awed tones.

They were engaged to be married and had planned to migrate to Canada, but fate intervened. Annie's mother became terminally ill. They decided Annie would remain and care for her mother. Robbie would go to Canada to prepare a home for them and she would join and marry him after her mother's passing.

But World War I began before their dream was realized. Robbie joined a kilted Canadian Scottish regiment. By chance, it bivouacked near Tillicoultry en route to France. During a 24-hour furlough they were married and spent one night together. The next day Robbie sailed for France and was killed in an assault on a mountain of coal slag a few days later.

Heartbroken Annie never remarried. She lived out her years in Tillicoultry, working in a woolen mill and cheerfully serving her church and community in volunteer work. She always claimed one night of love with the man she loved was enough to last a lifetime.

In a previous visit it finally dawned on us the villagers were talking about my kin. Robbie was the only brother of my mother, Barbara Hunter. Although I vaguely remembered the Canadian version of the American Purple Heart, a wreathed cross my mother wore on a purple ribbon around her neck at tearful Armistice Day celebrations, I had not realized the connection.

My mother and all other relatives were long dead. I had a treasured photo of Robbie in his uniform kilt, but there were no other family records of which unit Robbie had served or where he lay in final rest.

We decided to find out and complete the last chapter in their love story. It took a lot of doing, especially since we didn't know Robbie's Army serial number. But the Canadian government officials also became enamored with the love story and were very helpful.

We wrote to the Canadian Commonwealth War Graves Commission and received a call from Marlene Moffatt saying they were having difficulty finding Robbie's grave because there had been so many casualties in 1917, including several named Robert Hunter. Two days later she called again, triumphantly announcing: "We've found him. He was a member of Ontario's famed 115th Battalion."

She not only sent us maps of the cemetery and the location of his grave, but said she had contacted the curator of the battalion's museum at nearby Oshawa, and he was eager to help. He told us Robbie was indeed a member of the battalion's honored dead and his name was read every year in Remembrance Day ceremonies.

"But I am puzzled by the copy of the photo you sent of your Robbie in a Highland uniform kilt. The battalion was not a kilted unit," he wrote. "Because of the high number of casualties the battalion sustained, I assume he was transferred to us from his Scottish unit as a replacement. I have taken the liberty to contact our war department in your name to send you his official record. I am enclosing a history of the battalion that details the battle of the coal slag hill in which he died."

Within a week we received Robbie's record confirming the transfer and a letter of gratitude for our family's sacrifice from Maj. Gen. M.G. Cloutier on behalf of Gilbert Parent, speaker of the Canadian House of Commons. Included was a color photograph of the page bearing Robbie's name in the Book of Remembrances kept in the Chapel of the Peace Tower of the Canadian Parliament.

Marilyn and I then journeyed to Tillicoultry where residents, particularly George and Marjorie Grieve, owners of the Castle Craig Hotel, went all out to assist us.

The Grieves found a distant cousin of Annie who found a photograph of her and escorted us to her grave.

At the County of Clackmannan courthouse the deputy registrar of records, told us: "Oh! What a wonderful story. I'll keep researching the records and won't stop until I find what you are seeking." She then spent all day and a night to find and copy by hand an extract of Robbie and Annie's marriage license.

After a long search, Allan brings a touch of Scotland to his Uncle "Robbie's" French grave site.

Then, fortified by multiple toasts of whiskey to "a brave Highland soldier and his lassie" from other hotel guests, we headed for France.

At the cemetery Patrick Booth, our English chauffeur – who used to cross Nebraska on I-80 as a truck driver – was as moved as we were.

Borrowing Marilyn's manicure scissors, he trimmed the red roses alongside the grave before photos were taken.

We played a tape recording of Scot balladeer Alex Beaton lamenting a Scottish soldier dying in a foreign land with:

> *"Now he's dying, his heart is crying because these are foreign hills. They are not the hills of home."*

Then we planted a sprig of purple heather we'd brought from the hills of home.

Finally, we sprinkled an envelope of earth on Robbie's grave that we had dug from the front yard of the home in which he was born. We added another we'd brought from Annie's grave.

After bowing our heads in a silent prayer, Annie and her Highland laddie, at long last, were together again.

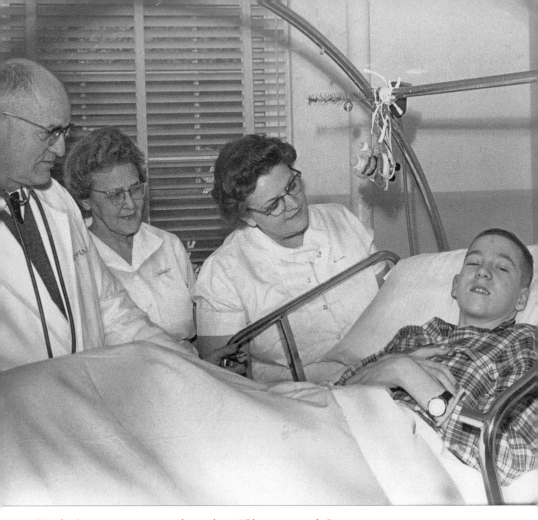

Douglas Stewart prepares to give his mother a "Christmas miracle."

CHAPTER TEN

MOTHERS' PRICELESS GIFTS

My favorite Christmas story was written Dec. 25, 1964.

Beatrice, Neb. – A miracle will have come to pass this Christmas Day at the Beatrice State Home (now known as the Beatrice State Development Center).

Mrs. John Stewart of Lynch will anxiously lean over a bed at the home's hospital to clutch the hand of her son, Douglas, 14.

Suddenly, she will feel the pressure of a hand clasping hers.

Douglas' eyes will open and from his lips will come three words, "Merry Christmas, Mother."

It will be the most priceless Christmas present a mother has ever known.

Douglas, believed by medical authorities to be doomed to a speechless, paralyzed "vegetative state" just a few short months ago, will surprise his mother with proof of a miraculous improvement.

His secret has been closely guarded for the past two weeks so he could surprise his mother and father on their Christmas Day visit.

Dr. Paul K. Mooring, Omaha pediatric cardiologist who gives some of his time and talent to the home, describes Douglas' improvement as a "dramatic change, a miracle."

Dr. H.M. Hepperlin, the home's clinical director, describes it as "fantastic."

Superintendent M.E. Wyant simply calls it "our Christmas miracle."

Last March 31, Douglas was an average, athletic-minded boy.

He and a friend decided to start a tractor in a farmyard near Monowi. It lurched forward, Douglas was thrown off and dragged under the wheels, and one wheel ran over his head.

He was rushed to a hospital with a severe brain injury. Major surgery was necessary. It was believed there had been irreparable brain damage, especially after several weeks with no improvement.

He was sent here to the home, arriving June 5.

A Million Miles of Memories   63

"He was a complete vegetable with paralysis of all extremities," Dr. Hepperlin said. "He had to be tube fed. We were told there was no hope for recovery.

"Then the remarkable recovery began. There was nothing special we did medically. I'm sure the main thing was tender, loving care and kindness, and having other youngsters around. The entire state took a special interest in this boy. Somehow he became inspired and motivated."

Both Superintendent Wyant and Dr. Hepperlin give much of the credit to two nurses aides, Mrs. Hazel Gaines and Mrs. Salome Pribyl, who provided much more than tender, loving care.

Mrs. Gaines, who works the day shift, "became a special mother to him," Dr. Hepperlin said.

Mrs. Gaines said: "We had been told there would be no response from Douglas. But every day I'd go to his room and talk to him. It must have been about three months before there was any indication that he was even aware of me. Then I noticed he followed me with his eyes.

"Later his only response was little whine-like sounds. I told him, 'Douglas, if you can make those sounds, you can make words instead.' We just kept working and slowly he did. It is still hard, but he's progressing rapidly.

"He told me he'd like to get back to school and is worried about the work he's missing. He said that because of all the kindness and things done for him here, he should be a doctor. But he thinks maybe he would like to be what he had his heart set on before, an architect.

"He decided a couple of weeks ago he wanted to surprise his mother and dad by telling them 'Merry Christmas.' Believe me, this really makes Christmas complete for me. I'm so very happy."

Thus the "miracle" came to pass this Christmas morning as his mother leaned over his bed expecting nothing but a silent, blank stare, Douglas' fingers suddenly squeezed her hand. Haltingly came the words, "Merry Christmas, Mother."

Dr. Hepperlin said it was still impossible to determine how complete his recovery will be.

"Most encouraging is his recovery of speech, usually the last to come back. His recovery has been so dramatic, I'm sure he'll be walking and I'm sure he'll be back in school one of these days."

When Wyant introduced me to Douglas on Christmas Eve and I had taken photos of him and his nursing aides, he seemed a little apprehensive. When I assured him the story and pictures of his surprise gift would be kept until Christmas Day, he smiled and placed thumb against forefinger in a traditional OK sign.

And then loud and clear, "Merry Christmas."

There were heartwarming follow-ups on Douglas, such as returning home, catching up on his school work and graduating from Lynch High School with his class in 1969.

In January 1971 I found him at the University of Nebraska-Lincoln working in the Abel Hall cafeteria. Although there was still a slight slowness of speech and a tilt of the head, he had fully recovered. He said he planned to become a nurse.

A few years later I found him teaching a special education class at Lincoln's Southeast High School. On my last visit with him, he had returned to Lynch where he was promoting his hometown as a member of its Community Improvement Committee.

A Mom's Agony Belonged to Someone Else

On March 4, 1968, I wrote a bittersweet story.

Grand Island, Neb. – "Hello, Mother!"

Those precious words uttered here Saturday night may never have sounded more heavenly to a woman.

For the words and a spontaneous bear hug were confirmation that could never be denied for Mrs. Rodney Johnson that her son, Marine Pfc. Michael (Mike) David, 20, was indeed alive and safe in her arms once more.

Pentagon officialdom had broken her heart Feb. 20 by erroneously reporting that Mike had died in a Japanese hospital from wounds suffered in Vietnam.

True, there had been a hurried correction and apologies that had turned grief to happiness for Mr. and Mrs. Johnson of Grand Island and their other children, Pam, 17, Gary, 13, and Craig, 18, who had been rushed home on emergency leave from his Air Force base in Homestead, Fla.

There had been heartwarming phone calls from Mike. First, that the wound in his shoulder was not serious; then an even better one Saturday morning.

"Mom, I'm at Oakland, California, and I'll be home tonight."

But nothing matched the complete happiness as Mrs. Johnson broke from the arms of her husband as her blond-haired son literally bounded down the steps of Frontier flight 564 – seven minutes late at 9:32 p.m. – and engulfed her in his arms.

They stood in that embrace for a moment as tears streamed down his

mother's face and the proud
Marine, looking much younger
than his 20 years, fought back
happy tears of his own.

"It feels great to be home,"
he said.

And as his father had done
before him, he indicated there was
no bitterness in the two errors that
had shaken his family with sorrow.
The first had been when he was
erroneously reported evacuated to
the Bethesda Naval Hospital and
the second when he was reported
dead.

"I'm just sorry it happened,"
Mike said. "I'm sorry for my folks
and now mainly for the other family involved."

*Mr. and Mrs. Rodney Johnson welcome their son,
Marine Pfc. Michael David Johnson, home after he was
erroneously reported killed in Vietnam.*

His father, a dairy employee
here, had purposely tried to stay in the background at the happy homecoming. He is an ex-Marine.

"This is a very happy occasion," he said. "You might call it a story-
book ending to a nightmare."

And then reflectively, he added, "Of course, our happiness means
someone else has heartbreak tonight."

Mike, showing no effects of his wounds, said he planned to spend a
30-day furlough "relaxing mostly" and then added: "At the end of my furlough, I'll go back to Oakland to see if I'm physically fit. If I am, I'll go to
Treasure Island for re-assignment."

The young Marine didn't hesitate when asked if he'd care to go back
to Vietnam, saying, "No, I wouldn't mind, if I could get back to my old unit,
C Company of the First Tank Battalion of the First Marine Division."

Parents' Sad News

There was a sadder story to cover on Oct. 24, 1983.

Dwight, Neb. – The bells tolled at Assumption Catholic Church
here and tears continued for Marvin and Maryann Helms as they tried to
accept the death of their son, Marine Pfc. Mark Helms.

Young Helms, just 20, died in the terrorist attack on the Marine barracks at Beirut early Sunday.

"I think there are no tears left, but they keep coming back," said the Marine's mother Tuesday morning. "I wonder if we'll ever get over this pain. It is such a waste when they die so young."

Holding his wife's hand and clutching a color portrait of his son, Helms smiled proudly through his tears and added: "Want to see an ideal American? Take a look at this picture."

The hours following the news of the bombing of the Marine barracks had been agonizing for the couple as they waited in their home on the edge of town. The wait ended Monday morning when two Marines from Omaha appeared at their front door.

The Helms said they had a premonition of the worst.

"We got up about 6:30 a.m. Sunday to get ready to go to church," Mrs. Helms said. "For some reason, I had this pain within me. Then Marv heard the news and said, 'Oh my God, the Marines have been hit.' I told him something tells me this is it for Mark. He's not coming home."

Helms, who retired in 1981 as a master sergeant after 20 years in the Air Force, said they knew from their son's detailed letters that he slept just above the front door of the demolished building.

"So we knew that if he was working, he was OK. If he was in the barracks, he was dead," he said.

Mrs. Helms added: "I had a feeling and sat up all night waiting for the news to come. It was strange, but a couple of months ago I had a dream Mark died and I saw him in his Marine uniform lying in a casket."

Word spreads quickly in small towns.

The Rev. Gerald Vap, pastor of the Helms' church, informed coffee drinkers at Cy's Cafe that a special Mass would be held at noon Monday.

"Everybody called everybody else. The bells began tolling at the church. The flag was lowered in front of the post office, and I think the whole town cried a little," said Cy Nemec, the cafe operator.

A Happier Return

It was a happier return to Loup City on Feb. 5, 1981, for Marine Staff Sgt. Michael Moeller and his parents, Mr. and Mrs. Keith Moeller.

He came to his yellow-ribbon-bedecked hometown for a welcoming parade attended by more than 3,000 after he and 51 other Americans were held hostage in Iran for 444 days.

There were no thoughts of revenge in his heart during the joyous occasion.

"I'm basically not a bitter person," he said. "They did some terrible things but, I believe, leave them to their own devices and they will harm themselves. We don't need to look for revenge.

In his first interview since his release, Moeller, with his wife, Elisa, and his parents by his side, said: "As a Marine I did a job, and I don't want anyone to make me a hero. I don't feel I am a victim as much or a hero. The biggest thing is I'm a U.S. Marine."

He told the crowd: "I now realize what's been on my mind and heart all along. That is that there is no greater feeling a man can feel than the one he gets when he comes home. This welcome brings tears to my eyes and true love in my heart."

CHAPTER ELEVEN

NIXON WAS AN ALRIGHT GUY

A reporter's fringe benefit is the opportunity to rub shoulders with nation-al figures, from presidents to ambassadors and assorted VIPs.

Such personal contacts often provide a different view than seen by the general public.

Such was my experience in a meeting on April 15, 1971, with President Richard M. Nixon at the White House. It happened a little more than three years before his Aug. 9, 1974, resignation in disgrace after Watergate revelations.

Nixon was widely lampooned by the news media as "Tricky Dick." But to 31-year-olds Robert and Richard Santin of Fullerton, who became nationally known as the "Try Harder Twins," Nixon was a warm, compas-sionate and humble "alright guy."

Perhaps no other president ever got down on his knees for visiting dignitaries, but Nixon did to pay homage to a couple of Nebraska farm-raised youth.

The President had to stoop to praise them eye-to-eye because the twins' bodies had been twisted by muscular dystrophy since birth, and they were held captive in their wheelchairs.

But the disease was no deterrent to the active minds of the fun-lov-ing twins. They were electronic geniuses, who as small boys established a communication system to learn their "3 R's." Their lessons were broadcast via radio transmission from a one-room school to their farm home by a sys-tem they had designed.

Then they established their own company. Driven by an aide, they went throughout Nebraska setting up the first radio communication systems for county sheriffs and the Civil Defense Administration.

The president knelt to present them a plaque and to honor them as the 1971 Handicapped Americans of the Year.

The twins had been disappointed the night before when Nixon, because of a meeting with the German and Moroccan ambassadors, was

Fullerton, Neb., Santin twins Richard (right) and Robert receive the 1971 Handicapped American of the Year award from President Richard Nixon in the White House Rose Garden.

unable to award them the honor at a banquet sponsored by the president's Committee on Employment of the Handicapped at Washington's Hilton Hotel.

They received a standing ovation by the 4,000 attendees, were honored by national TV commentator Howard K. Smith in a "Tribute To Courage" and presented the award by Labor Secretary James G. Hogsdson on behalf of the President.

Since I had written several stories on the twins and had become their close friend, they had invited me and my wife, Marilyn, to the banquet. The World-Herald made it an assignment.

The twins' big surprise came early the next morning when they were given a personal wake-up call by the president.

"We couldn't believe it," Richard said when he called me. "The president of the United States called to apologize for not being able to attend the banquet. He said he wanted a piece of the action and asked if we could meet him in the White House Rose Garden at 10:30 a.m. today. He invited our family and when I asked him if you could come, too, he said, 'Sure, bring him along.' "

When I got to the White House I discovered Jack Jarrell, The World-Herald's Washington bureau chief, not only had made arrangements for my admittance, but told me I was to be the only reporter present. I'd be the "pool reporter," reporting to the Washington press corps what happened in the Rose Garden.

It was a simple ceremony that became touching. Awaiting the president's arrival with the twins were their widowed father, Robert Santin Sr., a Nebraska farmer who "didn't mind a bit missing chores" on his farm eight miles north of Fullerton; the twins' sister, Marilyn, who had flown in from her teaching post in Venezuela for the occasion, and Miss Jennie Kreidler, their schoolteacher who had retired as Nance County's school superintendent.

Also present were Nebraska Sens. Carl Curtis and Roman Hruska, and the official White House photographer.

Nixon was quiet and formal when he praised the twins for their "courage and example" and first stooped to present them their plaque. Then he unwound in joyous laughter as he and the twins engaged in a "horse-trading session."

It began when Richard looked Nixon in the eye and said: "Mr. President, Nebraska is number one in agriculture, number one in livestock and, as of this year, number one in football. It was the first to have a Unicameral and the first in support of President Nixon in the last presidential election. So we want you to have this."

At the twins' bidding Nixon knelt so they could pin one of the new Nebraska No. 1 pins on his lapel.

"You've got it all in Nebraska, including you two. This is indeed Nebraska's year," said the delighted president before completing the "horse trade" by dispatching a Secret Service agent on the run to bring a special package. He completed the swap by saying, "I've got something for you," before presenting the twins a tie clasp and cuff links bearing the presidential seal.

Nixon sent the agent on the run again to get a similar gift for the twins' father after he was introduced. The puffing agent was dispatched again to get presidential seal pendants for their sister and teacher after Nixon met them.

When I was introduced by Sens. Curtis and Hruska, I told the president I was bringing best wishes from Fred Seaton, the Hastings publisher and old friend, who had served in the Eisenhower administration.

"Hey!" gasped Nixon. "Fred doesn't have a set of my cuff links." Then after dispatching the agent on the run again, Nixon added, "I'm giving you a presidential commission to personally deliver a set to Fred with my fondest regards."

I'll always remember the look of the sweating agent's face and the grin of the twins' faces when Nixon grabbed my hand and said, "You are a member of the press I like. You also need a set of my cuff links," and sent the agent sprinting again.

The twins summed it up with, "It has been the best day of our lives." We all agreed.

Late on the night Nixon made his resignation speech on national television I received a telephone call from Robert. He was crying.

"Tom," he said between sobs. "President Nixon can't be as bad as all the media reports say. He was an alright guy to us, wasn't he?"

I assured him with: "Yes. To us, Nixon was and always will be an alright guy."

Everybody Liked Ike – and Mamie

Thanks to the late Fred Seaton, publisher of the Hastings Tribune, who had been President Eisenhower's Secretary of Interior, I got to traipse along with Seaton and his wife on Ike and Mamie's first tour of the Eisenhower Presidential Library in Abilene, Kan., on May 1, 1962. I wrote:

Abilene, Kan. – Mamie Eisenhower had the last word here Tuesday. "I'm simply fascinated," she said.

She summed up the feelings of her husband, Dwight D. Eisenhower, and the crowd of 25,000 people who jammed this town of 7,130 for the dedication of the $3 million Eisenhower Presidential Library.

There was no doubt that Ike and Mamie had spent one of their happiest days as they combined a visit – his first as plain Mr. Eisenhower – to his hometown, with the ceremony at which the library, built by donations and the state of Kansas, was turned over to the federal government.

Ike, a picture of robust health, acted like a kid at a circus as he stood on the reviewing stand watching the parade, and later was given a tour of the building which houses papers and artifacts of his presidential years.

It was the first time he had a chance to visit his home without the restricting arms of Secret Service men. And it was the first time the home folks could break through the ranks of more understanding police to grab his hand, snap a picture or get autographs.

If he had any disappointment it was when a float of his old Lincoln Elementary School passed the reviewing stand. Sitting at her desk on the float was Miss Emma Hasshagen, his fifth-grade teacher, long retired.

"Oh, I wish I could get down there," said Ike, glancing at the review stand's high railing.

During his library tour he excitedly discovered old mementos and delightedly pointed them out to Mamie.

"Oh-oh," he said, looking at an old painting of him in his general's uniform. "I've never quite liked that as well as some others."

Mamie, looking as sparkling as an enthusiastic coed, acted like one.

She excitedly greeted Fred Seaton of Hastings, Ike's Secretary of Interior, with an affectionate hug and a kiss on the cheek.

Seaton wasn't sure which he liked better – the greeting or being escorted by Ike into a replica of the Oval Office to inspect his presidential desk. They laughed when Ike opened the bottom-right drawer and gasped, "What happened to the bottle of cough medicine I used to keep in here?"

There were some solemn moments. Ike and Mamie stole away from the crowd after lunch to visit his mother's grave. The dedication ceremonies marked the 100th anniversary of her birth.

Ike's Sad Farewell

I returned seven years later to write an April 3, 1969, story on the sad adieu by thousands to Ike at his last rites.

Abilene, Kan. – Chris Lindsay, an 11-year-old towhead from nearby Salina, climbed a light pole Wednesday, and despite a chilly north wind, clung to it for an hour and a half near the little Union Pacific Railroad station here.

Chris watched wide-eyed as another small-town boy long since grown to manhood and world renown, came home for the last time.

Chris was one of the estimated 100,000 persons who came to this prairie town of 7,000 to watch, if even from afar, the final rites for Dwight David Eisenhower – president, general and statesman.

A young Vietnam War veteran was in the Veterans of Foreign Wars section in the throng across town at Eisenhower Center. He stood throughout the solemn military ceremonies, teetering on his crutch as the wind whipped an empty trouser leg.

At better vantage points were President Richard M. Nixon and his predecessor, Lyndon B. Johnson, as well as other high governmental and military figures from throughout the nation and world.

Johnson, a surprise visitor, pulled up in a white sedan almost under little Chris' perch just before Ike's flag-draped steel coffin was removed from the 10-car special at the station.

There was a hurried shuffle to insert the Johnson car in the procession of black limousines in the brief period between the trainside ceremony and the start of the solemn procession to Eisenhower Center.

Chris Lindsay climbs a lamp post for a last look at a hometown hero.

Many Nebraskans were on hand to honor an outstanding neighbor.

They were led by Gen. Alfred M. Gruenther, formerly of Platte Center, who was Ike's former chief of staff. He was an honorary pallbearer.

Officially representing Nebraska were Gov. and Mrs. Norbert Tiemann, state Sen. Jerome Warner of Waverly, speaker of the Legislature, and Adj. Gen. Welch.

They sat among the 220 VIPs for the funeral service in front of the Eisenhower Presidential Library.

The library is a block down the flower-fringed mall from the tiny Chapel of Meditation, where a short, private service for the family, Nixon and Johnson, and close friends ended the five-day national farewell with a booming 21-gun salute and the mournful bugling of "Taps."

As the bugle stilled, the only sound was the splatter of water in the fountain in front of the chapel.

Then President Eisenhower, in the soldier's Ike jacket he loved, was laid to rest in the chapel's crypt just across the street from the two-story white home where he was raised.

The large crowd showed the public affection for the Abilene boy who now belongs to history. The dignified silence and tears many shed along the procession route and during the service showed their respect.

Little Chris described it just as eloquently after climbing down from his perch. "I'm a little guy and I wanted to see 'cause Ike was a pretty great man."

The ceremonies were strictly a military show. It was done with pomp, ceremony and split-second precision.

Most people were cordoned off by ranks of soldiers and kept about a block away. Few could hear the formal words of farewell, but they heard the military commands, the hymns played by the 5th Army Band, the booming guns and "Taps."

When the ceremony was over and the Army's regulatory grip was released, the crowd swarmed over the mall. Many stripped the red, white and blue carnations from the portico in front of the chapel. Men, women and children plucked flowers planted the night before from both sides of the block-long sidewalk leading to the chapel.

An Army sergeant, wearing the ribbons of three wars, said, "Now I've seen everything."

But there were those who felt it was unwitting desecration. They were seeking one last token, however fragile, of a man they loved and respected.

Like the flowers taken, that memory will fade. Remaining forever will be the recall of the dignity and beauty of a nation's farewell to Dwight David Eisenhower.

Harry Did Give 'Em Hell

President Harry Truman lived up to the "Give 'em hell, Harry" description in two visits to Omaha in his post-presidential years that I was privileged to cover.

The national news media had given him the moniker after he had angrily described a music critic as an "SOB" after a review panning daughter Margaret's concert singing debut.

The old World War I artillery battery captain was just as peppery and his language as salty in the two visits with an old Omaha Army buddy.

During his first visit, covered by the late photographer John Savage and me, he greeted us as we entered the presidential suite of Omaha's old Fontenelle Hotel, with: "Come on in boys. I've got to show you something funny as hell."

He led us to the bathroom where he had delightedly discovered a wall telephone had been installed next to the toilet.

"I've been sitting on the throne this morning calling all my old Republican adversaries and telling them to listen to my words of advice. Then I flush the john," he said.

On another visit, photographer Pat Hall and I accompanied him on one of his famous early morning walks straight up the Douglas Street hill at a fast pace.

Before we took out, he'd been greeted warmly by Democratic faithful in the hotel lobby. They roared, when after turning down a request for an autograph, Truman replied: "I ain't gonna do it and I'll tell you why. You let one dog pee on a fireplug and every other dog wants to do the same."

After the brisk hike, Hall, who had recently had the cast removed from a broken leg, gasped, "Mr. President, I hope when I'm as old as you are I'll be half as spry."

The grinning Truman replied: "Son, I'll tell you how to do it. Watch what you put in your gut and watch what you put your pecker in."

Naturally, neither comment made it into the family newspaper. I've often wondered if modern television would show the same restraint.

CHAPTER TWELVE

FOLKSY QUEEN

Queen Margarethe II of Denmark was beautiful and as comfortable as an old shoe during her visit to Blair's Dana College on May 19, 1976.

Her majesty came to the college, with its rich Danish heritage, to receive an honorary Doctor of Letters degree during graduation ceremonies at Viking Field. Her commencement address was her only public speech during a three-week visit to America. She was accompanied by her husband, Prince Henrik.

Blair was agog and all gussied up for the visit of the world's youngest reigning queen at age 36. Many in the crowd of 10,000 had helped turn Blair into Copenhagen, the Danish capital, for the day and applauded wildly as the queen praised the "free, independently minded" Danish immigrants who made America their home. Many in attendance were descendants of Danish immigrants who the queen said "helped make America great."

And they were delighted that despite all the protocol, the royal pomp and ceremony and the tight Danish and U.S. Secret Service security, the queen was no fairy tale.

She wore a commoner's dress and had trouble with her Nordic blonde hair in the stiff afternoon breeze before donning the mantle, cap and gown to receive her doctorate.

At the post-graduation reception, she had the same difficulty as a commoner trying to balance a cup of coffee, Danish cookies and a cigarette.

Despite her girlish laughter, she exuded an aura of dignified humbleness. How humble? It was best described by Dana's own "queen," Alice Laaker, the dean of women and "Mother Superior" of Mickelsen Hall coeds.

I had kidded Mrs. Laaker as being "Keeper of the Royal Privy Council" when she was assigned by the security forces to guard a powder room assigned to the queen. Mrs. Laaker supplied it with imported Danish soap and special hand towels she had sewn.

After the queen had used the facilities, Mrs. Laaker whispered to me: "Her Highness left me a sweet note of thanks. But instead of my soap and towels she used the regular soap dispenser and paper towels. She is indeed a wonderful, down-to-earth, folksy queen!"

Shunning a Prince

My wife, Marilyn, never forgave me for relating in my July 24, 1994, Byways column how she had not only shunned Great Britain's Prince Andrew, but had brushed him aside.

Her royal faux pas occurred at Scotland's Turnberry, a week before the famed golf resort hosted the 1994 British Open.

While seated in the parlor waiting to be called to dinner, I casually mentioned to her that two of the men standing at the bar were Nick Faldo, winner of three British Opens and Masters golf tourneys, and Prince Andrew. I knew they often played a round of golf together.

She recognized Faldo, but told me emphatically: "The other is not Prince Andrew. He's short and pudgy. The men of British royalty are skinny and have sharp facial features."

My "Why do you think they call Prince Andrew 'Teddy Bear'?" fell on deaf ears and I became engrossed in my cocktail.

Then I realized my mate, who always greeted everyone as a long-lost friend, was no longer by my side. I gasped as I saw her making a beeline for Faldo as he and the prince were being ushered into the dining room. I shook my head in dismay as she brushed the prince aside to grab Faldo's hand to say, "Good luck from America's heartland in the upcoming Open."

Then, brushing the Prince aside again, she led the grinning Faldo toward me, saying: "Mr. Faldo, I would like you to meet my husband. He is also a golfer!"

It was one of the nicest things she ever said about me. But I couldn't savor the moment of shaking hands with a real golfer as I looked over his shoulder at the prince left cooling his heels.

By the time we were led to the dining room, the entire hotel staff had heard about the royal slight and were smiling. So was Faldo, seated with the prince just a table away. He and Marilyn exchanged gay waves.

I didn't help when I said to Marilyn, "See those two gentlemen standing by the door? They are members of the British Service and I've been informed we're leaving in the morning because our visas have been canceled for slighting a member of the British royal family."

Still adamant, she summoned the maitre d' for confirmation of the man seated with Faldo. The smiling maitre d' bowed and whispered, "Madam, he is the Duke of York. He is the second son of Queen Elizabeth II.

He is, indeed, Prince Andrew."

Marilyn gasped and exclaimed: "Oh, my God. I'm going over to apologize!" It took all my strength to restrain her.

She got some consolation when the royal party left the dining room. The chuckling Faldo detoured past our table to greet her with: "Mrs. Allan, it was a distinct pleasure to meet you. Have a most pleasant evening and good night."

For some reason, Marilyn didn't appreciate it when I conned a distinguished fellow passenger on our homebound Queen Elizabeth II into posing as a U.S. State Department official. When he told her he was investigating a "recent breach of U.S.-British protocol," she replied, not so sweetly, "Get lost!"

CHAPTER THIRTEEN

DOWN-HOME AMBASSADOR

In 1970, when my wife and I were vacationing in Scotland, we made a detour to accept an invitation to be guests of Ambassador Val Peterson and his wife, Elizabeth, at the U.S. Embassy at Helsinki, Finland.

The following is my July 24, 1970, story:

Helsinki, Finland – The U.S. Ambassador to Finland a few months ago heard the sounds of a flag being lowered from the flagpole in the embassy courtyard.

The ambassador, seated with his wife on the patio, turned to see a young U.S. Marine performing the daily sunset ceremony.

Waiting until the Marine had folded the flag, the ambassador then called to him, "Son, I want you to do me a favor."

"Yes, sir!"

"I want you to never do that without first informing me. I want all of my guests, whatever we are doing at the time, to come out on the patio with me to stand at attention and pay respect to that flag of ours, whoever they may be or where they come from."

Since that day, officials of governments from around the world have participated in the simple but touching ceremony to pay respects not only to the U.S. flag, but to former Nebraska schoolteacher, newspaper editor, governor and President Eisenhower cabinet member, Val Peterson.

"Nothing I've done has created more comment," Peterson said. "I've seen grown men cry during the ceremony."

The ceremony is typical of the way Peterson has served as ambassador to two nations – Denmark from 1957 to 1961, and now Finland.

Also typical was the folksy "Welcome to Nebraska" greeting Peterson, who prefers to be called just Val, gave to Gerald Smith and his U.S. delegation to the Strategic Arms Limitation Talks (SALT) with Russia here last November.

So, too, was the cutting of red tape when, during the SALT conference, he proposed to his Russian counterpart, "Let's go Dutch," in hosting a joint reception, the first in history for the two nations.

"The Russian ambassador lives just down the street in a big palace, so I thought he could afford it," Peterson said. "After I explained to him that 'going Dutch' meant sharing the reception's expenses, he readily agreed. But it took several weeks before an OK came from his wary bosses at the Kremlin.

"It was a great success. It gave both sides a chance to relax and let their hair down during the strict protocol of the meetings," Peterson said, grinning and patting his balding pate.

Peterson also delighted Finnish officials – as well as those from other nations – by staging a Fourth of July celebration in his embassy's yard.

Peterson didn't forget his staff of 60 Americans and about 60 Finns, plus Americans from the local business community.

Wearing a cowboy shirt, Peterson staged the embassy's first old-fashioned picnic with hot dogs, hamburgers, bingo games, foot races and patriotic speeches.

In frequent trips around the country, Peterson also delights Finns, from mayors to waiters, with greetings in Finnish.

But the bicycle he pedaled around Copenhagen when he was ambassador to Denmark is gathering dust in the embassy garage.

"I discovered I'm getting older and Finnish motorists drive with more gusto and abandon," he explained.

Here he uses the dexterity he once used on his Danish bike to maintain the proper diplomatic balance between the U.S., Russia and the officially neutral Finns.

"The job is much more sensitive here because of Finland's 900-mile border with Russia. It is but 187 air miles to Leningrad. Since they cannot escape geography, the Finns chose to remain outside of Cold War tensions and alliances," Peterson said.

"They have had 42 wars in 970 years against the Swedes and Russians. Finland is the only country to have been defeated by Russia and still remain independent. It's like our old saying, 'If you don't whip them and still don't want to join them, you must at least be friendly and maintain a good neighbor policy.' They have to play it cool."

Strict neutrality is the official Finnish policy. But people in the street, still bitter about the 1939 Winter War with Russia and the stiff reparations demanded by the Russians, often do not disguise their feelings.

When I asked a Finn about the towering statue of a long-gowned woman alongside the waterfront, he replied: "It's supposed to be Mother Russia and was given to us by Russia as a 'gift of friendship,' but to us it is like having a wart on the end of your nose. We try to overlook it."
Mostly, there is a feeling of warmth for the Americans.

However, the ambassador said some embassy windows were broken during an anti-Vietnam War demonstration by about 50 students. Police still patrol the adjoining streets.

"But otherwise, here there is very little anti-Americanism, certainly in comparison to that in Sweden," Peterson said. "There is a great reservoir of good feeling toward Americans."

The ambassador assessed his relationship with Finland's officials and his Russian neighbors as both "excellent and extremely pleasant."

Peterson told a touring group from Scottsbluff's Hiram Scott College led by former Nebraska state Sen. Marvin Stromer, that he felt the most important task in his first year here was being co-host to the SALT conference. Although not a participant in the talks, he was responsible for the American arrangements.

"So far, the talks currently continuing in Vienna are running as well as they did here," he said. "So we'll be ready for them when they come back here, possibly in September or October. I think they are the most important talks in the world.

"Just think what it would mean if the two giants of the world got together on disarmament. Cold War tensions would be eased and," he paused and grinned, "it might even cut taxes back in Nebraska."

In addition to his official duties, Peterson helps his wife, Omaha-born Elizabeth, run the embassy which they have dubbed "The Helsinki Cornhusker." The Petersons have been hosts to scores of touring Nebraskans.

Shortage of space for formal receptions in the Williamsburg-style, two-story embassy upsets Mrs. Peterson. And she has the same housewife problem she had back in Nebraska – the ambassador is shocked by the grocery bills.

"I have to keep reminding him we only get groceries four times a year from a U.S. Army commissary in Germany," she said. "I also have to remind him I have to make the list big if he wants to eat and, believe me, he's a U.S. ambassador who likes to eat."

Ambassador Peterson diplomatically declined to reply.

Ambassadorial Status

Covering the Byways can lead to a lot of places – from deep in the Amazon jungle to the U.S. Embassy at Helsinki, Finland.

Once there you can find yourself pressed into extracurricular jobs.

After finding Fullerton's Dr. James Maly a thousand miles deep in the jungle at his clinic for Mundurucu Indians, he put me to work helping give immunizations.

But Ambassador Val Peterson gave me a more professional, if fleeting, job in Finland.

I became U.S. Ambassador to Finland for 10 seconds.

My wife and I were guests at the embassy while I wrote a story on his ambassadorship. He suggested I interview him at breakfast served on the patio. It was his favorite spot in bright, warm sunshine after six long months of winter.

Befitting his rank, I dressed in a suit and tie. Val, beloved for his folksy informality, showed up in pajamas, dressing gown and bare feet.

After we had munched and talked for a few moments, a busload of American tourists pulled up outside the embassy's garden wall.

"This is your American embassy," blared the tour director over the bus loudspeaker. "And, we are in luck. That must be your ambassador eating his breakfast!"

Val, his bare feet up on a chair, didn't miss a bite of toast as he whispered urgently to me, "Stand up and wave!"

"Ambassador" Allan did. The tourists cheered. Val, still munching his toast, grinned.

CHAPTER FOURTEEN

MOVIE STAR GAZING

I received a call in May 1967 from Marv Stromer, a former state senator who had become a political science professor at Scottsbluff's short-lived Hiram Scott College.

"We need you to come out and have a date with Broadway and Hollywood movie star Vivian Blaine," he said. "Our drama professor has lured her to replay her lead role of Lola in our campus production of 'Damn Yankees.' She's a history buff and we want you to take her to Fort Robinson State Park between performances."

Wow! Heeding the show's hit song, "What Lola Wants, Lola Gets," I sped out to make sure she got.

She was a delight.

Before leaving Scottsbluff for the fort she asked me, "Could we please stop for one of my very favorite double-dipped chocolate ice cream cones?" She explained that in New York City it was difficult for her to go to a soda fountain without having to stop and sign autographs.

Lickin' and slurpin' we sped north to the fort where I discovered she indeed was a frontier history buff. She was enthralled when we arrived at the very moment an archeological crew unearthed some original timbers from the old guard house where Crazy Horse was bayoneted by a nervous soldier when he balked at being led in the door.

Park Superintendent John Kurtz got a kiss on the cheek when he presented her a treasured sliver of historic wood. It was a reason he and other park employees turned a deaf ear when I said her director had promised to shoot me if I didn't get her back in time to get ready for the evening's performance.

Belatedly, we sped south singing a duet, "Home on the Range." Just at the moment Vivian asked, "Do antelope really play out here?" a buck and a doe antelope appeared on a bluff alongside the highway.

Before I could say, "Yep, take a look." Vivian yelled, "Stop the car!" and bounded out the door. She was so excited and enchanted she grabbed me and gave me a kiss. Despite the delay, I was the enchanted one because from that moment she began calling me "Luv" instead of Tom.

It was a much nicer name than the glares of Stromer and the director implied as we finally pulled up at her motel, especially since Lola wanted and got: "Please, Luv. One more double-dipped ice cream cone." Stromer and the director were speechless when we pulled up lickin' the cones. She made her curtain call with moments to spare. But the best was yet to come.

En route she had told me she longed for a "homey, family atmosphere where I can kick off my shoes and relax." It was an impossible wish in busy New York and Hollywood, she said.

Again, what Lola wanted, Lola got.

I asked Jack Lewis, publisher of the Gering Courier, and his wife to entertain Miss Blaine after the night's performance at their ranch southeast of town.

"Great," he replied. "But you better call Carol Ann and explain. She won't believe me."

When I called and asked Carol Ann, "How would you like to entertain a movie star tonight?" she curtly replied, "You and Jack cut the drinks and get out of that bar" and hung up.

She was speechless with her mouth gaping in disbelief, when after the show Jack and I pulled into their driveway in his pickup with Vivian between us in the front seat. Carol Ann was in the yard, barefoot, clad in an old smock and chasing baby ducklings back to their pen when we arrived.

Vivian was delighted and the two women immediately hit it off. Jack and I were ignored – except for initial angry glares from Carol Ann – as Vivian kicked off her shoes and helped tidy up the kitchen. The movie star even begged for a starring role in changing the diaper, feeding and burping Tamas, the Lewis' infant son, who is now a Lincoln painter and bartender.

Completely ignored as the women talked nonstop around the kitchen table, Jack and I fell asleep on living room sofas. They woke us up before dawn for a scrambled egg and bacon breakfast Vivian insisted on cooking.

She wrote me later thanking me for "the best day and night I'll remember."

Gordie Became a Nebraska Fan
Gordon MacRae, the Broadway and Hollywood star of "Oklahoma!" was perched on seed sacks chawing with farmers down at the elevator when I first met him at Sterling on Feb. 11, 1969.

The New York state native had "come home" for the first time with his wife, Elizabeth, and their 9-month-old daughter, Amanda Mercedes, to visit Mrs. MacRae's dad, E.R. Lambert, a retired superintendent of the Consumer's Public Power District, and her mom, of Sterling.

Mrs. MacRae had hoped to keep the visit a secret, forgetting you can't keep secrets in a small town. Within a few hours her husband met and became friends with everybody in town.

Among his favorites was Clara Podburg, a national star in her own right. My story on her being the nation's oldest soda jerk after 48 years tending Uncle Charlie Gordon's old-fashioned soda fountain, had made the front pages of the National Druggist Association's magazine.

"Clara not only makes the best sodas I've ever tasted, but she's the best information booth in town. She filled me in on everybody and everything going on for miles around," MacRae said.

Later, after a folksy stroll down the main street, he led his father-in-law and me into a local tavern with, "Watch, you got to see this to believe."

As the bartender served us glasses of beer, MacRae plunked down a $10 bill with another admonition to watch. He broke out in his well-remembered "Oklahoma" song, "Oh what a beautiful morning," when the bartender gave him $9.10 in change. "Can you believe that?" he said. "Thirty cents for a glass of beer. Back in New York City a bartender would have told me my 10 bucks wasn't enough."

Sterling has never been the same and neither was Nebraska or the MacRaes. They retired in Lincoln, where before his death "Gordie" became a rabid Husker football fan and led Memorial Stadium fans many times in singing the national anthem.

Never-to-Be-Forgotten Kiss

Screen star Robert Taylor, a Filley native, never forgot his home state and visited several times. The wife of Grand Island's Dick Kingman, still hasn't come down from blissful heaven after one visit.

Taylor, a graduate of Crete's Doane College, returned to the campus as an artist-in-residence for a week, and accepted a role as narrator for "The Grand Island Story," an annual Chamber of Commerce production. It was followed by a private party at Dreisbach's Steakhouse.

Kingman, the chamber president, announced it was a special night because he and his wife were celebrating their wedding anniversary.

Goaded by the crowd to "kiss her," Kingman gave her a husbandly peck on the cheek.

Taylor, shouted, "No, no!" and, gathering Mrs. Kingman in his arms, said: "That is not the proper way to kiss a beautiful woman. Greta Garbo would have killed me in 'Camile' if I had ever gotten my face in front of hers, blocking the camera. The eyes should be closed and the embrace tender.

Then he demonstrated the way several memorable screen queens liked him to kiss them. It was a difficult task because Mrs. Kingman was floating on Cloud Nine.

Red Cloud residents have never gotten over the "down-to-earth folksiness" of Julie Harris, one of America's most versatile actresses during her May 1987 visit to the Willa Cather Pioneer Memorial and Educational Foundation's annual Spring Conference.

Miss Harris said her first visit to Catherland was as rewarding as her two Emmy and five Tony awards. She came to Red Cloud, she said, because "Miss Cather has been my lifelong inspiration." Of her banquet speech before an overflow crowd, she said, "It will not be scholarly, just full of love and adoration."

I'd mistakenly thought Basil Rathbone, star of numerous Sherlock Holmes films as well as many Shakespearean productions, was a stuff-shirt Englishman.

That changed when he came to Hastings for an artist-in-residence appearance at Hastings College. I found him down on his knees, laughing in a bookstore while picking up greeting cards from a display that had been dumped on the floor during a rush by autograph hounds.

Since both he and his family were close friends of Britain's Sir Winston Churchill, he regaled a luncheon gathering with "Winnie" stories and said he "loved every minute" of his Nebraska visit.

The Power of the Press

Western movie actor Robert Fuller and Omaha theater producer, the late Don Romeo, both told me in the summer of 1966 that they would never again question the power of the press.

Fuller was the star and Romeo the producer of an outdoor pageant written by North Platte award-winning author Nellie Yost commemorating the centennial of frontier Fort McPherson at Maxwell.

As a capacity crowd gathered at the arena for the evening premier, so did ominous storm clouds. After hearing severe weather radio warnings Romeo said, "We may have to cancel the performance tonight."

I raged at him, "You can't cancel the show. Whatever happened to the old theatrical saying, 'The show must go on?' " Besides, having seen the rehearsals, I had already filed my story for the early World-Herald editions describing the show as a resounding success. "You can't stop the show and make me out a liar," I said.

Romeo warily relented. And just as the show began, the clouds parted and the crowd basked in a beautiful sunset and a starlit night.

Allan and fellow Scotlanders Andrew (left) and Will beneath the railing of West End House in Tillicoultry.

CHAPTER FIFTEEN

'HAME' ON A WING AND A PRAYER

Oh ye'll take the low road and I'll take the high road.
And I'll be in Scotland a-fore ye. Old Scottish song

In the summer of 1961 I went "hame" again to my native land on a wing and a prayer. I took the "high road" to return to bonnie Scotland. It took just nine hours flying high from Lincoln Air Force Base to bridge the 33 years since I had migrated to Oxford, Neb., as a 9-year-old laddie.

My wings were those of a Strategic Air Command B-47 bomber.

Howard Silber, the now-retired World-Herald's ace military writer, a World War II infantry combat veteran who tasted battle again in two assignments in war-torn Vietnam as a correspondent, arranged my flight.

Through his connections at SAC headquarters at Offutt Air Force Base, I was allowed to become the fourth member of a bomber crew to chronicle their Cold War ever-ready missions in Operation Reflex.

My prayers were twofold. First, remembering the questions often asked me by instructors during a week of mandatory training at Offutt, I prayed we would make it safe and sound and I wouldn't have to endure what they frequently reminded me: "Do you really want to do this? You know, if anything happens you don't have an ejection seat. Being the fourth man you will have to crawl out of the opening left by the ejected navigator/bombardier."

After surviving my cramped, hard seat on the bomb-bay door and the anxiety of not finding our refueling tanker in the dark of night high above Nova Scotia until the last minute, I said my second prayer: That the fairyland of my boyhood would be the same. Too often I'd been disappointed in looking back. Would my boyhood reveries be barren in adult reality?

I took a couple of days leave from covering the "loaded and ready for bear" exercises at the Royal Air Force Base at Upper Heyford, England, and took an overnight train to Glasgow to find out.

I wasn't disappointed.

I surprised Kit and Rachel, the two remaining aunts who had bid my brother, "Wee Willie," then 7, and me, "Wee Tommie," a tearful farewell as we embarked alone on a ship from a Clyde-side pier on a cold, foggy morning in January 1927 to join our father, the Rev. William Allan. He had migrated five years earlier, leaving us in our aunts' care after the death of our mother. He'd become a naturalized American citizen, remarried and established a home for us at Oxford.

I confessed to Auntie Kit we had not obeyed her tearful farewell plea to "Nae look because ye're gaein' to a strange land o' painted savages and wild naked women."

I told her that not only were her impressions of America (gained from seeing too many Hollywood movies) false, but on arrival we had been the most "wide-eyed and disappointed immigrants ever to land in America."

I found my old school in Springburn just as I had left it, although doomed to be razed for a new housing development. I wrote in a World-Herald story:

Glasgow, Scotland – I came back to my old school today and was saddened.

Like so many other well-remembered parts of Glasgow, old Hyde Park School was just the same – untouched by World War II and three decades.

With its dirty stone face it stood still, stern and foreboding as the well-remembered strictness of the discipline inside. Around it was the same steel-spiked fence with the gate that clanked shut with finality when classes began.

The students were on summer holiday so it stood silent and empty. Workmen repairing a sewer line were out to lunch.

When I crossed the threshold, the timidity of a boy returned. Almost instinctively I thrust out my hand for the never-to-be-forgotten and almost automatic lash of the headmaster's black leather strap for being late.

I smiled at finding myself instinctively rubbing my palm on the seam of my trousers to ease the sting. I remembered what was more feared than the lash for being late or being unable to recite when called upon – the curt order to 'go sit with the girls!' The school had separate entrances and playgrounds for boys and girls, and the ultimate punishment was being ordered to sit on the girls' side of the classroom.

For fear of raising the wrath of the absent schoolmaster, I found myself tiptoeing down the hall ... till I stopped short at my old classroom door.

It was the same. Nothing had changed. I had just come back from a 33-year recess.

Maybe it was the mood instilled by the silence. But it was as if my old classmates – Hugh, Alex, Peter and the rest – were still there, all of us ramrod straight at our desks.

Then I remembered the day Hughie broke his leg in a fall from a wall on his way home from school. We had been playing soldiers. In those days World War I was just yesterday, and even closer still because, as is common here, nearly all of us had lost close relatives in the trenches.

Hughie was the bravest of the brave 8-year-old soldiers that day. His face white and biting his lips to prevent disgraceful tears, he said, "Remember, we promised we'd never cry – even if we're dead."

We didn't know then that we were boys ripening for World War II. We didn't know our class would be ripe for the picking in 1939 when Hitler struck.

I wondered if they remembered me on the ill-fated H.M.S. Repulse, Prince of Wales and the H.M.S. Hood or at Dunkirk and Tobruk.

I was the lucky one. I went to America, became a Yank. They fought – and died – three years before I became a GI. I came back from the Alcan Highway and South Pacific theater unscathed.

Standing there in the silence of the old room, I had a feeling of guilt. I had left and broken those boyish vows we made "to be together forever." Now, I was a trespasser.

There was a lump in my throat as I turned to leave. Then I heard Hughie again, "Remember, we promised we'd never cry – even if we're dead."

At least I kept that promise, Hughie. But it was hard.

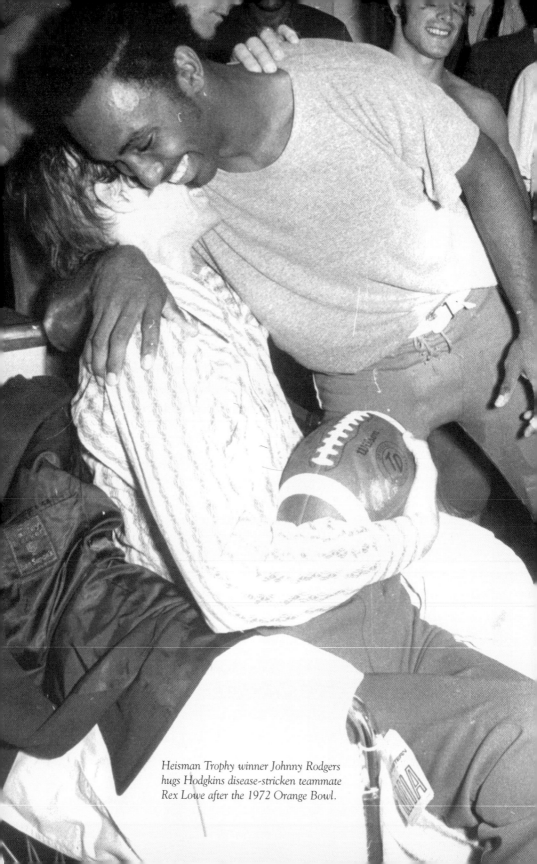

Heisman Trophy winner Johnny Rodgers hugs Hodgkins disease-stricken teammate Rex Lowe after the 1972 Orange Bowl.

CHAPTER SIXTEEN

HUSKER FOOTBALL

Being a Husker football nut, I volunteered in 1955 to be a sideline reporter-photographer at Nebraska Cornhusker games.

It was a labor of love that lasted for 29 years – from the last year of Coach Bill Glassford's tenure, the one-year stint of Coach Pete Elliott, the five-year agonizing "winning the impossible but losing to the patsies" term of the late Coach Bill Jennings, the 11-year resurrection of Go Big Red pride resulting in two national championships under Coach Bob Devaney, and the continued dominance during Coach Tom Osborne's first 11 years.

In covering the regular seasons and 21 bowl games on the sidelines – from the 1962 Gotham Bowl to the 1985 Sugar Bowl – I usually had my back to the playing field. I aimed my camera and story-finding to the sidelines, stands and locker rooms, seeking the overlooked "little daisies" that often proved more poignant and dramatic than the battles on the field.

Perhaps most poignant was a story I called, "Tears fell on the game ball."

I found it overlooked in a quiet corner of the riotous locker room after the Huskers nailed down their second consecutive national championship in the 1972 Orange Bowl by humbling Alabama's Crimson Tide by the lopsided score of 38-6.

Heisman Trophy winner Johnny Rodgers rightfully held center stage in the joyously mad locker room. On the field he had displayed some of his most electrifying moments in one of his finest gridiron efforts. But it wasn't his finest moment.

"Johnny R," a once-troubled youth, demonstrated the compassionate man he had become when he spotted Rex Lowe, a former teammate, seated alone in a wheelchair in the quiet corner.

Rex, who had played split end before being diagnosed with Hodgkin's disease, had been brought to the game by his family and trundled into the locker room to share the elation of victory.

What happened next was Johnny's finest moment.

Joe Garagiola of NBC Sports read my story of what happened and asked permission to use it on his nationally broadcast Jan. 30, 1972, show.

This is how he told it:

"It's doubtful if a college football game ever got more coverage than the meeting between Nebraska and Alabama in the Orange Bowl New Year's night. Still, there was something that happened that night that you might not have heard about. If you didn't, I think there is something in this story for all of us.

"I learned about it from the Nebraska Byways of Tom Allan of the Omaha World-Herald. It's the story of two men. One is the former Nebraska split end Rex Lowe. He sat on the sidelines in his wheelchair, which has been his means of transportation since he was stricken by Hodgkin's disease.

"The men on the field had been his teammates, and he was proud of all of them, as they nailed down the lid on their rating as the nation's Number One team. It had to be a thrill for him. It was a thrill to me, as I sat in the stands that night. The whole Nebraska team was exciting to watch, especially Johnny Rodgers.

"In writing about that night, Tom Allan said: 'In future years, cold statistics in sports record books will show Johnny's biggest moment in the Orange Bowl was his game-breaking 77-yard punt return for a touchdown.

'But such 'impossible' scampers have become a tradition for Johnny R. He pulls stadium crowds to their feet in expectancy every time he fields the ball. It has become the trademark of an extremely talented athlete. What moment could be finer?'

"Then Tom Allan tells us of an even finer moment. After the game the Nebraska dressing room was crowded and noisy. Off to one side, quietly enjoying it all, was Rex Lowe in his wheelchair. In the middle all of the attention was Johnny Rodgers holding the game ball.

"Suddenly Rodgers jumped up on a bench. Over the noise, he started to yell. He said: 'Hey, guys, give me your attention. I know we always put it to a vote to see who gets the game ball. But I say it should go by acclamation to one of the greatest guys there is, Rex Lowe.'

"The approval came quick and loud, and Johnny Rodgers slipped through the crowd as gracefully as he had gone through the Alabama team. He gave the ball to Lowe. They embraced and tears began to come."

I ended my story with, "This is for you, Rex, from all the guys. You are the greatest and nobody deserves it more," Johnny said.

Then they embraced. And tears fell on the game ball.

Garagiola ended his broadcast with: "In these days when we hear so much of hate, I might point out that Johnny Rodgers is black, and Rex Lowe is white. Although in that beautiful moment in the Nebraska dressing room, neither man seemed to notice that."

To Bucktail and Back . . .

A sad footnote: Rex Lowe died a month later on Feb. 2, 1972.

Another Tear-Stained Game Ball

On Oct. 2, 1976, the Huskers showed another display of affection for a fallen teammate in Memorial Stadium after beating Miami 17-9.

In my post-game story I wrote:

The "real winner" in Saturday's Nebraska-Miami game sat near the end of the bench in a wheelchair.

Scott Porter, a third-generation Husker who is better known to his teammates as Budge, proved by just being there he is "winning the biggest game of his life."

His courage was the reason behind the heart-gripping scene in the Husker locker room as the players awarded him the game ball.

Porter is the Nebraska City athlete whose promising Husker career was ended by a critical neck injury during spring drills. A broken vertebra bruised his spinal column and paralyzed him.

Cheers echoed through the locker room and tears fell freely for several emotion-packed moments.

Choking back tears, blackshirts coach Monte Kiffin said: "It means everything to me to win games. But I don't care if I ever win another game if it would mean Budge Porter would walk again. His courage exemplified what our team had out there today."

Budge hugged the tear-stained ball.

"I'd have thrown in the towel," said his father, Morton, a guard on the 1943 Husker team. "But this kid refuses to quit. He's a winner, and I'm more proud of him now than when he was making touchdowns and being an all-around athlete.

"He's now in the biggest game in his life and he's winning it. The dedication and determination he learned as an athlete is helping him win now."

Budge has made a slow but steady recovery. He gets therapeutic leaves every football weekend from Omaha's Immanuel Hospital.

"And you bet I'm making all the home games," he said on the sidelines before the kickoff. "I'm as nervous as if I were out there with my teammates."

He added wistfully, "It has always been a dream to play down here. My grandfather, Grover, played here under Jumbo Stiehm in 1915-16 and dad played here in '43.

"I know I can never again be out there on the field. It remains a dream. But I can be here pulling for my teammates. If I can't play I want to be one of the good Husker backers and spectators."

Covering the Foe

I also was allowed to cover the opposing team's locker room until the sports desk decided in 1984 that participation in sports by a news sider was not appreciated.

In those frequent-winning days I always had a hard time knowing what to ask the opposing coach after another bashing by the Huskers.

In a 1975 article, Buck Turnbull, who was the football writer for the Des Moines Register, wrote a story about my sympathetic approach, saying: "Tom Allan has become an expert at consoling losers. There may not be a newspaperman anywhere who has matched his dismal record.

"Allan is the roving reporter for the Omaha World-Herald and on weekends in the fall he doubles covering Nebraska's football team. His job: Report on the opposition's dressing room.

"Well, ever since 1962 you know what that has entailed. The more winners produced by Bob Devaney and his successor, Tom Osborne, the more losers Allan gets to visit.

"The combined Devaney-Osborne winning record now stands at better than 80 percent, meaning Allan has talked to 136 losing coaches in Nebraska's last 168 games."

Buck must have been setting a trap for me by his praise, because the next Saturday I covered a winning locker room, Iowa State's after they upset the Huskers 37-28.

Target For a Beef

I thought I was at my sympathetic best when I entered the Kansas locker room after the Huskers beat the Jayhawks in a last-minute, come-from-behind 21-17 victory on Oct. 18, 1969.

The game that launched an unbeaten Husker victory streak, leading to consecutive national championships in 1971 and 1972, was bitterly fought. It was even more bitterly rehashed afterward in the KU dressing room.

In those days Nebraska had the lousiest dressing room in the conference, or perhaps even in college football. The tiny quarters were tucked in the southeast corner of the stadium.

But even in the small confines I had trouble finding Pepper Rodgers, the KU coach. I finally found him sitting on the floor with his head in his hands in a corner of a tiny cubicle.

Salty Pepper was still peppery hot after the heat of battle. I knelt beside him and offered consolingly, "Coach, that was a tough way to lose a ball game."

Pepper snarled and hurled a four-letter obscenity at me, adding, "Let's see you print that in your family newspaper!" It only inflamed him more when I answered, "OK, Pepper. How do you spell that?"

He cooled a little when an assistant handed him a sack lunch. Pepper's teams were the only ones I ever knew to partake of such a post-game snack. Most teams had a bottle of pop or slices of orange or lemon.

After savagely biting into a sandwich, he snapped: "I will not volunteer information. I will answer questions."

The first question, naturally, was on the questionable pass interference call in the winning Husker drive. It was a 31-yard error that was compounded when Jayhawk captain Emory Hicks challenged the heredity of the mother of the official who'd made the call. Head linesman Glenn Bowles of Des Moines gave the Huskers an additional 15-yard bonus for the indiscretion.

Through his mouthful of sandwich Pepper grunted: "No comment. I said all I'm going to say about that to the squad and you missed it. I said last week all officials are wonderful."

Taking another bite, Pepper added that he didn't know which player got the 15-yard penalty because "the officials didn't tell me." He then volunteered: "You have to understand the way I feel when kids work that hard and come back and play a very fine Nebraska team and then lose it not in their play. I want that emphasized, NOT their play. Then you have to feel somewhat emotional for the players."

Pepper declined to expand on the remark and later, in a more gracious mood, he added: "Everybody in the whole world is nice. Officials are nice. Nebraska is nice. It has great fans and I'm very happy to participate in the great sport of college football. I feel we were beaten by a very fine team."

In later years the salty coach always accused me of asking the next question, which really added pepper to his wounds. It didn't make any difference that I swore it was a former Topeka Daily Capital colleague who was leaning over my shoulder who asked, "Are you feeling a little snakebit after losing two weeks in a row in the final moments?"

Pepper snarled and said angrily: "We lost every Big Eight game we ever lost by four points. How about that, (bleep)!

Then, grabbing the lunch sack, he disgorged the remainder of his sandwich into it, rolled it into a ball and hurled it at me. I ducked. It barely missed one of his assistant coaches before smashing with a thud on the wall.

"How about that?" he shouted. "There's your story. Rodgers throws sandwich against the wall with vengeance – and by the way, it was beef!"

The next year after the NU-KU game at Lawrence, Rodgers demanded all Nebraska scribes stand and introduce themselves. After the press conference I asked him: "Why? We've known each other for years."

"Because you (bleep bleeps) made an ass out of me last year," he snarled.

When I reminded him it was he who not only gave us the story but the headline with his beef sandwich-tossing, he had two of his biggest linemen unceremoniously escort me out the door.

No, Sir. Yes, Sir. Sir!

At least I didn't come up as empty-handed as the late Jim "Rags" Raglin of the Lincoln Journal after the 14-9 upset victory by the Huskers over a highly rated 1960 Army team.

Although rival news hounds, Raglin and I were the best of friends and we decided to ease an unusual assignment each of us was given of covering both teams' dressing rooms.

Since Rags had boasted he was the boyhood pal of the Army coach and they had double-dated to the Independence, Kan., high school junior-senior prom, I agreed to job-sharing. While he covered the Army dressing room, I would cover the Husker locker room and Coach Bill Jennings, and we'd meet in the center of the field afterward and exchange notes.

It never took long to interview the taciturn Jennings. So I took my time talking to Husker players before heading to meet Rags. I finally found him enraged and still waiting outside the door to the Army dressing room.

"Don't ask," Rags snarled. "Just watch what has been going on for half an hour," and then pounded on the door. It was opened by an impassive-faced cadet standing at attention with his arm in a sling that he used as an additional barrier.

"Sirs!" he yelled in a parade ground shout. "No one is allowed in the dressing room until the coach gives his expressed permission. He has not. Thank-you, Sirs!" Then slammed the door in our face.

Finally, we were allowed to enter and made a beeline for the Army coach, standing glum-faced in a corner. After his opening statement: "We were surprised by Nebraska's winning pass. They don't usually pass." The coach added, "Otherwise, I have no comment and I have ordered my players to talk to no one from the press."

Rags was speechless until he got on his knees and with his hands held in supplication begged, "I'm Rags, your old Kansas bosom friend and classmate. Talk to me, old buddy!"

Hall gave a glimmer of a smile when he replied only with, "Hi Rags."

And it didn't help, nor did I get an answer, when I pleaded, "Can you at least tell us what happened to you and Rags at the junior-senior prom?"

'Gobble-De-Gook' Helps Missouri Upset Huskers

"Gobble-de-gook" doesn't make sense. It's usually a phrase used to describe indecipherable bureaucratic red tape.

But it made sense to the Missouri Tigers in their 17-7 upset of the highly favored Huskers in 1969 at Columbia, Mo.

A sign reading: "What you give you have. What you do not give you've lost forever" had been placed on a wall of the Tiger locker room.

Amid the joyous bedlam of the Missouri victory celebration, I asked Missouri Coach Dan Devine, a close friend but staunch competitor of Bob Devaney since they were assistant coaches at Michigan State, "What does that mean?"

"It's the reason we upset Nebraska today," Devine replied. "My players gave more of themselves today than they thought they had in an all-out effort and have a victory to remember forever. If they had not given more than they thought they had, they'd have lost the chance forever. The sign was our rallying cry, and it worked."

He's Not With Us!

Big 8 official Glenn Bowles of Des Moines and I were old Army buddies and I used to kid him unmercifully during games, especially when he was head linesman and therefore close enough to the sidelines to hear me.

After I had baited him with, "Thank God, Glenn, you are so bow-legged, you give us an unobstructed view of the game," Bowles turned to the Nebraska bench and ordered, "Get that guy outta here or I'll give you a 15-yard penalty!"

Paul Schneider, a Husker trainer known for his excitable nature and high-pitched voice, dashed on to the field shouting: "He's not with us. He's definitely not with us. He's with the Des Moines Register!"

Bowles laughed so hard he fell to his knees.

Schnitz the Parrot

I was always amazed Bob Devaney never received a penalty for the salty language he used debating calls against the Huskers. It didn't take investigative reporting to find out why.

Paul Schneider, affectionately known as "Schnitz" by generations of players, had a squeaky voice that carried farther than Devaney's. And he parroted every word of Devaney's heated laments.

When the officials looked for the offender, Schnitz scurried behind a wall of players. Devaney, upon hearing his own words from Schneider's lips, would then exclaim, "Oh, that was bad, really bad."

Bleeding for the Huskers

In 1996 I received the Nebraska Football Hall of Fame's Lyell Bremser Merit Award, named for the late, great radio football announcer famed for his, "Man, Woman and Child!" broadcasts.

With tongue-in-cheek I told the banquet crowd, "I deserve this for no other reason than I may be the only member of the media to have actually bled for the Huskers."

The sidelines are a dangerous spot to be, especially during sweeps around the end. I used to duck behind giant Carl Samuelson, who guarded the left end of the Nebraska bench. He threw a lot better blocks protecting me than he ever did as a Husker or with the Pittsburgh Steelers from 1948 to 1951.

Samuelson perhaps threw his greatest block at Missouri when he dashed across the field to wipe out a bevy of Tiger students who had ripped a banner from Husker cheerleaders.

I dashed after Samuelson to defend him as he was escorted by police to a spot under the south end zone bleachers. But he didn't need any defense. The cops explained they had to put him under arrest temporarily to prevent a Missouri student body riot. Then they shook his hand and asked, "Please wait a bit and then sneak back to the Nebraska bench."

But my giant protector wasn't on hand at Manhattan, Kan., in 1969 when the Huskers eked out a 10-7 victory over the Kansas State Wildcats with a last-minute field goal.

As the ball sailed through the goal posts a burly Husker lineman at

To Bucktail and Back . . .

the end of the bench jumped high in the air flinging his arms wildly in unbridled elation. A fist caught me squarely in the face and cartwheeled me back over the bench.

Dazed and bleeding profusely from my battered nose, I staggered into the Husker dressing room to interview Coach Devaney.

When Devaney asked: "What the hell happened to you? You're bleeding all over my locker room. Did you get hit by a truck?" I explained what happened and Devaney added: "Who was it? I'll talk to him."

I told Devaney, "It might be hard to identify the player because there's a whole line of them waiting outside your door to joyfully confess they decked a member of the press."

Devaney, laughing, then called on Dr. Paul Goetowski, a team physician, to stanch my bleeding. The big Doc grabbed my nose between thumb and forefinger and wrenched it down, up and then sideways. His trademark white suspenders suddenly became red, my blood red.

"The good news," he said, is that the nose ain't busted. The bad news is that I'm turning you over to Sully and Schnitz to fix it up."

Trainers George Sullivan and Paul Schneider were eagerly awaiting me and summarily ordered, "Take off your pants." To my howls that it was my nose that needed tending, Sullivan told me that if I had paid attention in high school physics class I would know about possible torque damage.

"Torque," Sully explained, "happens when a force is inflicted in one spot but is expended in other. So drop your pants. We have to check your other extremities."

More dazed than ever, I did. After stanching the blood flow, the grinning medics began applying a bandage, a lot of bandage. When they got through, I looked like a mummy. Then I looked like a ghost after they answered my pleas, "How am I gonna write my story?" by snipping two eye holes. Only then did they finally release me and allow me to put on my pants.

I scared the hell out of my colleagues when I showed up in the press box. En route home I began unwinding the bandages to see to drive. They must have used an entire season of bandages because the front seat of the car was engulfed in gauze.

Wife Marilyn screamed when I got home. A Band-Aid covered a cut on my swollen nose and I looked like a banshee with two giant black eyes.

Beware of Flying Objects

I can vouch for the asininity of rabid fans tossing oranges on the field signaling hopes of another Husker Orange Bowl trip.

I was standing alongside the stadium employee who got hit on the back of the neck with a frozen orange and later became paralyzed. I was only nicked on the leg by another errant missile.

I suffered more at the November 1968 Colorado game at snow-shrouded Boulder. Beer-drinking Colorado students drove their own band and Nebraska's off the field in a halftime snowball barrage. When Colorado's athletic director Eddie Crowder pleaded for sanity from midfield, he also was sent scurrying for a bomb shelter.

I didn't duck very well because I got one smack dab between the eyes – as a wedding gift. I recovered enough to make Marilyn my wife at a Loveland, Colo., chapel the next day.

Right Song, Wrong Tempo

The 1971 and '72 Orange Bowl national championship games will be remembered for the absence of the Huskers' famed fight song the first year and listening to it played as a stately waltz the second year.

Both occurrences came at the Orange Bowl committee's gala New Year's Eve parties attended by representatives of the competing schools and the press.

In 1971, before the Louisiana State game, the big dance band played the Tigers' fight song. When they didn't play Nebraska's, my wife Marilyn, who was dancing with Gov. Jim Exon, went to the bandstand for an explanation of the omission.

"We don't have the music," said the bandleader despite Marilyn's and Exon's threat to sit on the edge of the bandstand until the fight song was played.

When the desperate maestro asked if they had any musicians who could play it, they rounded up Don "Fat Fox" Bryant, the Husker sports information director and trumpet player, and Bill Fischer, the piano-playing Husker business manager, and the band played a rousing rendition.

The next year on the eve of the game with Alabama, the same maestro proudly announced, "And now the Nebraska fight song!" – and the band played it in waltz time!

Husker faithful, standing ready to sing accompanied by the traditional clapping, stood silent and aghast. The maestro was ready for Marilyn and the governor's angry raid on the bandstand.

"Lady, this year we went to a lot of trouble and dug up the music," the maestro said triumphantly. Then handing them the sheet music, he added: "Here it is. Note that it is meant to be in three-quarter waltz time."

I had to eat crow after a Byways column blasting the band's error. Ken R. Keller, then NU's assistant public relations director, and others in letters sadly informed me the song originally was written to be played in waltz time.

Keller wrote me, "Don't shoot the piano player. He was doing the best he could because the original score was written by Harry Plecha, class of 1924, in three-quarter waltz time for an ROTC dance at Camp Ashland."

Keller added that our only consolation was that someone had scribbled in pencil on a corner of the original score, "Speed up tempo!" and that Husker bandmasters later did so with gusto.

A Sad Post-Bowl Game Refrain

I've always been saddened that the media all but ignores the Husker marching band in game coverage. The music and precision drills of the 200 to 300 kids who give the biggest toot for the Huskers has always provided much color of the game – as well as providing some choice "little daisy" stories.

There is total dedication by the kids – who have four pre-season daily drills under a broiling sun to the football team's two – and among the old-timers who return each year to march and play at the Alumni Band Day game.

Such was Gordon Watkins, of Auburn, who hoofed and gave a toot one last time for the Huskers at the Oct. 5, 1980, Band Day game halftime performance.

"Although I can still play sweet and cool," said the longtime school administrator at Fairmont, Red Cloud, Palisades and Lyman before retirement, "this winds it up. Being 80, I'm old enough to quit now. But I'll sure miss it."

A Discordant Note in the Finale

Don "Fat Fox" Bryant, the now-retired veteran Husker sports information director and later assistant athletic director, and I arranged with the band to play "Auld Lang Syne" as a farewell salute to Bob Devaney, the man who painted Nebraska red, at the end of his final game as coach in Memorial Stadium on Nov. 23, 1972.

But the game ended with a heartbreaking 17-14 defeat at the hands of arch-rival Oklahoma. As the final seconds of the game ticked away and the loss was inevitable, Bryant tried desperately to have the band change the musical selection.

But the band had its orders and dutifully played the song famed for its "Should auld acquaintance be forgot and never brought to nigh" lyrics.

Instead of a rollicking New Year's Eve song, it sounded like a dirge. Dark clouds and approaching darkness added to the solemnity.

The crowd stood silent, many wiping away tears, as Devaney, with head bowed, headed for the dressing room alone.

Another Sad But Magnificent Refrain

Perhaps the saddest but most magnificent note of them all was played at the Orange Bowl in 1984.

A Gothenburg family – dad, mom, brothers and sisters – who all had played for the marching band, had driven to Miami to see the youngest daughter play for the first time in the Bowl's pre-game and halftime pageantry.

Carrying on the family tradition was especially important because mom was fighting cancer and it could be her last chance to see her daughter play.

Mom died the afternoon of the game in her hotel room.

"I was given the hardest task I ever had in directing the band for 37 years," said Band Director Jack Snider. "Carol's dad called me before the game and said it was their wish that she not be robbed of the chance to play in the Orange Bowl. He asked that I wait until after the game to tell Carol of her mother's passing.

"It was a beautiful gesture with a sad refrain. I had a hard time telling the daughter of her mother's wish after she had happily performed in the halftime show. Then we arranged for her to join her family at the hotel."

'Game of the Century' Memories

These things linger in memory besides Johnny Rodgers' unbelievable punt return of the 1971 "Game of the Century" 35-31 win over Oklahoma.

The pre-game atmosphere in the Sooners' sold-out stadium was so intense on the sidelines you could have lit a match simply by holding it up in the air.

Rich Glover, who later won both the Lombardi and Outland trophies as America's outstanding lineman, may have won the game before the kickoff when a national television crew arranged to have him take a three-point stance facing a Sooner All-America offensive lineman.

When the nervous Sooner tried to make small talk, the glowering Glover didn't answer, simply stared menacingly into his eyes and then, cat-like, reached across and cuffed the Sooner on the side of his helmet. The completely surprised Sooner wasn't worth a tinker's damn against the ferocious Glover during the game.

Two-Bit Expense Account

When the Huskers defeated Mississippi State in the 1980 Sun Bowl at El Paso, Texas, there was a change in the then merry-go-round of World-Herald sports editors.

The new editor had never covered the Huskers or a bowl game, but he was eager and developed a cost-cutting "Battle Plan" for the newspaper's coverage at El Paso.

I was given orders to fly with photographers arriving on the eve of the game, share a hotel room with one, and was allocated $25 for meals and incidentals. I was assigned to write two of my usual pre-game stories and to cover the opponent's dressing room after the game.

The post-game chore was impossible since the "Battle Plan" called for me to accompany some of the photographers on a flight home at the end of the third quarter. When I couldn't figure out how to cover the Mississippi State locker room while homeward bound at 31,000 feet, I obtained permission from Executive Editor G. Woodson Howe to take a week's vacation time. Then I took my wife, Marilyn, and drove her car to El Paso so I could complete my assignments.

Afterward, I turned in an expense report reading:

TRAVEL: Used wife's car. Cost – nothing.

HOTEL: Jealous wife objected to me sleeping with a
photographer; insisted I share a bed with her. Cost – nothing.

MEALS: Wife brought me doggy bags. Cost – nothing.

INCIDENTALS: Bought copy of El Paso Sun Times
newspaper for orientation. Cost – 25 cents.

TOTAL COST TO WORLD-HERALD: Befitting a two-bit
operation, 25 cents.

Howe, better known as Woody, later paid me in full with a quarter.

Now that the statute of limitations has expired I have a confession to make. Woody, I hid my actual costs in subsequent expense reports stretched over a year. Although they are in there somewhere, I defy you or the sharpest of CPAs to find them. Besides, I'm retired and it's too late to fire me now.

The Jens Marie Chicken Truck Rescue

The late Coach Bill Jennings chalked up a 15-34-1 record during his 1957-'61 tenure as the University of Nebraska's football coach.

But the .310 record of the quiet-spoken native Oklahoman included two of the Huskers' most memorable upset victories and an unforgettable trek to Oklahoma State at Stillwater via Ponca City. I'm sure before Jennings' death in June 2002, the recall of all three brought a smile to his lips. They helped in his induction into the Nebraska Football Hall of Fame in 1996.

At homecoming in Memorial Stadium on Oct. 31, 1959, the heavily underdog Huskers ended the 74 consecutive conference winning streak of Oklahoma, where Jennings had been a star player and an assistant coach, with a startling 31-25 upset that shook the collegiate football world.

The partisan crowd of 32,765 went wild with delirious joy. Most of the students rushed the field to tear down the goal posts and parade them through downtown Lincoln. NU President Clifford Hardin got caught up in the delirium. He canceled Monday classes so the celebration could continue unabated over the weekend.

Ron Meade, who intercepted a desperate last-minute Sooner pass in the end zone to seal the improbable victory, also went wild, hugging the football while repeatedly leaping high in unbridled ecstasy to shout: "We did it! I can't believe it! We finally did it!" before being carried off the field on fans' shoulders.

Back at The World-Herald, Editor Fred Ware, who'd been one of the most colorful of sports editors, also went wild. He sent an "urgent" message to Gregg McBride in the press box via Western Union ticker tape, our mode of communication in those days, reading, "Suggest you work as a team!"

McBride, who treasured the ticker tape in his billfold for years, beat out a reply on his battered typewriter and handed it over his shoulder to the telegraph operator seated on a bench behind him. It read: "Will try, but it might be hard. Phipps (longtime sports writer Bob) is trapped in the crowd trying to get to the Husker locker room. The last time I spotted Allan he was being trampled in the mud on the field."

I remember Husker halfback Noel Martin, who was married to Jennings' daughter, Vicki, picking me up from the quagmire of mud and bodies to bid me to look at a Husker flag flying over the stadium.

"Look at it! It has never waved so proudly!" he shouted.

Somehow, McBride, Phipps and I worked as a team and survived, and "Work as a team!" became our battle cry for coverage down the years.

The victory over Oklahoma was compounded the next year with another improbable 17-14 win over the revenge-bent Sooners at Norman. It was sweetened because furious Sooner fans blamed Jennings for blowing the whistle on their legendary Coach Bud Wilkinson for alleged NCAA rule violations. Security guards escorted him on and off the field.

Jennings' final year as coach provided the saga of "The Jens Marie Chicken Truck Rescue."

Oklahoma State in 1960 had beaten Nebraska 7-6 in Lincoln. Jennings wasn't about to have his team stay overnight in rambunctious Stillwater the night before the Oct. 21, 1961, rematch. He chose instead to stay at the Jens Marie Hotel in Ponca City.

Travel budgets were slim in those days and Nebraska had used Purdue University Airline, which consisted of two World War II surplus C-47s. En route, the aged planes ran into headwinds forcing the use of burp bags and a refueling stop at Wichita.

Having driven, McBride and I arrived at the Jens Marie before the team. We discovered it was an historic, stuccoed hotel. A famed statue, "Pioneer Mother," stood outside by the street. Later we discovered the Jens Marie was famous for something else on the Oklahoma-Texas oil circuit.

The tiny elevator barely had room for a portly bellhop, McBride, and me as it shook, screeched and trembled to our top-floor suite. The room also trembled when I turned on an unbalanced ceiling fan.

When the bellhop returned with a bucket of ice, he tarried, first on one foot then the other. McBride, pouring us a trail's end, dust-cutting drink, asked him: "What's the matter? Didn't we tip you enough?"

"Oh, no sir," the beaming bellhop replied. "I am kinda thirsty and that looks like mighty fine booze you are pouring."

"Well, get yourself a glass, pull up a chair and join us," McBride bid him. After drinking his fill the bellhop, who identified himself as "George Number One," said, "Ah can see you are real gentlemen. I'll go back down and send the girls up right away."

After gulping in disbelief, we declined female companionship.

"No problem," said George Number One. "George Number Two comes on duty at 8 o'clock. I'll tell him what gentlemen you are and he'll see you are not lonely."

That evening we bumped into "Colonel" Floyd Bottorff, the Huskers' legendary equipment manager with a gruff voice and an ever-ready, but unlit cigar in his jaw.

"Ain't this a friendly place?" he asked as he introduced me to an Indian maiden named Juanita Allan he claimed had to be my cousin. She had stopped overnight while driving a flatbed truck loaded with crates of live chickens to Oklahoma City.

We spent a noisy night listening to more than clucking chicks, which fortunately were in the parking lot.

As the team prepared to board the bus to Stillwater the next morning, the equipment van wouldn't start. After a hurried consultation with Juanita, the Colonel shouted: "No problem! Lend me a hand!" Team members helped him unload the crates of chickens and then threw their bags on the truck. Only halfback Willie Ross' bag bounced off and was lost en route.

Whether the lost bag had any bearing on Nebraska losing the game 14-6 is debatable.

Pat Quinn, Oklahoma State's jovial sports information director, couldn't believe the Huskers actually had stayed at the Jens Marie. For years afterward he sent a telegram to the press box where ever McBride was celebrating his birthday. It read: – "Happy birthday, Gregg. With love from all the girls at the Jens Marie."

Colonel Bottorff's daughter, Bonnie Walker, longtime manager of Lincoln's Nebraska Club, didn't share her father's love of football. When I asked her why, she replied: "It was tough sledding in the early days for our family when I and my sisters were young. It was also lean budget years for the Cornhuskers.

"Dad helped by bringing the team uniforms home for our mother and us to wash. If you think young girls like having to wash and hang out to dry on a clothesline a bunch of jockstraps everyday, you have another guess coming."

To Bucktail and Back . . .

CHAPTER SEVENTEEN

DEVANEY, THE GREATEST

Wily Irishman Bob Devaney wove his leprechaun magic during the 11 years he was the football coach and the 26 years he was the University of Nebraska's athletic director.

During his 1962 to 1972 coaching tenure, he united the state and painted it from border to border with a happy "Go Big Red" glow while twice dragging the Cornhuskers from ignominy to national championship fame. Then as athletic director from 1967 to 1993, he built one of the NCAA's top sports programs with the best of facilities.

I consider myself most fortunate to have known Devaney while helping The World-Herald cover Husker football for 29 years.

Devaney was the best, and his coaching years, including back-to-back national championships in 1970 and '71, were fun years. They were spiced by the jolly Irishman's football mastery, accessibility and fierce competitiveness, all balanced with wit, a sense of humor and hijinks.

The sometimes profane Devaney, who was known to hoist a drink or two, had a summa cum laude degree in plain old barnyard, horse-sense psychology.

In his first game at Nebraska in 1962, a 58-0 win over South Dakota, Warren Powers fumbled the ball.

Devaney met Powers 10 yards into the field, grabbed him by his shoulder pads and pulled him close as he snarled: "You are too good a football player for that kind of (bleep). Now go sit on the bench and ram those press clippings of yours where they'll do the most good and think about it. When we get the ball back you are going back in and show me."

A couple of plays later the Huskers got the ball back and Devaney again grabbed Powers and snarled, "OK, (bleep), show me!"

Powers got the full benefit of Devaney's basic psychology: He was chewed out, as he fully expected to be, was flattered by being called "too good an athlete" for his mishap, was given a promise of playing again and then a dare.

Powers responded by carrying the ball for five yards behind blockers and then went for extra yardage carrying half the South Dakota team.

Powers later "showed" Nebraska during the tenure of Devaney successor Tom Osborne. Miffed at not being considered heir apparent to Devaney, Powers jumped at the chance to leave the Husker coaching staff to become head coach at Washington State and later Missouri where he beat Nebraska in two crucial games.

Carl Selmer, who was a Devaney assistant at Wyoming as well as Nebraska, didn't have the same success. He got beat by Osborne when he brought his Miami team to Lincoln.

The press loved Devaney because he always came up with good quotes and stories, and didn't hold a grudge against reporters whose stories he didn't like.

The late World-Herald sports editor Wally Provost told me that Devaney, not liking one of his columns, waited until the middle of the night to call him and ask: "You having a good sleep, Wally? Well, good. I just wanted to let you know I didn't like what you wrote yesterday. You are a (bleep bleep). Good night, pleasant dreams."

The next day he greeted Wally warmly and never mentioned the incident.

I always questioned Devaney's claim that the 25-13 upset victory over Michigan at Ann Arbor in the second game of his Husker tenure was the game that turned Nebraska's football fortunes around and established them as a potential national power.

Devaney didn't argue with my claim that the turning point came in the season-ending 36-34 cliff-hanger victory over Miami in the Gotham Bowl. It was played in below-freezing temperatures at 10 a.m., Dec. 15, 1962, in a near-empty Yankee Stadium before an official crowd of 6,166.

A veteran New York City Irish cop gave another attendance figure, saying: "That's blarney. I've patrolled Yankee Stadium for 20 years. If there is more than 3,000, I'll eat me hat."

Devaney didn't argue with my reasoning that the game was the most important because for the first time the Eastern press discovered Nebraska, and him in particular, as a salty, jolly Irishman as well as an outstanding coach.

When reporters awaiting the Huskers' arrival at the New York airport asked me what kind of a guy Devaney was, I told them, "Hold on to your hats!"

And Devaney hit them like a hurricane of fresh air with his wit and candid talk, telling them: "We were raring to go, but had to sit on our butts for hours at the Lincoln airport until a $35,000 guarantee check from the Gotham Bowl cleared the bank. We thought about passing the hat and taking up a collection for the team to raise enough money to get the plane off the ground."

When a Manhattan scribe greeted Devaney saying, "We never thought we'd see you in New York." Devaney quipped: "Well, I'll tell you right now, if I had to do it over, you wouldn't. That's for damned sure."

The financial confusion and the dismal attendance ended the Gotham Bowl's reign. But not before it went out with one of the most exciting games in post-season game history.

Husker assistant coach George Kelly, who later became defensive coordinator at Notre Dame, summed it up eloquently with: "The people in New York missed a helluva show today. They really blew it."

Devaney's humor shone through during a visit by Frank Leahy, the Notre Dame coaching legend, who had come home to O'Neill during a St. Patrick's Day celebration.

It was the first time many Nebraskans, including a few O'Neill Irishmen, realized that Leahy was a hometown boy, losing bar bets that Devaney was not the first "Nebraskan" to win a national football championship. Devaney, a Michigan native, won two. The O'Neill-raised Leahy won five during the 1940s and early '50s.

Leahy had returned to his home state to be honored at an evening banquet. He told me the next morning as I drove him to Omaha to catch a flight, that his only disappointment was not getting to see Devaney, who had to cancel at the last minute.

On learning that Leahy planned to stay overnight in Omaha to visit his mother, I suggested we call Devaney and detour to Lincoln for lunch.

Devaney was delighted, and both were at their story- and joke-telling best during the luncheon that stretched to three hours at Lincoln's University Club. My only regret was not having a tape recorder.

Leahy confessed that during a last minute, come-from-behind victory over Southern Methodist at New York's Polo Grounds, his quarterback called a time out and came to the sidelines to ask what play to call.

"Millions of radio listeners heard Graham MacNamee tell them I was whispering in my quarterback's ear the play that led to victory," Leahy said. "But actually what I said during those tense moments was, 'Kid, never take up coaching as a career.' "

Devaney countered with a story of his advice to quarterback Jerry Tagge in a similar situation during the winning drive in the "Game of the Century" amid the bedlam in the Sooners' stadium. "All I could say was,

'Whatever you do, Jerry, don't make a mistake! Just don't make a mistake!' "

Devaney was at his devilish best during a 1966 game with Missouri, coached by Dan Devine. Although they were the best of friends, having been assistant coaches under Duffy Daugherty at Michigan State, their rivalry was intense.

During the tight game Devine thought the chain gang crew on Nebraska's side of the field was cheating in the Husker's favor. He sent his assistant coach, "Black Jack" Harry Smith, a hulking ex-Detroit Lions player, over to "referee" the chain crew.

"Gee, Harry," Devaney said in greeting. "It's always nice to see you, but this isn't the time or place. Get your big butt over to the other side of the field where you belong!"

With the officiating crew seconding the motion, Harry scampered across the field to the roaring delight of Husker fans.

Devaney had a temper, too.

He never forgave Alabama Coach Paul "Bear" Bryant for what happened in the Crimson Tide's 34-7 victory in the 1967 Sugar Bowl at New Orleans. It was the first time Alabama had played against a team with black players. New Orleans was flooded with postcards picturing Bryant walking on water with faces of Nebraska's black players superimposed and the inscription, "Ah, believes!"

Devaney felt Bryant went too far in having his players, whenever they tackled a black Nebraska back, pick him up, put their arms around him and lead him back toward the Husker huddle.

Devaney got even in the 1972 Orange Bowl with the Huskers' 38-6 shellacking of Alabama and their All-America star, Johnny Musso, who had been touted as the "Italian Stallion."

When the black Husker players decked Musso, they picked him up, put their arms around him and led him back toward the huddle whispering, "How do you like that, you Italian gelding?"

It was reported that Musso was so frustrated by the Huskers' complete dominance of the game that he ripped his jersey to shreds after the final whistle.

I saw Devaney also show his temper in the Husker lair. He'd been in a joyous mood after dominating Alabama and being thrown into the shower by his players celebrating their second consecutive national championship.

He had stripped to his shorts when bowl and national television officials strode in to order: "Coach, get dressed right now! We need you for the MacArthur Bowl presentation and we don't have much time to waste."

That did it. The fiery Irishman glared at them shouting: "Are you sure? Are you damn sure? Don't you want us to play the Green Bay Packers and the Chicago Bears first?"

He was referring to a slight by The Associated Press, the sponsor of the MacArthur Bowl. The United Press had named Nebraska No. 1 at the end of the regular season. Devaney was furious when the AP broke its similar long tradition by deciding to conduct its poll after the bowl game because Nebraska was rated No. 1 and was playing Alabama, rated No. 2 at the regular season's end.

"Get out of here and stuff your damned trophy!" Devaney roared.

The harried AP and bowl officials scrambled and finally found NU President Woody Varner and Chancellor James H. Zumberge to accept the trophy.

Devaney stayed with his boys, relishing the finest of unbeaten seasons, including the "Game of the Century" win over Oklahoma.

There was sadness when Devaney had to walk alone to the locker room in the blue funk of defeat after a 17-14 loss to Oklahoma ended the regular 1972 season in his final game as coach in Memorial Stadium. Fans and players alike had hung back, feeling they had let the Great One down. He felt he had let the fans down in their hopes for a third consecutive national championship.

But the joy and pride returned on New Year's night in the 1973 Orange Bowl with a 40-6 thrashing of Notre Dame in his coaching finale.

It was such an overwhelming defeat with the outcome evident as early as the second quarter, the Miami-area press focused on a pre-game police raid on a Bicardi Rum-sponsored buffet in the press box and the confiscation of all alcoholic beverages.

The sergeant who led the raid must still be walking a beat in the Miami's Cuban quarter because he barely missed the governors of Nebraska, Indiana and Florida, and his own chief of police!

Fort Lauderdale columnist Bill Bondurant featured the raid throughout his hilarious game story in which he called the game a "gasser." He ended his column with: "After the game when Notre Dame Coach Ara Parseghian was asked what happened to his Fighting Irish, he replied, 'I just don't know. I'll have to study the game film to find out.'

"My sentiments exactly! I want to check the film to see if those dirty cops pulled an old Statue of Liberty play to sneak up the back elevator to steal our booze when we needed it most."

The late Ernie Seiler, longtime head of the Orange Bowl, was so incensed by the police raid he threatened to make citizen arrests in similar raids at every Miami Dolphins home game.

Miami's mayor and other officials apologized profusely and the liquor was returned the next day – too late for the thirsty press.

Former Nebraska Coach Bob Devaney chats with an official about penalties.

Bob Elliot of the Miami Herald mused in his game story that there had been "some sleep-producing affairs" in Orange Bowl history, before adding: "However, it is doubtful that any brought a deeper slumber than did Monday night's 39th offering that saw Nebraska's Cornhuskers smash Notre Dame's Fighting Irish in a 40-6 slaughter."

By the middle of the third quarter the only people left and joyously awake in the stadium were the 20,000 Husker faithful relishing every moment.

And when it was over, no one basked more in joyful pride of a job well done than Devaney.

Although he hadn't reached his goal of a third straight national crown, he was proud Johnny Rodgers had won the Heisman Trophy and that Rich Glover had won both the Lombardi and Outland trophies as the nation's outstanding lineman. And with hugs he let his players know how much he thought of them.

Since I had covered Devaney so long, I was assigned to cover his swan song. I wrote:

Miami, Fla. – A golden era in Cornhuskerdom ended late Monday night in the sauna bath-like heat of the Orange Bowl with the man who made it all possible riding high on the shoulders of his players and even higher in the hearts of all Nebraskans.

Bob Devaney, a jolly Irishman this night, closed out his collegiate

To Bucktail and Back . . .

coaching career as his Huskers, romping like the national champions they were for two years, took the fight out of the Fighting Irish of Notre Dame, 40-6. At the end he was the winningest coach in the nation with 101 victories in 11 seasons at Nebraska.

Sports scribes had called the 39th Orange Bowl one that lacked prestige since neither team was in the running for the national crown. Looking to the football heritage of both schools, they tagged it as a game rich in tradition.

That they got, as Devaney put an exclamation mark behind his name in the annals alongside such coaching immortals as Knute Rockne, Frank Leahy, Jock Sutherland, Bernie Bierman and Nebraska's other greats, D.X. Bible and Biff Jones.

Stealing a page from Notre Dame's legendary "Win one for the Gipper," the Huskers, who felt they had "let the man down" in the Oklahoma defeat, kept their vow to win the last one for the coach.

And his brightest star, Heisman Trophy winner Johnny Rodgers, a prancing pinto on the poly-turf Monday night, proved his right to gallop through the pages of football history with the fabled Four Horsemen of Notre Dame with four touchdowns and a 52-yard "special" pass for another.

In the locker room after the game Devaney, grinning widely and at his impish Irish best, turned serious long enough to emphatically call it quits as a collegiate coach after his Jan. 7 American Bowl assignment at Tampa. But he left the door open to "listen" to any pro-football offer.

He surprised veteran writers by revealing, "I'd been thinking of quitting at the end of 1969." He didn't give a reason why he didn't other than, "Well, you get to thinking let's try one more year."

Pressed by some if he could really stand on the sidelines and watch the Big Red as an onlooker, Devaney replied: "I can manage. If I can't, I can always find a coaching job somewhere else. I'll listen to anyone if they want to talk. You guys know that. But I'm not interested in any other college."

Then grinning and with a wink, the 59-year-old coach added: "I don't think I have the maturity to go into pro football. Owners very seldom go for a coach who's just 29."

He said he had no direct pro offers. "Some guy up in Philadelphia was supposed to have made a contact with me, but I never heard from him. I'm a little put out 'cause I heard he's here in Miami and he didn't give me a call," he joshed.

Then turning serious, he emphasized, "My next goal is a new sports center at Nebraska." He got what was later named the Bob Devaney Sports Center after a memorable poker game in the old Cornhusker Hotel that included state Sen. "Terrible Terry" Carpenter, who spearheaded a special

5-cents-a-pack cigarette tax to finance it.

Devaney had been pummeled by his players and given a victory ride on their shoulders to midfield to greet Irish coach Parseghian.

"He's a gentleman. He told me we had a fine football team and congratulated me in every way he could," Devaney said.

Parseghian told the scribes: "Nebraska just played an outstanding game. Their execution was super. I have nothing but praise for the kind of football they played."

Before leaving the field, he'd slapped Husker players on the back with, "You guys played a heckuva ball game."

Devaney was engulfed by players and fans alike as he walked off the field to be closeted with his team for a few moments.

"I didn't tell them anything special," he said. "I just ran around thanking the boys and was so busy trying to reach them all, I almost forgot our after-game prayer. We got it in though."

It was obvious he still wanted to be with his boys when NU President Woody Varner and Chancellor James Zumberge rushed in with congratulations followed by the press.

He often interrupted interviews to hug a player or grab an assistant's hands with, "Thanks, it's been great!"

That it was! For Devaney was the greatest.

Devaney also was an undisputed champion storyteller.

Playing golf one day at Denver's Cherry Hills course, a partner told me he not only knew Devaney well, but had been chairman of a national church convention held in Louisiana and had arranged for Devaney to be the main banquet speaker.

"Having heard Devaney wow audiences on several occasions, I knew how he loved to tell salty jokes," he recalled. "So the banquet committee and I had a special meeting with him before the dinner and got his promise to clean up his act. But once Devaney hit the podium, he forgot, to the utter delight of the audience. He got a standing ovation."

Recalled was one joke, a favorite at banquets throughout Nebraska. Devaney related how as a young coach in Michigan he and another coach were hired to drum up votes for Ole Olsen, the keeper of a drawbridge over the river, who was running for a county commissioner's seat.

"We were doing just great until we got to the house of a farmer," Devaney said. "He was aghast when we told him he ought to vote for Ole and exclaimed, 'You want me to vote for that dumb politician? He's the dumbest blankety-blank there is and I'll tell you why."

Then the farmer proceeded to tell how he once had a prized bull that suffered a severe case of constipation. His vet provided him with a laxative, instructing him to mix a pailful and pour it through a funnel into the bull's rectum.

"But I couldn't find a funnel," the farmer said. "But I ain't dumb like that Ole Olsen. I looked around and found my son's old Boy Scout bugle and used it instead. It worked just fine except just when I finished pouring it a train roared by spooking my bull. He took off down the road toward the drawbridge a tootin' and a fartin', a tootin' and a fartin'.

"And that dumb Ole opens up the drawbridge. My bull falls in the river and drowns. Now you two guys want me to vote for some dumb son-of-a-gun who don't know the difference between a bull with a bugle up his fanny from a tugboat!"

The one speech the United South Platte Chambers of Commerce remember most was the grace reluctantly given by Devaney at Red Cloud's packed Veteran's Memorial Building.

I had been drafted to introduce Devaney before his speech, so I was seated beside him at the head table when a retired missionary was called upon to give the invocation.

Instead of walking to the podium, the missionary strode to the middle of the audience. Waving his walking cane, which was studded with coins from his missions in the Middle East, he loudly proclaimed: "In ancient times there was a hero son. David was his name. But in Nebraska we, too, have a hero son. Devaney is his name. I deem it fitting our hero son give the blessing." Then he pointed his cane at Devaney and bid him say grace.

Devaney, chomping a mouthful of salad, asked me, "What the hell did he say?"

"Bob, I hate to tell you this," I replied. "In addition to a speech, you are about to say grace." Devaney gulped and whispered, "Well, I'll give 'em one," and strode to the podium. After asking all to bow their heads, in hallowed tones he said: "The Good Lord giveth and the Good Lord taketh away. Now, if you don't think that isn't a square deal, I'll kiss your fanny. Amen."

There was utter silence among the packed crowd before it suddenly exploded in roaring laughter. Don Seacrest, who was president of the Red Cloud Chamber of Commerce, laughed so hard he fell out of his chair.

Again, Devaney was the greatest!

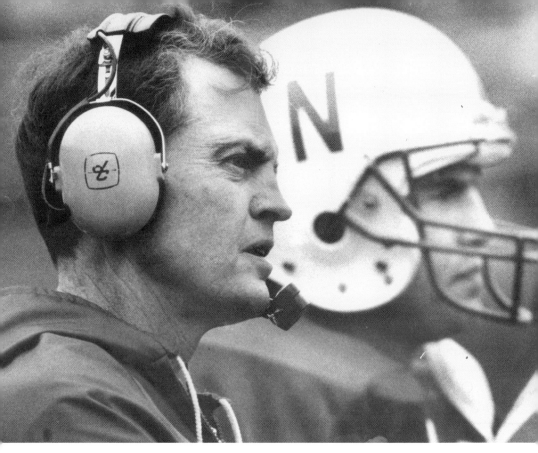

Former Nebraska Coach Tom Osborne surveys the action on the field.

To Bucktail and Back . . .

CHAPTER EIGHTEEN

An Enigma, But Also One of the Best

Tom Osborne was Bob Devaney's personal choice in 1973 to take over the football dynasty he had created.

He confessed it was a difficult task to choose the tall, lanky Hastings native over longtime assistants Carl Selmer, Mike Corrigan and John Melton who went back to his years at Wyoming, and Warren Powers, one of his former Husker players. All had helped him turn the Husker football fortunes around.

But Devaney was positive Osborne was the right man for the job.

Osborne had turned his back on a Nebraska scholarship when he was named Nebraska high school athlete of the year. He became an all-star, all-sports athlete instead at Hastings College. He began his Husker coaching career after playing professional football for two years with the Washington Redskins and one year with the San Francisco 49ers. He joined the Huskers as a graduate assistant after completing his master's and doctorate degrees in educational psychology at UNL.

Devaney was so sure he had picked the right man for the job he made him assistant head coach in 1972, his final year, after crediting him as his victory strategist.

Devaney's choice proved him so right! Osborne's brilliant 25-year career of 255 victories, 49 losses and three ties included three national championships. When he retired after the 1997 season-ending national championship 47-17 victory over Tennessee, he was the nation's winningest active coach with an .836 winning percentage and, like Devaney, was elected to the Coaches Hall of Fame.

He was so popular he was a shoo-in as the Republican candidate for the third district Congressional seat where he is still "coaching" with vigor in 2002.

I was privileged to help cover the first 11 years of Osborne's head coaching career, although I had gotten to know him during his graduate assistant years and when he was a sergeant in the Nebraska National Guard.

I considered him an enigma during his initial years as head coach.

How could a man so dedicated to Christian principles coach big-time collegiate football which essentially is a dirty war in which players get so fired up they'd cut down their own mother with a savage tackle if she was wearing an enemy uniform?

He was the direct opposite of Devaney. He was quiet, almost shy. He didn't smoke or drink or, like Devaney, stay up late dancing at Lincoln's Legionnaire Club. He was a devout Christian gentleman, a lay leader in his church and the Fellowship of Christian Athletes. He was scholarly. His only cussin' was "Dad Gum!"

Glenn Bowles of Des Moines, a veteran Big 8 official, told me, "The big difference in officiating a Devaney and a Dr. Tom-coached game was that we were in utter shock after the language Devaney used to berate us on questionable calls, to suddenly be addressed as 'Mr. Official' by Osborne."

Another major difference was that Osborne was gun-shy of the press at first and woefully uneducated in press relations. At one of his first Extra Point Club luncheons in Lincoln, Osborne announced that he had canceled his World-Herald subscription because he didn't like what was said about him in its sports columns. Then he added, "I don't want this to appear in the press."

He didn't realize he'd made big news that would be aired everywhere anyway. The 250 businessmen in attendance went back to their offices and told their employees and then told their wives at dinner that evening. Reporters did their jobs and by the next day it was all over the state. Osborne greeted reporters coldly for several days.

It got so reporters would pay a cursory visit to Osborne's post-game interviews and then go find more talkative assistants or players because he seldom had anything interesting to say.

In his early years Osborne, unlike the fiery Devaney, was stone-faced and seemed utterly devoid of emotion.

I often turned my back to the field and focused my camera on Osborne's face when the Huskers were close to the opposing end zone, hoping to capture his reaction. But there was none. I had to rely on the roar of the crowd or look at the scoreboard to see whether the Huskers had scored.

After the 1976 Astro-Bluebonnet Bowl in Houston, a 34-27 victory for the Huskers over Texas Tech, I started to take a photo of the glum-faced Osborne accepting the trophy.

"Damn it, Tom. Smile! You won!" I shouted in desperation at him. My camera set at 500th of a second was able to barely catch but a small glimmer of elation.

At the 1974 Sugar Bowl in New Orleans Osborne was particularly upset at the charges of a disgruntled agent he'd banned from the Husker campus. The charge was regarded by the press as "asinine and completely unfounded" against Osborne who was dubbed by many as "Mr. Clean."

But Osborne voluntarily kept bringing it up at pre-bowl press conferences. One day he even went so far as to announce he had gone to the New Orleans police department and had asked for a lie detector test that proved he was telling the truth in his denial of the charge.

He finally heeded the advice of family and friends who asked when he was going to quit stewing over an unfounded charge and start concentrating on his team's preparations for the Sugar Bowl.

The Huskers got his full attention and defeated the Florida Gators 13-10 in a thrilling come-from-behind victory.

After heart bypass surgery in February 1985, he went on a strict diet and exercise regime, and learned to relax and even tell a joke or two in speeches around the state.

My always cordial relations with Osborne as a coach ended when I quit covering the Huskers' sidelines after Nebraska's 28-10 Sugar Bowl victory over Louisiana State in 1985. By then he had gained my heartfelt respect as a man as well as a coach.

My respect, as well as that of much of the press, was bolstered by what he described as his most disappointing loss – the 30-31 defeat by Miami in the 1984 Orange Bowl. It ended the Huskers' national championship hopes.

Instead of going for a chip-shot point after a touchdown that could have assured a tie and the national title, Osborne chose to go for a victory with a two-point pass play by Turner Gill that was barely batted off the fingertips of Jeff Smith by Hurricane strong safety Ken Calhoun.

Osborne was praised by the national media for his gutsy call. Perhaps never had the words inscribed on Memorial Stadium been more appropriate: "Courage, Generosity, Fairness, Honor – In these are the true awards of manly sports."

In January 1995, an anguished year, while en route to his second of three national championships, Osborne had plenty of reasons to be leery of the news media. Few coaches or teams have had to weather the adversity Osborne, his staff and the 1995 team had to endure on and off the field.

Despite repeated proof to the contrary, Osborne was labeled a "win at all costs" coach by the national media.

The focal point of the attack was Osborne reinstating Lawrence Phillips as I-back two games before the bowl appearance after his arrest for assaulting a former girlfriend.

As a journalist, I cringed at the attack by CBS and the low curve, surprise question of its Bernard Goldberg at a press conference. It was what I call "wolf-pack" journalism at its worst.

Osborne was at his emotional best, but restrained his anger when he halted Goldberg, who had unexpectedly interrupted the press conference.

Osborne in his book, "On Solid Ground," recalled the incident and Goldberg's questioning this way: "Coach, I understand this may not be the most popular subject to bring up in Lincoln, but let me try anyway. If one of your players had roughed up a member of your family and then dragged her down a flight of steps ..."

Osborne cut him off, asking his identity before Goldberg completed his question with, "Would you have reinstated that player on your team?"

Osborne said, "I kind of resent the question to be very honest with you." When Goldberg asked, "Can you tell me why?" Osborne replied: "Yes, but I don't think this is the right place or time. If you want to talk in the hall, I'll talk."

Osborne, relating how he had a hard time keeping his temper in check, completed the press conference before meeting Goldberg who was waiting in the hall with a cameraman. After asking the camera be turned off, Osborne answered the question saying he would play Phillips even if he assaulted a member of his family. Then he quickly walked away.

In a CBS news broadcast, Goldberg began his segment with, "America, are athletes allowed to play the game of life by a different set of rules?"

Reinstating Phillips after the troubled youth had undergone counseling was part of Osborne's philosophy of giving youth a second chance if the situation warrants.

He ended his book, "On Solid Ground" with: "I believe we all need to be more forgiving and understanding of each other. What each of us does with a second chance is up to us."

Osborne and his wife, Nancy, exemplified their philosophy of caring for not just football players but all youth with their Teammates program, matching mentors in the community with local middle school students. He also urged his players to give back to the community as evidenced by the more than 800,000 students his players reached annually in community outreach activities.

It's a reason the 1995 season ended with Osborne being awarded the National Football Foundation and College Hall of Fame Distinguished American Award.

Like Devaney, he also is the best.

CHAPTER NINETEEN

AUTHORS AND THE POET

I was blessed to know Nebraska author Mari Sandoz and the state's poet laureate in perpetuity, John G. Neihardt, as friends.

They were my inspiration. Both told me on separate occasions in the exact same words, "You can write a good story when you hear it in your heart."

I felt a deep sense of loss at their passing. Following are the stories I wrote after Mari's death on March 10, 1966, and Doc's on Nov. 3, 1973.

The Hills Were Alive at Mari's Death

March 13, 1966 – It saddened me.

Yet I'm glad when I heard the news on my World-Herald car radio that Mari Sandoz had died I was rolling through a stretch of Sand Hills – the land she loved best.

It could have been ironic that she said good-bye on a day that the hills were becoming alive again under the warm spring sun.

But it was a day like those she must have remembered best about her beloved Nebraska during her long illness amid the concrete and asphalt of New York City.

The ducks were on the fly. The Sandhill cranes were settling on the Platte River bottoms, resting for their last leg home. There were wide areas of ice-free water on in the lakes and creeks.

It was a day that softened the hurt of farewell.

I had long been an admirer of her books when I went to Alliance in June 1959 for the first reunion of Mari and the other children of Old Jules. It was a thrill as one of America's best-known authors introduced me to many main characters and made her book, "Old Jules," come excitingly alive.

There were more than 100 of Old Jules' kinfolk at that picnic in the city park, but I'll always remember Suzi (Mrs. Suzzett) Grossendacher, Old Jules' fourth wife.

Mari, her rugged face alive with happiness, hugged the tiny woman and told me: "This is our good Aunt Suzi. She bought me my first pair of shoes. She brought all the flowers today because she knew Old Jules loved them. He often came home with a wildflower stuck in the button hole of his greasy old jacket."

After that wonderful day we became good friends. Good enough that she would give me hell – she had enough of cantankerous Old Jules in her to know how – for something I did or something I forgot to write. Sometimes she would give me a pat on the back for a story she thought had merit.

Last Christmas was most memorable. My wife had obtained a copy of Mari's latest, "Old Jules Country," an anthology of some of her finest work.

Mari, in the sand-colored ink she liked so well, had scribbled across the flyleaf: "To Tom Allan. Greetings to one who has seen the sun rise over the green hills of spring."

Perhaps that was the reason the beauty of the Sand Hills softened the sadness on the day she died. It was a day to remember and the best day for a good-bye.

Nebraska lost an illustrious daughter.

Like hundreds of other lucky ones who knew her, I lost a friend and an inspiration.

On April 3, 1966, after a visit to her lonesome grave site I wrote:

Gordon, Neb. – It is a fitting spot for her last resting place.

Only a meadowlark's trill breaks the tranquillity, and not even a road mars the natural beauty of the valley. It was what she wanted, this woman who alone stood shoulders above all the others in chronicling the heartbeat of her beloved Sand Hills and the state she cherished.

Mari Sandoz, the barefoot girl who reached international fame as an author before her death on March 10 at age 65, lies alone just beneath the brow of a knoll overlooking the picturesque valley of home.

A small, simple monument, the one she wanted, will be added soon.

The place is on the Sandoz fruit farm and ranch buried deep in the hills off Highway 27, some 40 miles south of town. Down the valley near the house are some of the fruit trees her father planted. Old Jules, made famous in her book by that name, was the Luther Burbank of the hills who defied scoffers to plant fruit trees in the treeless range.

Just beneath her grave, row on row, is the new orchard planted by her sister, Flora, heir to Old Jules' green thumb. There are 30 varieties of apples in the grove.

Deep in the valley is a lake and the greening hay is home to pheasant, grouse and deer as well as white-faced cattle.

And above all is the ever-changing sky.

Mari Sandoz, whose heartbeat was expressed best in her "Love Song To the Plains," is home.

Her heritage, her works and memorabilia are being preserved for all eternity in the Sandoz Center at Chadron State College.

Gone on Life's Greatest Adventure

I was finishing writing a story in Nebraska's Memorial Stadium press box after the Cornhuskers' victory over Colorado on Nov. 3, 1973, when I received a call from my wife notifying me simply with the words, "Gaki has left us," of the death of Nebraska's Poet Laureate John G. Neihardt. I put a fresh sheet of paper in my typewriter and wrote:

John G. Neihardt, 92, known to the world as the Poet Laureate of the Prairies, has gone on his "last great adventure."

Doc, known as Gaki to his close friends, died Saturday afternoon at the home of his daughter, Mrs. Hilda Petri, at the Skyrim Ranch near Columbia, Mo., that he loved so well.

"His heart just gave out," Hilda said. "But he was Dr. Neihardt until the end."

Having known the little guy with the white mane and amazing vitality so well over the years, I knew Hilda meant Neihardt was the same old Doc who once, when I expressed concern when he was about the embark on a long trip abroad, scoffed: "Ho! You think something might happen to me? Death cannot rob me of my life. I've already lived it. Oh, how I have loved. I do not fear it. I look forward to it as my last great adventure."

Surely there was that last twinkle in those always merry eyes and a bit of triumph in his heart in those last moments. For Doc said good-bye the way he wanted to. He'd expressed it best in one of his poems that he always liked to recite in his booming, resonant voice. It says in part:

Let me live out my years in the heat of blood.
Let me die drunken with the dreamer's dream.

Let me go quickly like a candlelight snuffed out in the
heyday of its glow.
And grant me, when I face the grisly thing, one haughty
cry to pierce the gray perhaps!
O let me be a tune-swept fiddle string that feels the
Master Melody – and snaps!

Nebraska won't be the same without its poet laureate and neither will Bancroft, the site of his Sioux Prayer Garden and the "little shack" where he wrote much of his epic "Cycle of the West" and many of his poems, now translated into a score of languages.

Neither will I, his legions of other friends, Nebraska and the literary world. We are all better for knowing him.

Somehow we knew in our hearts, and I think he did, too, last August at the annual Neihardt Day at Bancroft that it would be his last pilgrimage to the park whose giant trees he'd planted as a young man.

I was honored to be part of all the programs sponsored by the Neihardt Foundation, which is making plans for completion of the Neihardt Historical and Cultural Center at Bancroft.

"Hoy!" he exclaimed using the term of joy of his beloved Sioux Indians in his world-famous "Black Elk Speaks" and "Cycle of the West" as he confided in me after his last appearance in August. "This was the best of them all, wasn't it? Did the crowd know that I love them all?"

It had to be, Doc.

I know the crowd had roared its delight at the down-to-earth poet on one occasion during the hot afternoon in which he insisted in sitting in the searing sun to recite to the crowd in the shade.

Knowing his love for a cold beer, I had arranged with Marie Vogt of Bancroft, one of the founders of the foundation, to get him one disguised in a thermal mug.

Remembering the wrath of Mrs. J.D. Young of Lincoln, at whose home Neihardt stayed during his last years, for mentioning in a story that Doc loved two beers a day, I told him, "I will tell the audience you are taking a break to wet your whistle with a glass of lemonade. Please remember it is l-e-m-o-n-a-d-e."

Doc, forgetting the microphone in front of him, took a long swig, wiped his lips with the back of his hand and in a voice that echoed throughout the park gasped, "Damn! That's good beer!"

I was finishing up covering the Nebraska-Colorado game in the press box of darkened Memorial Stadium when the word of his passing came.

His oft-repeated, "It'll be my last great adventure," had prepared me

To Bucktail and Back . . .

for it. But I was crushed by the irony of the day. En route to the game, my wife had reminded me of a recent letter from Mrs. Young saying Doc wished to see me. I had promised to visit him the next Monday.

"I'd lost the chance to say 'so long' to the little guy who, despite his greatness, was not a poet in the ordinary sense.

He'd paddled the length of the Missouri, lived off the land with Indians, sat by a thousand campfires and, until recent years, out-walked and out-shot with a rifle any man, knocking off the beer bottles we'd emptied.

He taught the world about love: "It's the only thing that gains in value by being given away."

And on a golden October 1964 day to remember, he taught me and two Dana College students, who had accompanied him back to Bancroft for the first time in years, the place he called "paradise," about the best things in life.

I had asked him before driving him back to Omaha for his flight back to Missouri, "What's the best thing in life?" He answered without hesitation: "There are four. Love, not just the affection of boy-girl, man-wife, mother-child but the all-inclusive love that makes one willing to die for a cause or his country; the joy of craftsmanship which we are losing in the world today; a deep spiritual insight and deep sleep."

He laughed when I blinked at the last, figuring he needed a nap because we had worn the old man out after the boundless energy he had displayed during the tour of his hometown.

"Got you on that one, didn't I?" he chuckled. "Deep sleep may be the most important of all. I am not talking about the restless sleep of dreams or the fitful sleep of exhaustion. I mean the deep, restful sleep of complete oblivion. It is most important because you cannot have it unless first you have in your heart love, that joy of craftsmanship and a deep spiritual insight."

Doc, I wish as in that poem of yours you used to kid me about, "I knew some slow, soft sound to call you. I cannot shape the sound, tho I have heard it."

But for now.

Deep sleep, and as we always said, "So long for a while."

Willa Cather Was 'One of Ours'

I was not privileged to know Willa Cather, Nebraska's Pulitzer Prize-winning author of "One of Ours" and other best-loved novels such as "O Pioneers!"

Red Cloud boosters burn copies of Pageant magazine after the publication called their town "a rural community dying on the vine."

But I got to know and love Red Cloud, her childhood home used as a setting for many of her novels. And I got to know and admire the late Mildred Bennett and the late Helen Obitz, two of the women who did the most to promote the Willa Cather Pioneer Memorial and Educational Foundation and Webster County as "Catherland."

Mildred, an author and Cather authority, was the wife of Red Cloud's country doctor. Helen, known affectionately as "Butch," was the wife of Harry Obitz, a professional golfer.

The two women were "beautiful" when I first met them. Their faces, hands and grubby jeans were smeared with dirt when I found them on their knees cleaning out the cellar of the old Silas Garber Bank building before turning it into a museum.

Mrs. Bennett had persuaded her husband to help her purchase the home the Cather family had lived in after moving to Nebraska from Virginia.

With the help of donors and Cather admirers, the busy duo-led foundation obtained the Garber bank, the railroad depot, the Anna Pavelka farmhouse of "My Antonia" fame as well as other buildings that were locales in Cather's novels.

They were a determined duet, telling the suddenly interested state of Nebraska to "keep your bureaucratic cotton-pickin' hands off our project!"

They later relented, after establishing the foundation on firm ground, and let the Nebraska State Historical Society take over the buildings as historical sites.

Pageant magazine felt the two women's wrath when it re-printed an article describing Red Cloud as Exhibit A of small, rural communities dying on the vine.

They staged a middle-of-main-street bonfire, burning every Pageant magazine they could find, with the Red Cloud High School band, cheerleaders and town fathers in attendance. Then they launched a letter-writing campaign to Pageant editors listing all the progressive development projects in Red Cloud, including making it a shrine to a world-renown author.

Pageant editors wrote a profuse apology. Whether the Red Cloud protest was a factor is not known, but the once-popular magazine ceased publication a few months later.

The two women also helped launch the annual Cather Spring Conference that draws Cather scholars worldwide and has had famed actress Julie Harris and leading educators as its banquet speakers.

The foundation currently is completing restoration of Red Cloud's opera house, where Cather gave her high school graduation speech.

I also got to know and write about Red Cloud's late Carrie Sherwood.

As one of Cather's best friends, she provided much of Cather lore.

She also provided me with a classic photo as well as a classic one-word quote when she was chosen to unveil the bronze bust of Cather in the Nebraska Hall of Fame in the state Capitol.

The photo showed the delight in her face as she first viewed the bronze likeness of her childhood friend. Her heartfelt utterance of one word, "Willie!" made the story.

Mrs. Sherwood later told me: "I was the only one Willa ever allowed to call her Willie. She fussed at me at first, but secretly liked me calling her that name the rest of her life."

CHAPTER TWENTY

NEBRASKA CENTENNIAL
AND THE U.S. BICENTENNIAL

Without a doubt, Gov. Frank Morrison is the father of tourism in Nebraska.

But I'm sure even he'll agree Nebraska's centennial in 1967 provided much of the impetus for what is now the state's third largest industry.

Morrison began promoting Nebraska with a series of "Know Nebraska" tours for state leaders and national and foreign journalists to prove the state had much to offer and was not part of the erroneous report in Stephen Long's 1819 Yellowstone Expedition journey that as part of the Great American Desert it was unfit for habitation.

In speeches throughout the state, Gov. Morrison urged communities to develop a sense of pride in their heritage and hometowns. They did in hometown celebrations honoring not only the state's 100th birthday, but also their own colorful pasts.

The John B. Rogers company of Fostoria, Ohio, proved a godsend for inspired but lazy communities to dramatize their history in pageant form.

A company representative, usually advertised as a Hollywood director (but more often actually a vacationing high school drama teacher), moved in to direct a town's observance.

He directed the "Brothers of the Brush" beard contests and the "Daughters of the Swish" hoopskirted style shows, sold souvenirs – from buttons to centennial mugs and plates – and directed the historical pageant, usually hailed as being produced on the "world's largest stage" (the town football field) "with a cast of hundreds."

Boy and Girl Scouts, 4-Hers, Future Farmers and Sunday school kids were given flags to carry in colorful opening and closing scenes, which ensured that mom and dad and grandma and grandpa bought tickets. A local banker was named chairman of the finance committee in charge of ticket sales. The newspaper editor headed the publicity campaign. The local preacher with the best voice narrated the pageant.

Writing the scripts for the "Hollywood" pageants, usually titled "Plowshares to Missiles" or "Arrows to Rockets," was easy. Every town had the same basic history – Indians, the coming of the white man, arrival of the railroad, the Gay Nineties, Depression and drought years, with World Wars I and II providing a patriotic finale. All the "Hollywood scriptwriter" had to do was fill in the blanks with local names and places.

Locally, they were great successes. But for me, covering the entire state, they were repetitious – and boring. Towns that staged their own celebrations were the bright spots.

The best observances were those celebrating a town's ethnic heritage. The centennial provided major boosts to O'Neill's Irish celebration, Czech festivals at Wilber, Verdigre, Clarkson and Dwight, Swedish festivals at Stromsburg, Oakland, Wausa and Gothenburg, a Norwegian celebration at Meadow Grove and an annual Greek picnic at Bridgeport.

Launched was Nebraskaland Days, a statewide celebration of Nebraska's frontier heritage, held for the first three years at Lincoln and now held annually at North Platte, the home of Buffalo Bill, in a new Wild West Show Arena.

Best remembered for its novelty was Milford's centennial and the hijinks led by Hilton L. "Pete" Petersen. Pete enlisted the aid of Lexington's mounted Plum Creek Posse to stage a raid on Seward to "steal back the courthouse the dastardly Sewardites swiped from Milford."

Pete, a Marine veteran, led the raid brandishing a Samari sword he'd taken from a Japanese officer on Iwo Jima. He had arranged with the District Court judge to swipe a couple of law books, but Pete misjudged the enthusiasm of his posse.

They galloped into the courthouse square, then stormed through the doors firing their blank pistols. The shots, echoing off the dome, deafened startled spectators and the powder smoke blinded them. And instead of swiping the two law books, they kidnapped two District Court secretaries and took them to Milford.

The judge issued a Writ of Habeus Corpus (deliver the bodies) ordering his secretaries be returned. But neither Pete, the posse or the two pretty secretaries obeyed. The girls phoned the judge they were having such a good time at the festival they didn't wish to come back that day.

When I got to Milford the next day, a member of the Lexington posse told me The World-Herald and I had gotten him in deep trouble with his wife by running a photo I had taken of him firing his pistol with one hand while carrying one of the secretaries around the waist with the other.

"Nope. We actually saved your hide," I replied while presenting him with a copy of the original picture. World-Herald artist Homer Schlei had spent two hours moving the man's arm to a more appropriate place on the secretary's anatomy for family newspaper consumption.

"Gee!" the posse man gasped. "Is there any way I can get a couple of extra copies of the original?"

Lonesome Charlie

Petersen also was the culprit responsible for one of the most colorful hijinks in Nebraska's 1976 centennial observance.

Petersen, then a building arts "professor" at the Milford campus of Southeastern Community College, first "prescribed" Milford druggist Charles Samuelson as Nebraska's "most handsome bachelor."

Then he coaxed Samuelson into wearing bib-overalls and growing a gigantic beard. Pete then conned the state's Centennial Commission into recording Samuelson's beard as the No. 1 entry in its beard-growing contest.

That set the stage for an historical lawsuit that echoed from border-to-border to the state Capitol. Pete filed a District Court suit on Samuelson's behalf against the centennial commission and the state for "breach of companionship."

Pete claimed the defendants were guilty of making Samuelson "Lonesome Charlie," reasoning, "He's lonesome because girls shun him, claiming his centennial beard tickles them too much."

Signs went up around Milford claiming it "The Home of Lonesome Charlie." A statewide contest was held "to find suitable companionship" for Charlie. It was climaxed by a banquet and a panel of judges, including state senators, selecting "Lonesome Charlie's Centennial Girfriend" from a bevy of queens from throughout the state.

Ten years later, on the eve of America's bicentennial celebration, I stopped in Samuelson's drugstore. He ducked behind the counter and peered warily out the door to see if Pete was following me.

"Pete was the culprit and you were his publicity agent and I thought I told you I never wanted to see you guys ever again," he said with a grin. "I want it clearly understood I'm now a conservative, respectable businessman and I'm definitely not Lonesome Charlie any more."

He told me he had married the former Kathy Bauer of Benkelman, "the girl I'd always been lonesome for," and they were the proud parents of three children, Karla, 6, Paul, 4, and Eric, 4 months.

Bicentennial Observance

Perhaps no single event drew more publicity and controversy than the Interstate 80 bicentennial sculptures.

The 10 sculptures located at rest stops from the Platte River to Sidney allow Nebraska to lay claim to the "World's Longest Sculpture Garden."

As a member of the Nebraska America Bicentennial Commission, I can take a share of the credit – and the blame – for the sculptures.

The commission had plenty of funds to allocate to worthy projects. The Franklin Mint supplied us thousands of dollars as Nebraska's share of the brisk sales of bicentennial coins and medallions. All we had to do was determine which of the worthy projects got funded.

We readily approved and financed the sculpture project presented by a committee headed by Norman Geske, curator of the University of Nebraska's Sheldon Art Gallery.

The commission made a mistake allowing the committee to run the show, inviting national artists to submit their ideas and then selecting the winners.

Most of us were aghast when all of the accepted entries were "What is it?" abstract sculptures. Not one was a realistic interpretation of Nebraska's role in the development of the nation. Perhaps worse, no Nebraska artist was selected.

Rancher Gerald McGinley of Ogallala was so furious he resigned his seat on the commission.

The flames of a "What's art?" controversy were fanned the most by the steel sculpture at the eastbound I-80 Grand Island rest stop, mostly because of its name, "Erma's Desire."

The artist, John Raimondi, then 28, of Boston, a suave, handsome swinger who described himself as "absolutely of Sicilian Italian heritage," proved popular in his artist-in-residence classes at Grand Island and Hastings while completing his work.

And he couldn't wait until the July 4th dedication of what he called his "largest and best work." He revealed he had named the sculpture after his mother, Erma, and said its pointed beams jutting skyward was every mother reaching in supplication for the best for her children.

He planned the unveiling to be a special surprise for his mother and sneaked her into Grand Island from the west so she wouldn't see it until the magic moment she unveiled it. And he arranged for me to meet the "Erma" everyone was talking about on the eve of the unveiling.

When Raimondi led me into her motel suite I was delightfully astounded to discover Erma was gorgeous – a slim, vivacious ash blonde.

Catching my raised eyebrows aimed at her son, Erma said: "I know just what you're thinking. You expected a little old, fat Italian woman sweating over a hot stove making a pot of spaghetti. Well, I'm here to tell you John Raimondi is my son of whom I am very proud and I'm the mother of some more just like him."

Immediately, the abstract "Erma's Desire" sculpture took on new meaning.

CHAPTER TWENTY-ONE

NEBRASKA'S ORATORICAL CAPITAL

On April 24, 1997, I named McCook the "Oratorical Capital" of Nebraska. "It is the speechiest city in the state," I said in a speech before the George W. Norris Foundation's annual recognition dinner.

The Red Willow County seat is famed as the home of U.S. Sen. Norris, father of Nebraska's Unicameral legislature and the Tennessee Valley Authority. It's also home to Govs. Frank Morrison, Ralph Brooks and Ben Nelson, the fiery publisher and dam-creating conservationist of the McCook Gazette, Harry Strunk, and former state fair board president and state Sen. Don Thompson.

Being home to so many politicians helped make it the Oratorical Capital. I dubbed it the "speechiest city" after listening to so many of their speeches over 50 years.

I never had to take notes on the opening remarks of Govs. Morrison or Brooks. I knew them by heart.

Morrison, in countless speeches throughout the state always began, "In 1819, Major Stephen Long, leader of the Yellowstone Expedition wrote in his journal that Nebraska was the Great American Desert, devoid of vegetation and totally unfit for habitation. But look at it today. Its lush, verdant fields make it the breadbasket of the entire world!"

Brooks, a former school superintendent, opened his orations with, "In school I learned the Appian Way of Ancient Rome was the most important road in the world. Then in World War II, I was taught the most important roads were really the Burma Road and the Alcan Highway. But here tonight in (whatever town he was speaking) I have discovered my education has been sadly lacking. I have been both educated and enlightened, thanks to you folks – the single most important road in the world is – – – – – !" Then he'd name the highway or spur that the town was pushing for construction or modernization.

Morrison's "Breadbasket of the World speech" once was the subject of the wrath of Thompson, his McCook neighbor who was president of the Nebraska State Fair board.

Gov. Morrison asked the fair board to allow him to present an admiralship in the Great Navy of Nebraska to Irish tenor Dennis Day during the evening show.

Morrison was left cooling his heels while the board went into executive session. After stewing for several long moments, the governor was called before the board and Thompson began his memorable speech, saying: "The fair has a time-honored tradition of not allowing politicians to make speeches during our all-star night shows. Sir, we have decided to make an exception. You can give an admiralship this one and only time, provided you promise not to give a political speech."

Morrison humbly accepted the terms.

In rushing to add the historical ultimatum to my morning story, I missed the opening of the presentation. When I arrived I was almost knocked down by Thompson as he rushed from the grandstand, red-faced and furious, shouting, "That (bleep bleep) Frank is giving his damned old Great American Desert speech!"

It was the first time I ever heard the usually soft-spoken Thompson, a staunch Republican, cuss.

Most historic was a speech at McCook's Norris Centennial celebration during a hot July 1961. It reverberated all the way to the Oval Office in Washington, D.C.

It was the ill-famed "Nebraska is the place to come from or a place to die" speech by Nebraska native Ted Sorensen, who was a top aide, speech writer and the personal representative of President John F. Kennedy at the centennial banquet.

Sorensen's speech was the last of five banquet orations after midmorning speeches, including a tape recording of one by the late Norris at his grave site, speeches at a noon luncheon at the Elks Club and several more midafternoon speeches in the park.

The "speechiest city's" banquet audience was not only speeched out, but was almost asleep when Sorensen got up to speak in the sauna-like heat of the high school's non-air-conditioned gymnasium. And he compounded the lethargy by reading his lengthy address in a quiet monotone.

The fateful passage, near the end of the speech, was given without voice inflection.

And few, if anybody, in the audience heard it!

Jack Jarrell, The World-Herald's Washington bureau chief, had received advance copies of the speech from the White House, and early editions of the paper already had headlined the offending passage. Jarrell had sent me a copy of the speech and I was assigned to get comments after Sorensen's delivery.

Knowing what was coming, I turned in my front row seat to witness the crowd's reaction when Sorensen delivered the words that would doom any political hopes he had in his home state. There wasn't any from the lethargic crowd!

When the speech ended, Sorensen got a standing ovation. But a seat partner voiced the crowd sentiments, "Thank God this oratorical smorgasbord of a day is over!"

When I reached Gov. Morrison, who had his eyes closed during the speech, and asked for a comment, he replied, "Great speech!"

But when I asked specifically for a comment on the "place to be from or die" passage, he choked, "He didn't say that!" When I showed him the script and assured him Sorensen had indeed mumbled the words, Morrison asked for a few moments to reply. Then I saw him in an angry tirade with the offender.

I chased Sorensen to the McCook airport and asked him for a comment as he was boarding a private plane back to Washington. "I was hoping the press would miss those lines," he said.

The next morning at the popular McCook coffee shop the crowd was aghast after reading The World-Herald. Many asked, "Did he really say that?"

After the McCook Gazette headlined the passage in its evening edition, Dr. F.M. Karrer, then McCook's mayor, became so incensed he sent telegrams to Nebraska U.S. Sens. Roman Hruska and Carl Curtis, U.S. Rep. Phil Weaver and Gov. Morrison.

"We do not believe Nebraska is a depressed area," Karrer declared, adding, "Less federal waste would allow us to take care of our own problems." The Gazette also received several calls from Time magazine staffers, who wrote extensively about the "old, outmoded" slam by Sorensen.

And President Kennedy, attempting to cool the storm of protests, told Time, "This is what you get when you let your speech writer make a speech."

Actually forgotten in the speech was Sorensen's glowing praise for Norris when he said, "Norris became famous for the battles he lost, but he lived to see his every cause prevail.

"He was a politician without guile or ambition, an elder statesman with aspirations of youth and a widely hailed hero who most often walked alone.

"He was both praised and condemned, both sought after and

shunned. He was capable of soft words and righteous wrath, of sincere humility and stubborn conviction. His speech and dress were of the old frontier, but his ideals are found on the new frontier."

Many Nebraskans thought it was a great speech, but one spoiled by a line of misguided words.

CHAPTER TWENTY-TWO

GREGG MCBRIDE WAS MY 'FATHER'

Gregg McBride and his wife, Evelyn, were childless. But the wily Scot, who is best known as "Nebraska's Mr. Sports," and by legislative resolution the "Ambassador of Goodwill to Every Community in Nebraska," surprised me by revealing to me I was indeed his "son!"

The revelation came while we were driving a long, round-about way home from New Orleans after Nebraska had been humbled by Alabama 34-7 in the 1967 Sugar Bowl.

Gregg was 67 and it was his last hurrah, his last game before retiring after nearly a half-century of service to The World-Herald and its readers, preceded by chores as the University of Nebraska tennis coach, its athletic department public relations assistant and reporter for the Lincoln Star.

Working out of The World-Herald's Lincoln bureau, he pioneered high school team ratings, selected the first All-State teams, wrote about the state trapshoot championships for 49 years although he'd never fired a shotgun, and covered every Husker football game after the Nebraska-Notre Dame game in 1923.

At his death in 1977, then World-Herald publisher Harold Andersen lauded him as "one of the greatest assets The World-Herald ever had."

I was privileged to be his "road partner," driving to cover most Husker road games. Our last trip home was nostalgic and special, especially since the old Scotsman got us into Civil War battlefields and other Southern attractions free by telling gatekeepers, "My grandpappy was a Southern gentleman and a captain in the First Virginia Militia fighting the damn Yankees."

I had become used to Gregg's shenanigans, but I was shocked when he made his paternal announcement. We were almost back to Lincoln when he awoke from a nap and made the startling disclosure.

"Ha! You thought you were pretty special at all the away games this year," he began. "You lorded it over me when bellhops almost knocked you down in eagerness to carry your luggage but not mine. You were insufferably smug when maids kept knocking on our hotel room door to ask if you were

OK and could they do anything for you. You had a happy smirk on your face when waitresses offered to cut your steak and hovered over you like mother hens.

"Well," Gregg continued, "I just want you to know in making our reservations I asked the hotel management to provide extra special care for you. I told them you were a family cross to bear and that you would go into terrible, embarrassing tantrums if you thought you were not treated nicely."

Then he added the astonishing clincher: "I told them you were my backward son!"

I deem being Gregg's "backward son" to be my greatest honor. Even my kids loved the man I called "a wily old coot." They called him "Grandpa Gregg."

It began when my late daughter, Susie, was chosen by her Ralston High School journalism class to interview Gregg on why he didn't have Ralston's undefeated basketball team as No. 1.

I stood outside the door as Susie made her pitch and asked her afterward, "Did you sell him?" Susie replied, "No, but he was so nice explaining his ratings to me he made me feel he was a cuddly old grandpa!"

Daughter Mary, a cheerleader, felt the same way after she talked Gregg into being Ralston's victory banquet speaker after the Rams proved him wrong by winning the state championship and his belated No. 1 rating. Gregg even spent the evening cuddling and bottle-feeding a lamb the school had given him.

Later that night I didn't agree with son, Tam, that "Grandpa Gregg was the greatest" when I was awakened by the lambs baa-ing and found Tam sitting in the middle of the kitchen floor bottle-feeding the "special gift" Gregg had sneaked to him. The lamb, named Gregg naturally, grew into a fat ram and became the Ralston mascot.

I should have known living with Gregg was full of surprises and even his wife was not immune.

We had taken her along on a trip to Norman, Okla., for a Husker game against the Sooners. We stopped for lunch at a roadside cafe in Kansas where the proprietor stood with his arms protectively around his cash register and double-checked his waitresses' addition.

When Evelyn went to the powder room, Gregg said, "Watch this – I'll show that old tightwad." I couldn't hear the conversation, but noted Gregg shook hands with the proprietor, who was anxiously watching the powder room door.

Chuckling, Gregg explained: "I told him my wife is a kleptomaniac who has just one sin – stealing toilet paper. I told him the only reason I was telling him was it might be embarrassing for other lady customers at finding no tissue paper after Evelyn left.

"And I begged him, 'Please, please don't say anything to my wife or she'll become hysterical and cause a disturbing scene in front of your other customers.' He agreed he wouldn't say a thing and we shook hands on my suggestion that he just add the price of two rolls of Charmin to our lunch bill."

I almost choked trying to keep a straight face when Evelyn returned, angrily exclaiming: "Did you see that cashier staring at me? He was trying to undress me with his eyes!"

Evelyn fumed all during lunch and then sped out the door glaring at the proprietor leaning around the cashier trying to spot where she was hiding the stolen loot.

He and Gregg dutifully shook hands and we drove 100 miles down the road with Evelyn still furious at the "lecherous cafe owner" before the chuckling Gregg told her of his prank.

For some reason, Evelyn refused to speak to either of us the rest of the trip. But she remembered it with fond laughter in later years.

The late Bill Madden, longtime sports editor of the Scottsbluff Star-Herald, columnist for the Gering Courier and a Gregg admirer, even forgave Gregg for making him an "assault-and-battery" victim.

It happened, Madden recalled, when he and Gregg were seated side-by-side at press row, which used to be courtside during boys state basketball tournaments in the NU Coliseum.

They were busy pounding out game stories on their typewriters when Gregg was approached by a sweet-looking little old lady who turned out to be not so sweet. Her grandson's team had just upset the team Gregg had picked as No. 1.

Elated by the upset but more mightily upset with Gregg, the grandma began heatedly berating him and questioning his sports mentality.

"Gregg knew I was hard of hearing and wore two hearing aids that I blessedly turned off to cut the bedlam of games in the Coliseum," Madden recalled. "So I didn't hear Gregg tell the irate woman: "Madam, you are mistaken. I'm not Gregg McBride. The gentleman on my left is."

"I remember the woman suddenly turned her attention to me. I couldn't hear a word she was saying, so I just kept pounding away on my typewriter and saying 'Yes, ma'am to everything she said. I must have irritated her more because she suddenly began beating me over the head with her umbrella. Gregg just sat there pounding away and chuckling."

Gregg was hanged in effigy at Ord and Omaha, fed crow at Grant and given a skunk at Lexington, but he loved every moment, especially because he was at his best in fending off criticism and insults.

Seward fans, angry at him for not picking their team No. 1, presented him with a typewriter that had all its keys removed except S-E-W-A-R-D. Gregg quickly quipped to the banquet crowd: "I sincerely want to thank you for this wonderful gift. It spells out Dewars, which is my favorite brand of Scotch whiskey."

He quickly tossed away letters that praised him and treasured those panning him, explaining, "If you only receive love letters, that means only half the people are reading you."

He was an indefatigable worker and was exacting in figures.

Many is the time after a long day covering a Husker road game I'd awaken in our hotel room to the clicking of his typewriter. He was busy writing stories about his Top 10 high school teams for the Monday morning paper.

I've always considered Gregg as the best newspaperman I ever knew. And I loved the old coot.

I had to. After all, I was his "backward son."

CHAPTER TWENTY-THREE

COWBOY-LOVIN' AUNTIE RACHEL

When I received an honorary Doctorate of Letters from Dana College in May 1979, my wife, Marilyn, arranged for my widowed Aunt Rachel MacMeekin to fly in from Scotland.

The tiny bundle of energy was the last survivor of the three aunts who took care of my brother and me when my father migrated to America after my mother's death.

Always the life of a party, Auntie Rachel received an admiralship in the Great Navy of Nebraska, a key to the city of Lincoln and won the hearts of all she met.

But I knew her heart's desire was to meet a genuine cowboy. Western movies had long been her favorites.

Marilyn arranged a trek to Chet Paxton's ranch south of Thedford. The timing was perfect. Chet's daughter, Jessica, her husband, John Warren, John's brother, Jerry, and neighboring cowhands would be driving a cattle herd to summer pasture in the Nebraska National Forest range.

En route to Thedford, during what seemed to Auntie Rachel to be endless miles, she kept asking, "Lad, how soon until we get to the Pacific Ocean?"

She purred with delight when we entered a roadside cafe at Ansley for lunch. Her dream had come true. Seated at a table were four "cowpokes" wearing Stetsons and cowboy boots.

I was puzzled, and so were they, when she slowly walked around the table to see what they were eating. She shook her head after checking the blue plate special on a slate on the wall and then turning the menu over and back.

"What are you looking for – Scottish haggis?" I asked.

"Don't be cheeky," she admonished. "Those cowboys are not eating beans and there's no beans on the slate or menu," she replied. "Cowboys always eat beans. John Wayne is always walking over to the campfire to scoop up a plate of beans."

I didn't have the heart to tell her the "cowpokes" at the table were actually truck drivers, who dress more like Hollywood cowboys than do

Nebraska ranch hands.

The next day, after warm greetings by Jessica and John, and meeting genuine cowboys, she was delighted, exclaiming repeatedly, "Lovely. Lovely!"

She was enthralled following the herd in a pickup during the cattle drive that included fording what she called the "bonnie" Dismal River.

She delighted the cowhands by calling the calves "little beasties" and they howled with glee when she chastised them for kidding young Jerry for providing her with tender, loving care when he gave her a lift to his saddle.

"You cowboys shush!" she said. "Jerry is much more than a pretty face, you know!"

And Auntie Rachel had her heaven on earth during the pause for lunch. Ranch wives put out a smorgasbord of everything from prime rib to Caesar salad plus all the trimmings.

And, thank God, one brought a pot of beans!

Auntie Rachel beamed as she swaggered over to the table, scooped up a plateful and sat on the ground, John Wayne style, among genuine cowboys and relishing every morsel and moment.

At trail's end, after a bounteous supper that also included cowpoke beans, all of us wearily hit the sack. But not Auntie Rachel.

She and "much more than a pretty face" Jerry watched a late, late movie on TV – a John Wayne special.

The next year my son, Tam, arranged a family picnic at East Killbride, Scotland, complete with charcoal-grilled steaks and a pot of beans in the front yard of Auntie's son, Allan MacMeekin, and his wife, Lillian.

At age 88, Auntie Rachel was ailing and said she couldn't possibly come, but she arrived to become the life of the party again.

She told me during the party that the photo I took of her eating beans with genuine Nebraska cowboys was one of her most treasured keepsakes.

"The girls in my church group were all so jealous that I had proof I had indeed met real cowboys," she said.

Late that night when we bid her goodnight, she told us: "The day I was a trail-herding cowboy was one of the two happiest days of my life. The other is today. I was together with all of my family!"

The next afternoon as we pre-pared to play golf at St. Andrews, we received a call from Lillian.

Allan with Auntie Rachel at a family picnic in Scotland.

Auntie Rachel had died happily in her sleep during the night.

CHAPTER TWENTY-FOUR

PUBLISHERS AND EDITORS

I had one brief experience with the late Henry Doorly, son-in-law of The World-Herald's founder, Sen. Gilbert Hitchcock, who became the newspaper's second publisher.

But it was a memorable one.

In his later years Doorly, an Englishman born in Barbados, British West Indies, spent his winters in Arizona. He kept in touch and almost drove editors crazy with daily memos.

One year in the late 1950s when Doorly returned to Omaha in early March, I was summoned by Editor Fred Ware to report to him immediately because Mr. Doorly wished to see me.

Ware did not know what Doorly wanted, but he spent several minutes informing me Mr. Doorly was the grandson of a meticulous British Army major and warned me, "He won't put up with your usual shenanigans."

Ware accompanied me to Doorly's office and we both stood at attention in front of his desk.

"Mr. Allan, I understand you are our police beat reporter. I also started here as our police reporter," Doorly said in greeting.

Ware gripped my arm in warning because he knew that I knew Doorly, who was called "The Duke" by cops because of his English accent, didn't last long. Luckily, he switched to the business side of newspapering and both he and the paper prospered.

I stood mum – and then astonished – when Doorly continued: "I understand you know Police Traffic Inspector Jean Whinnery quite well. I have a question for him. Why have the traffic lanes on Dodge Street not been repainted? I want a full report tomorrow."

Ware tightened his grip on my arm, preventing me from waving out the window at the ice-glazed streets before he led me speechless out of the office.

Ware told me Doorly "meant a full report and I'll edit it before we report to Mr. Doorly tomorrow."

I went back to Central police station and confronted Whinnery with: "We, both you and me, are in deep trouble. Mr. Doorly wants to know why the traffic lanes haven't been repainted." Before the astonished Whinnery could point out the window, I added, "No, that's not good enough."

Whinnery and I, with the help of street department maintenance officials, spent the afternoon and evening compiling reports ranging from national and local paint and engineering companies to science professors at both the universities of Nebraska and Omaha.

Ware hadn't stressed his usual "keep it short and make it sing" admonition given news writers. So the next morning I turned in an eight-page, single-spaced report. I heeded his advice only in the summation: "All the experts say outdoor temperatures must be 50 degrees or higher for at least 48 hours for paint to adhere to concrete or asphalt."

Ware edited it with a worried look on his face before leading me back to Doorly's office where Mr. Doorly, without comment, read every word as he slowly turned the pages.

Then the publisher, responsible for much of the growth of the paper and Omaha, and who helped establish Children's Memorial Hospital and the Henry Doorly Zoo, leaned back, looked me in the eye and said, "Tell Mr. Whinnery to get them painted anyway!"

The next day city paint crews began repainting the driving lanes on Dodge Street – starting outside The World-Herald building.

Setting 'Terrible Terry' Straight

I had two short but memorable meetings with Peter Kiewit, who purchased The World-Herald in 1962 to preserve its independent newspaper status. He later sold it to employees.

The brief encounters were brought to mind when state Sen. Terry Carpenter of Scottsbluff, who loved the nickname "Terrible Terry" and tried to live up to it, repeated his oft-stated claim during a speech at Gering, "Pete Kiewit leans over the shoulder of every World-Herald reporter and dictates what they write."

I knew Kiewit had told the newspaper's board of directors he knew a lot about building military bases, defense systems, highways and bridges throughout the world, but knew little about publishing a newspaper, adding the admonition, "But I do know the difference between red ink and black ink, and the paper better be in the black." He then gave them free reign.

So I accosted the senator after the speech: "Terry, that is a damn lie and you know it. Let me tell you just how much Pete Kiewit controls what I write." Then I told him of my two brief contacts.

The first was in July 1940 at the headquarters of Force 6968 at Fort St. John, British Columbia, on the Alcan Highway. Kiewit's company was among a cartel contracted by the Public Roads Administration to help the Army complete the highway. I was a technical sergeant at the headquarters, and recognized him but didn't get a chance to speak to him when he arrived to attend a conference.

After the meeting Kiewit paused by my desk, asking what a cow-udder-like object hanging from a tripod was. When I told him it was a Lister bag and contained our drinking water, he said he could sure use a drink and asked for a paper cup.

Those were the days when Army privates, earning $21 a month, drove bulldozers alongside civilian contractor drivers making more than that in an hour. GIs bitterly called the Public Roads Administration employees "members of the Paupers Relief Association."

I told Kiewit only the PRA could afford paper cups and offered him the use of my canteen cup, filling it to the brim for him. There was only one catch. The handle on the canteen cup didn't hold. Water spewed all over Kiewit's jacket and pants. Kiewit, thinking I had done it on purpose, glared and me and left without saying a word.

"Terry, if you think the paper's owner and I have had long conversations about that incident, you have another guess coming," I told the senator.

My next and last encounter with Kiewit occurred at a cocktail party at the Omaha Club after he had purchased the newspaper.

Hugh Fogarty, then managing editor, introduced us. At that moment a friend tapped Kiewit on the shoulder and he turned to greet him. Then turning back to me, he said: "Nice to know you, Mr. Ringler. You are doing a good job. Keep up the good work."

After I told the senator, "Kiewit still doesn't know me from Don Ringler, our farm editor," Terry laughed and said: "Aw, you know me. I kid a lot. Let me buy you a drink." I let him.

Other Great Bosses

The World-Herald has been blessed by other great executive officers such as Walter E. Christensen and Harold W. Andersen and, currently, John Gottschalk.

I recall Christensen as a tall, soft-spoken gentleman who took time to come to reporters' desks to give words of praise or advice. Andersen, better known as "Andy," was a colleague who came up through the ranks as a superb general assignment reporter, head of the state capitol bureau and news editor before moving to what we called "The Ivory Tower."

I first knew Gottschalk, current president and CEO, as a runny-nosed little kid and the son of Phil Gottschalk, publisher of Rushville's Sheridan

County Star who is one of my all-time favorite country editors.

After Phil and I returned to the Gottschalk home – via the bar at the American Legion Club – after long days covering the second Grandsinger trial for the murder of a state patrolman, John and his brother entertained us with their magic trick show.

I later got to see John ply his magic as editor-publisher of the Sidney Telegraph and as the Panhandle city's town-promoting mayor. I've never quite forgiven him for telling me, when I interviewed him following his surprise announcement that he was leaving Sidney, that he "wished to seek new challenges" and "was not sure of his future plans."

Two weeks after my story appeared, I bumped into him in a hallway at The World-Herald. When I asked him if he was looking for a job with the paper, he grinned and replied: "I've got one. I'm the new World-Herald vice-president."

A few years later I bumped into him at the bar of Lincoln's Nebraska Club and introduced him to the cute bartender, Karen Nemec of Dwight.

"John," I said, "would you believe I took a photo of this gorgeous creature wearing nothing but lace panties and it appeared on the front page of The World-Herald?"

Before John could answer, the blushing Karen said, "I was only six months old and was ringing the fire bell at the Dwight Czech Festival" and then asked John, "Does Tom embarrass you all the time, too?"

Before the speechless John could answer, I asked Karen, "Would you believe this once runny-nosed little kid could grow up to become the vice-president of The World-Herald?"

John, after regaining his voice, poked me in the chest with a finger and said: "Mr. Allan, I suggest you read The World-Herald more carefully. I am no longer a vice-president. I am the president and chief executive officer!"

I replied, "Sir, let me buy you a drink." He did – even though I told him I'd include it in my expense account.

Frederick Rhetoric

My all-time favorite editor was the late Frederick Ware. He was one of The World-Herald's most colorful sports editors before becoming editor and a vice-president. I knew him as "Frederick Rhetoric" because of his exacting demands for proper grammar and wordsmanship. He wrote the newspaper's stylebook which was required reading for all new reporters.

Forever echoing in my ears was his often-shouted admonition: "Sophomore journalists! Keep it short and make it sing!"

But as stern as he was, he also was a fun-loving prankster. Jim

Denney, the retired writer-photographer for the now-defunct Magazine of the Midlands, recalls the day he was called into Ware's office and loudly berated for spending too much money on meals. Ware then handed him a case of Army C rations and told him: "We're cutting expenses. From now on eat these while outstate on assignments."

Ware was a Cambridge native, and I drove him into a tizzy by going out of my way to get the names of some of his high school sweethearts as well as learn of his boyhood hijinks. Then I'd use their names on "Freddie Dear" letters reminding him of when he put Limburger cheese on a hot high school study hall radiator or charged kid customers a nickel to read the magazines in his father's drugstore.

But the sly Ware turned two of my top pranks into personal plusses.

Once, he sent me to cover a trek to Mexico City and Acapulco by eastern Nebraska and western Iowa Rotarians heeding President Eisenhower's plea for a people-to-people crusade. I spent an extra hour making out my expense report in the highly inflated Mexican pesos.

"Can't you see I'm busy?" he snarled at me when I knocked on his office door immediately upon my return. "Yes, Mr. Ware," I replied. "You are indeed always a busy man, but I also know you demand expense accounts to turned in immediately."

Fuming, he grabbed the report and quickly scanned the daily sheets – and then really fumed when he spotted a luncheon listed as $60 in pesos.

"My God! If I knew it was going to be this expensive I'd have never sent you," he gasped. It didn't help when I apologized and asked, "What did you want me to do, buy a taco from a street vendor and eat it on the curb while waiting for the meeting to get over so I could interview the participants?"

Mumbling incoherently, he quickly turned the pages, not noticing the $150 for dinner or the $400-a-night hotel room. But he didn't miss the total of several thousand dollars in pesos. He gasped, turn white and then beet red, pounding his fist on the report. He came at me from around his desk shouting: "It just can't be. Is that right? Is that correct?"

I thought he was about to have a heart attack after I replied, "Yes, sir, Mr. Ware. It is absolutely correct in Mexican pesos." He fought for breath before angrily telling me, "Get out of my office and don't ever come back."

I figured I had gone too far when a moment later he stormed out of his office, put on his coat and hat and left, detouring past my desk to glare at me.

An hour later Managing Editor Hugh Fogarty, a prankster in his own right, asked me: "What did you do to Fred this time? He set a staff meeting for half an hour ago and we can't find him."

When I told Fogarty what happened, he grinned but said: "Damn you. He's been a bearcat all morning and then you have to pull this. It's been nice having you around."

I figured my days of newspapering were numbered, especially when Ware finally arrived and after another glaring detour past my desk, went in and slammed his office door.

I was sure I would be joining the unemployed ranks when I noticed he'd summoned his secretary, Irene Provost. I was certain a moment later when Irene approached with a small envelope in her hand and said, "Mr. Ware told me to deliver this to you personally." Why did she have to add, "I'm sorry, Tom."

I opened the envelope and, sure enough, inside was a traditional pink slip. But attached to it was a tattered, stinking two-peso bill that Ware must have searched every Omaha alley to find.

On the pink slip Ware had written: "Mr. Allan, you cannot add any better than you can write. You shortchanged yourself two pesos. Full payment herewith." It was signed with his trademark "F.W."

I felt better when I spotted him grinning mischievously from his office door.

One Last Release

I also should have been fired for my "last release" from the 1969 Nebraska State Fair.

After the fair's first day, State Editor Irv Baker called to report an angry reader had phoned complaining that her blue ribbon cabochon was not listed among the initial winners.

He didn't know what a "cabochon" was, curtly telling me, "You are covering the fair and are supposed to know." Neither did the fair manager, Ed Schultz, in a shouting, "You're gonna get me fired" confrontation. His longtime secretary, Helen Wadhams, solved the mystery. With dictionary in hand, she sweetly told us, "It's a semi-precious rock and won in lapidary competition."

Every day of the fair a wary Baker called after I had sent my last dispatch, asking, "Are you sure we have everything?"

When Baker called the last day of the fair with the same question, I replied: "Nope. I'm sending a special dispatch by bus." I then scurried down to the horse barn to collect and send two "road apples" with a note reading: "This is the final release from The World-Herald's State Fair bureau."

I cringed when I returned to the newsroom Monday morning and found the two horse barn deposits sitting on my typewriter atop another pink slip. It read: "Mr. Allan, this is by far the best output we have ever received from you." It was signed "F.W."

CHAPTER TWENTY-FIVE

EDITORS FINALLY CAME CLEAN

The biggest change in newspapering since the invention of the Gutenberg printing press came with the beginning of the computerized era.

After sweating through the days of hot-lead Linotypes and greasy, old flatbed presses Nebraska's community editors suddenly came clean.

I didn't recognize them when they came to annual Nebraska Press Association conventions. Instead of having ink and grease-smeared faces and clothing, they looked like gussied up white-shirted, small-town bankers or preachers.

When Al Zinc and Terry Beaver, fugitives from The World-Herald's press room and typographical union, made their Tekamah Burt County Plaindealer the first community newspaper to go offset, they met me at the door and ordered me to take my shoes off. They didn't want me tracking mud on their fancy tiled and carpeted floors.

But despite coming clean, rural weekly editors act the same. They still strut up to the podium to receive The World-Herald's coveted Service to Community and to Agriculture and Better Newspaper contest awards instead of allowing their wives to take the glory. Many know full well their wives do most of the reporting, writing, typesetting and layout work.

Once I almost caused a relapse for Alton "Mook" Wilhelms, the now-retired publisher of the Stromsburg Headlight, Shelby Sun, Gresham Gazette and the Polk Progress, when he was hospitalized for a couple of weeks and left his wife, Ardis, in charge.

I wrote notes and postcards to their Stromsburg headquarters under assumed names from all over the state asking, "What happened to your newspapers? They look so much better and are much more interesting to read than ever before. Did you fire your old publisher?"

Mook, a Dutchman famous for his "Mutterings by Mook" column and making Stromsburg Nebraska's Swede Capital, did relent and share the glory with Ardis when he received the 2002 NPA's highest honor, the Master-Publisher-Editor Award at the NPA banquet.

"I wouldn't be standing here accepting this award if it wasn't for my beautiful wife, Ardis," he said.

He had to. I'd threatened to tell the rest of the story.

Among the many other working powers behind the thrones are such queens as:

■ Bev Pollock, wife of Jack Pollock, retired publisher of Ogallala's Keith County News. She's also the author of a whimsical column, "The Beach Bum."

■ Helen Evans, wife of the late Jim Evans, publisher of the Clarkson Colfax County Press and Genoa Times Leader as well as mayor of Clarkson. Although their print shop is computerized, Helen prefers to use ancient Linotype for advertisements.

■ Shirley Bogue, wife of Bob Bogue, retired publisher of the Oakland Independent and Lyons Mirror-Sun. She also wrote a prize-winning column.

■ The late Carol Ann Lewis, wife of Jack Lewis, retired publisher of the Gering Courier. She gained fame for the impromptu hosting of Broadway and Hollywood actress Vivian Blaine, star of "Damn Yankees."

■ Betty Tarr, wife of Jack Tarr, publisher of the David City Banner-Press. She not only shouldered a heavy load at the paper, but also in civic volunteering. I took a photo of her lugging heavy circus tent poles for a Chautauqua appearance while Jack took pictures, laden only with a small camera and claiming he was over-worked.

■ Doris Kuhn, the late first wife of retired Hemingford Ledger publisher Arnie Kuhn. She not only "mother-henned" the Ledger, but wrote a column. In one I remember she chastised me in poetic lyrics for being a "dumb big-city reporter from the East who doesn't know Mountain time is an hour earlier than Central time." During an all-night drive to cover a threatened Indian takeover at Fort Robinson State Historical Park I had roused her and Arnie out of bed for a cup of coffee at 6 a.m. instead of 7 a.m.

■ Carol Pinkerton, wife of retired Kimball's Western Nebraska's Observer Bob Pinkerton. Bob not only had the expertise of his wife but "tailor made" his successor, daughter Sherri Blanche, to become a prize-winning editor-publisher.

■ Elna Johnson, not only co-published the Imperial Republican, Grant Tribune Sentinel, Wauneta Breeze and a Holyoke, Colo., newspaper with her late husband, Loral, but is continuing his legacy of church and community service.

■ Beverly Puhalla, of the Pawnee City Republican, runs an all-woman operation while her jack-of-all trades co-publisher husband, Ronald, considers himself to be "the luckiest of men."

Wrong-Day Visits

Rural publishers rued my drop-in visits because I always shouted my battle cry when I hit the door, "Everybody gets a raise and the rest of the week off!"

It didn't help that too often I arrived in the midst of a hectic press day.

Ducking a Printer's Wrath

Back before air-conditioning, I paused on a hot August afternoon at the Hooper Sentinel, published by the late Morris Payne, who boasted of being Dodge County's "Only True Democrat." An autographed photo of President Harry Truman dominated his front office.

Payne was the lone occupant in the stifling office and print shop. Thanks to his Truman-like cussin', I found him deep in the greasy pit beneath his old flatbed press. It had conked out during the press run.

I knew better than say anything. I just walked to one end of the pit, squatted, with my chin in the palms of my hands. Ink, grease and sweat-drenched Payne, wrestling with a big wrench, didn't say a word either. He just glared at me.

After five minutes of silence I asked, "Morris, can I ask you something? Have you got a problem?"

For some reason his heavy wrench sailed past my head to clank against a wall.

"Let's go have a cold one," Morris finally uttered.

Salute to the General

The late Warren C. Wood, publisher of the Gering Courier, always got my respectful attention and a brisk salute when I arrived and stood at attention in front of his desk.

I had to! He was a major general commanding the 34th Infantry division of the Nebraska and Iowa National Guard. I was a lowly major on his headquarters staff.

Thus there was no hesitation on my part when I'd drop in on press day and the general would bark: "Good. We need an extra hand. Go back to the press room and start stuffing papers with advertising inserts and help with the mailing."

"Yes sir, General!"

Once Wood called me into his office during summer training at

"What do the men call me?" he barked. He never spoke. He always barked or bellowed.

"Sir, they call you General or the Old Man," I lied.

"Damn it! I want a straight answer," he bellowed.

Sure I was facing a court martial for disrespect to a superior officer, I confessed, "Sir, some call you Hose Nose." Then pausing for breath while he glared at me, I quickly added, "But most of them call you Palladin!"

I should have received a cluster to my good conduct medal, for a big smile arched like a rainbow beneath his mustache and big nose that made him a spitting image of Richard Boone, star of the "Palladin – Have Gun Will Travel" television series.

Wood's daughter, Carol Ann Lewis, later confided in me: "You couldn't have said anything nicer about my father. Whenever we invite him over for dinner, we have to wait until the Palladin show is over before he'll sit down to eat."

Beneath his gruff exterior, Woods was a patsy. He's undoubtedly the only general to halt a war for "I Love Lucy."

Once during night maneuvers at Camp Ripley he called a halt to operations for an hour when I informed him we were receiving complaints from a Brainerd television station that our line-of-site battle radar was causing interference with the popular show.

"What channel is it on?" he asked while heading for a respite in his command post van.

Other Admired Editors and Reporters

Phil Gottschalk was the epitome of country editing when he published the Rushville Sheridan County Star.

I remember him best as the "Squire of Rushville" holding forth on world problems at the late afternoon "personality adjustment hours" in the back room of Fritz Wefsco's drug store.

Phil and Fritz tutored Bob Kerrey on the "facts of life" when he worked for Fritz as a fledgling pharmacist before becoming a Medal of Honor-winning Navy Seal in Vietnam, Nebraska governor, U.S. senator and New York City college president.

When Phil returned to his native Missouri he wrote a popular "Fan In the Stands" sports column for the Columbia newspaper and became a national award-winning author of the book, "In Dead Earnest," a detailed story of the Missouri Brigade, which had the longest and most decorated

Southern combat record in the Civil War.

Jack Lowe was much more than the publisher-editor of the Sidney Telegraph and author of its best-read column, "The Lowe Down." He was "Mr. Sidney" and Lowe's battery never ran low.

He served as his hometown's mayor and city councilman, and he wore me out writing stories on his retirement as interim city manager. He was back whenever the need arose and served as the city's boss three times. He was Sidney's and the Nebraska Panhandle's biggest promoter.

When Western Nebraska honored him for his 60 years of service to journalism, community and state, Lowe titled a collection of his columns, printed in a special edition of The Telegraph, "The Lowe Down – Sixty Years of the American Dream, With An Occasional Nightmare."

J. Alan Cramer is the suave longtime publisher of the Wayne Herald and other newspapers in Nebraska, Iowa, Colorado and Montana, who had sense enough to retire and play golf year-round at Scottsdale, Ariz. He's the donor of the annual "Maggie Award" given to the Nebraska weekly that wins the sweepstakes in the Better Newspaper Contest.

The late Jim "Rags" Raglin worked for the Lincoln Journal and thus was "the opposition," but we were the closest of friends.

We covered Nebraska Cornhusker football games as well as the Nebraska State Fair together, but we continually had to watch out for each other's pranks.

He learned one hot day at the State Fair that I had obtained a ladder to climb to the top of the Administration Building to take a panoramic photo of a record crowd jamming the carnival midway.

After taking the photo and chuckling at scooping Rags, I headed for the ladder and relief from the heat. The ladder had disappeared! There was Rags, smirking on the sidewalk below. He broke into a wide grin as I began ranting and raving at him to return the ladder.

The wily Rags not only turned a deaf ear to my pleadings, but told the crowd staring up at me in wonder: "Don't be alarmed and whatever you do, don't excite him. He's an escapee from a mental hospital. But have no fear. Help is on the way."

He finally brought the ladder after I swore and sweltered for an hour.

I later got even by suggesting it was getting hard to write new story leads after covering the fair, day after day and year after year.

Rags readily accepted my proposal that we swap stories and bylines. I'd send his lead story to The World-Herald and he'd send mine to the Journal.

The next day I showed him a note I had received from Irv Baker, the Herald's state editor, that read: "This morning's story was terrible. Allan, who was your English grammar teacher? Who taught you how to spell?"

It took a lot of persuasion, but he finally showed me a note he received from Journal publisher Joe R. Seacrest. It read: "Mr. Raglin, your story today was one of your finest pieces of journalistic endeavors. It was refreshing and outstanding!"

Later, I confessed I'd had one of the Journal photographers swipe a page from Joe R.'s note pads and I was the happy author of both notes.

World-Herald Colleagues

Carl Keith, the retired longtime night editor of The World-Herald, was a soft-spoken but exacting taskmaster with music in his soul. An avid big band record and tape collector, he made cassettes of Glenn Miller and Hal Kemp hits to make my long treks in World-Herald Car No. 18 shorter and harmonious.

Hollis Limprecht was editor of The World-Herald's Magazine of the Midlands. I miss both his work and the magazine. Both were favorites of Midlanders.

Harold Cowan, my predecessor on the Byways, had a lot tougher roads to drive than I ever did.

Bill Billotte, the late gruff-talking, cigar-chomping World-Herald South Pacific war correspondent, became the paper's ace investigative crime reporter.

Bob Dorr, the Herald's retired investigative reporter supreme, went after a story like a bloodhound and dug for facts and the truth like a beaver. He was a bearcat in telephone interviews.

Before his retirement, Bob McMorris' whimsical column was a reader's unmatched delight. I am eagerly awaiting his promised book, which he said will begin, "It was a dark and stormy night ..."

In my estimation, Tom Ash, Conde Sargent and Larry Porter were the best of sports scribes when I helped them cover the Huskers. Tom left to become the executive director of the Nebraska Cornhusker State Games. He made it nationally known. Conde became a top executive of the Nebraska High School Activities Association before his retirement. Larry is The World-Herald's outdoor reporter.

Ash and I always knew Porter would be a fishing expert. He gave up golf after losing all his golf balls when we played Miami's Doral Resort "Blue Monster" course after our Orange Bowl coverage. We later found him fishing for bass in one of the course's numerous lakes. He'd happily discovered that fishermen who can cast better than swing may rent tackle and bait at the course pro shop.

Photographers Bob Paskach, Buddy Bunker, John Savage, Larry "Robbie" Robinson, Rudy Smith and Yano Melangagio taught me how to flip flashbulbs while surviving an aching back carrying a heavy Speed Graphic. Jim Burnett helped me master easier-to-carry-and-shoot Nikons and Canons.

Mary McGrath, is a bashful retired sweetheart who was one of the first women to leave The World-Herald's society desk to become one of the nation's best medical reporters. I incurred the wrath of the late Molly Simpson, then the society editor, when I accompanied Mary to Valentine for a story on Western fashions.

I thought I had heeded Molly's admonition, "Now you be nice to Mary, she's a sweet little girl," when I took her wading in a creek. But I over-did it when I called the night desk staff and asked them to leave a note for Molly that read: "Sorry, we can't make it back tonight. Took Mary wading in a creek and discovered she has cherubic knees. Then we got lost in the Sand Hills. But don't worry, Mary and I are sleeping safe and sound in the Kennedy post office!"

Molly met me at the door when we returned late the next afternoon with: "Buster! You've got some explaining to do."

I was saved by Mary's blushing explanation that Kennedy was the ranch house post office in the home of Jerry and Marianne Beel. Mary helped more by adding, "And Tom was a perfect gentleman at all times."

Hugh Fogarty, Lou Gerdes and G. Woodson "Woodie" Howe were editors who gave me leeway to rove the Byways and forgave – I think – my indiscretions.

Irv Baker, Len Propst and Gene Beran were regional and state editors, who in me, had to put up with a helluva lot with good grace.

Deanna Sands and Joanne Stewart were the first women to become managing editor and assistant managing editor, respectively, of The World-Herald.

Thus, they are the first editors I ever stole a kiss and hug from. Come to think about it, they are the only editors I ever had a yen to smooch.

Grand Island boys dive off a Platte River backwater bridge near Alda.

CHAPTER TWENTY-SIX

Skinny-Dipping Memories

Picking another daisy was easy on a hot summer day. I had gone to Nelson, near the Kansas border, to report the heartbreak of local kids at long storm-caused work delays and State Health Department requirements on the construction of a modern swimming pool.

In the midsummer's heat all the kids could do was sit and sweat and hope the pool would be completed before summer ended. But four old men refused to wait. While sitting at a town cafe they recalled old skinny-dipping days in Elk Creek and literally stripped for action.

I chronicled the result in a July 16, 1961, story under the headline, "Muddy Waters Wash Years Away."

Nelson, Neb. – The muddy waters of Elk Creek swept four men back to boyhood last week.

They were caught in a flood of memories, and for a few hilarious hours they were cleansed of worries and cynicism.

Turning into happy, carefree boys again down at the old skinny dippin' swimming hole were Vernon "Tuffy" Wade, Nelson's barber for more than 50 years; Vic Scherzinger, editor of the Nelson Gazette; Harlan "Zim" Zimmerman, postmaster, and this reporter, just old enough to remember horse tank splashes and furtive Stink Creek dunkings.

"It's been all of 50 years since I slid down a mudslide or threw a bunch of cockleburs on it just as a buddy started down," Tuffy said with a laugh that shook the table.

Memories and stories roared back, and the first liar never had a chance. Then Tuffy held up two fingers and cut loose with an ear-splitting whistle.

"That was the signal. Every kid in town knew it meant 'Let's go swimming and the last one in's a horn-toed monkey,' " Tuffy explained.

That did it! It was hot. It was near quitting time anyway. Minutes later four usually dignified men were whooping like banshees in the muddy but cool waters.

The intent was to hit the water in traditional birthday attire at the remote spot until editor Vic remembered: "Geeze! There were 300 Girl Scouts camped across the way yesterday."

Tuffy stopped unbuttoning his old-fashioned BVDs. We stopped at shorts. But all the rest was the same.

Rushing back in mind's recall was the forgotten caress of mud squishing between toes, the taste – surprisingly pleasant – of cool muddy water uncontaminated by Health Department-required chlorine and filters, the wild horseplay, the old forgotten jests and jokes and the feeling of becoming wonderfully alive and young again.

Two bald heads float majestically like lily pads in the Elk Creek.

True, there were some differences. As we remembered it, the boys in the old days were all skinny and didn't sport pot bellies.

And last week even the frogs croaked in surprise when the white-hair-fringed bald heads of the nearly submerged Vic and Zim floated majestically by.

Perhaps best of all was the warm afterglow of happiness and comradeship as we scraped off the mud under a convenient pump and headed back up town.

Tuffy, who figured he lost "at least 60 years back in the muddy waters," summed up the afternoon best. "Sure makes a fella feel good all over, don't it?"

The story led to national publicity and surprising response.

Editor Vic established the Elk Creek Skinny Dip Association "to preserve ol' swimmin' hole memories."

He printed up membership cards, featuring the classic prize-winning photo of his and Zim's floating bald heads, and sold them for a buck.

Postmaster Zim said his post office was flooded with membership requests from throughout the world.

And Vic had the last laugh as he told me just before he passed into the most heavenly swimming hole of them all in the sky, "How do you think I financed my new Olds?"

Cool Water Ecstasy

I and other motorists did a double-take driving east on I-80 near Alda on a hot, humid June 14, 1995, day.

A dozen Grand Island Catholic High School boys were experiencing the ecstasy of hot sunshine and cool water diving off a county bridge into one of the channels of the Platte River alongside the superhighway.

I couldn't wait to get down a back road to snap a photo of their joyous abandon, and they were all too glad to oblige with another kersplash!

The World-Herald ran the color photo on the front page of the June 16, 1995, edition. I caught hell from a reader for picturing "an act of extreme foolhardiness" in the most dangerous of situations – headlong diving into a moving river."

It wasn't! Having been a Red Cross swimming instructor in college, I made sure they knew what they were doing. I first ascertained it was not a fast-running river, but a deep backwater channel. Then I checked and found all the boys were excellent, experienced swimmers and divers.

A Nebraska Highway Patrol officer, who'd pulled off the highway to watch, did not stop them for safety's sake. He must have been jealous.

And remembering my young and carefree days, I darn near joined them. It was a sight to recall and remember.

CHAPTER TWENTY-SEVEN

ANIMAL FEST

A wise old editor always demanded a good dog story for every edition, reasoning that almost everybody loves a dog.

I got some.

While visiting the late John G. Neihardt, Nebraska's poet laureate in perpetuity, at his Skyrim Ranch in Missouri, he told me love is one of the best things in the world because it is the only thing that increases in value by being given to someone else.

Then patting the head of a collie that had her head on his knee and looked up at him adoringly, he added, "Webster's Dictionary has a very poor definition of love. Let me live in this dog's heart for a week and I'll be able to write a beautiful, all-consuming definition of love."

But can the love of a dog for his master live on through untold generations of pups?

That's the question I asked Neihardt a couple of years later when J.D. Young and his wife, Myrtle, of Lincoln told me the story of "John's Ghost Dog."

Neihardt spent the last years of his life at the Young home where he wrote "All Is But a Beginning." J.D., a longtime high school science teacher who delved into facts and not theory, and his wife swear the story is true. They were eyewitnesses.

They said they were astounded while taking the poet back to Spearfish, S.D., after his absence of over 60 years to suddenly see a shepherd dog rush toward Neihardt and leap into his arms with unbounded joy, licking his face and yipping with delight.

"I can't believe it. That's the meanest dog I ever had and he never took to strangers like this," gasped the dog's owner, a rancher. He had to put a rope around the dog's neck to pull him back to his pickup.

En route back to town, Doc told the Youngs the dog was similar to the one that had adopted him and a girlfriend when, as a young man, he had spent the summer in a shack alongside the railroad tracks at Spearfish.

His owner, like the rancher, had expressed astonishment that his "meanest dog around," had shown such affection for a stranger.

"I remember back those 60 years when the dog first came to me," Neihardt told the Youngs. He ran up and told me, 'I'm your dog.' I told him, 'No, you are not.' But even though I handed him back to his master, he wouldn't take 'no' for an answer. So we became good companions."

Neihardt said the dog became a constant companion. At summer's end when Neihardt headed back to his studies at Wayne State College, the girl accepted his good-bye. But the dog refused. He attacked the engine of the train bearing the poet away and was killed. The girl buried the dog alongside the tracks and placed a marker bearing the words "John's Dog" over its grave.

The Youngs said they were astounded again when they traveled several miles back to a cafe at Spearfish.

"We saw the door bouncing back and forth, a dog's nose appeared and suddenly the dog we had left rushed in and again launched himself with unbridled joy at Doc," J.D. recalled. "He had chewed through the rope the rancher used as a leash.

"Doc laughingly called it 'the return of his ghost dog.' Regretfully, we had to return him to his doubly astounded owner."

I already knew Neihardt had a mystical relationship with animals. In October 1964 while taking Neihardt "home" to Bancroft for the first time in years, we tried to find his old home that had been moved to a farmstead outside of town.

Pulling into a farmyard I noticed a "Beware. Mean Dog" sign. Before I could stop him, Neihardt, with his usual boundless energy, jumped from the car and into the path of a huge, snarling dog rushing at him. Neihardt responded with a few soft words and knelt before the attacker. Suddenly the dog rolled over and with moans of joy allowed the poet to scratch his belly to the astonishment of both me and the dog's owner.

Neihardt chuckled when I asked him about the Youngs' story and then said, "Animals have always made me ashamed. They teach us humans more about love than most learn by the regular process. I believe there is a close relationship between mystical awareness and animals."

Neihardt chuckled again and his eyes sparkled when I asked him, "But do you really believe a dog's love for his master can live through generations of pups?"

Befitting the great teacher he was, he made me give an answer, by asking, "What do you think?" I told him I believed it, if for no other reason than I wanted to believe it with all my heart.

Neihardt replied, "There's your answer. It's a great story and should be told."

Proving the Honesty of a Madrid Farmer

In September 1968 I received a telephone call from Mrs. Mary Nutt asking me to save the good name of her son, Bob, a Madrid-area farmer, by driving out to take pictures proving he wasn't a liar as his morning coffee friends at the local cafe claimed.

It was followed by a letter from Nutt's sister, Mrs. Harold Peterson of Curtis, with a similar anguished plea.

They said Nutt had a wild pheasant he'd named Sport who chased him for hours in his field, playfully bouncing back and forth over the front tractor wheels.

I raised my eyebrows when both added, "but only if Bob drives his old 1952 yellow Minneapolis Moline tractor instead of his new green John Deere model."

Sure. Unlike his coffee shop buddies, this old cynic believed them. Or was it just a nice day for a drive to the farthest southwest corner of the state?

To my surprise, Sport, a cock pheasant, was for real. And I thanked my lucky stars I snapped photos to prove to my equally astonished editors that neither Nutt nor I were liars.

In my Sept. 29, 1968, "seeing-is-believing-story" accompanied by a photo spread, I wrote:

"The Nebraska pheasant season is scheduled to open Nov. 2. But good sports, Sport, the cockiest, doggondest cock pheasant you'll ever see, is strictly off limits.

"To Sport, all other pheasants are mere peasants. He's a frivolous fowl that has to be seen to be believed. Sport is a cock pheasant who thinks he's a dog.

"For three years now Sport has followed farmer Bob Nutt up and down his fields, running and hopping gaily between the front wheels of his old yellow Minneapolis Moline tractor. He keeps it up for hours until he's bushed and panting like a dog.

"But even then he's still cocky enough to crow in triumph or defiance if his tag-playing game is interrupted by a stranger."

I related how Nutt conceded he "couldn't believe it either when all of a sudden Sport had dashed out of a shelterbelt three years ago and started bouncing in, out and over my tractor's front wheels.

"At first I told the boys at Madrid about Sport, but they gave me that look or laughed at me and called me a liar. This summer I visited an old

Army buddy and took in the Hemis-Fair down in Texas. When I told those Texans about Sport, they just threw up their hands and said, 'OK, you win. You tell bigger stories than we do.' "

Thus his joy and that of his mother when I arrived. Nutt immediately stopped putting up silage in a field 2-1/2 miles south. I smiled politely, wondering if the long trip had really been necessary, while Nutt explained why he'd have to go back to the farmstead and pick up "Old Yellar" before Sport would perform.

There also were anxious moments as we putt-putted up and down the field until Nutt suddenly whooped, "He's here!" and there running toward us was the cocky pheasant. When I got out of the tractor cab, Sport dashed back to the shelterbelt.

"Get back in the cab. He don't like strangers," Nutt shouted.

Sport came rushing back before I got settled and for more than an hour he played tag with the front wheels while we zipped along at speeds estimated by Nutt at up to 18 mph.

We quit when Sport stood "panting" with his head cocked to one side, his beak agape but still raring to go.

I ended the story with, "An hour later after Mom Nutt's delicious coffee and cookies, I pulled out of the yard. As I did, down the farm lane echoed Sport's farewell – a loud and joyous, cocky crow.

"Yes, Sport. I believe you."

Wild Grouse Struts on Main Street

"Art the Grouse" delights Hayes Center residents and stumps hunting dogs by strutting Main Street.

I also had to see it to believe it for a story I did Nov. 22, 1959, at Hayes Center on "Art the Grouse," who almost daily strutted down Main Street like a peacock.

I heeded frantic telephone calls from several residents when the local Lutheran minister vouched the story of Art's urban strut was "the God's truth."

But I thought I'd been had when residents glumly reported Art hadn't been seen for several days and feared he'd been a target for an eager hunter.

"We'll shoot the hunter when we learn who he is," vowed an Art lover.

When I searched in vain in a pasture where

170   *To Bucktail and Back . . .*

Art had been reportedly last seen and was ready to call it quits, hope sprung eternal when a pickup roared up and the driver exhorted, "Get back to town. Art's back!"

I began my story with:

Hayes Center, Neb. – "An unruffled grouse has ruffled this usually quiet southwestern Nebraska town.

"The wild game bird fluttered in a week ago and became king of the roost to the delight of townsfolk and the utter bewilderment of hunting dogs.

"He gained a name, Art, and took over Main Street as his domain."

Then I related how most mornings Art flutters in from a secret field nest for a crushed corn breakfast served between the gas pumps at Stan Rucker's service station.

When the crowd gathers at 10:30 a.m. when the mail comes in, Art fluffs his feathers and crosses the street with proud disdain and goes to the post office. The usual collection of dogs get an "I dare you" stare and a flaunting flick of the tail.

Art the Grouse strutted his stuff with obvious delight for my picture taking, even letting Mrs. Hershel Evans pet his feathers.

"I never saw anything like it," said J.R. Garrett. "Hunting dogs ignore him, apparently thinking, 'This just can't be. There just can't be a grouse on Main Street.' "

Garrett demonstrated by calling Spud, his Chesapeake. Then he had to drag the big dog over to where Art was placidly eating lunch in the middle of the street.

Not until Art was almost under his nose did the truth dawn for Spud: "Art is real." As the leashed dog lunged, Art fluffed his tail feathers and slowly walked away like a matador taunting a mad bull.

"I still can't believe it," said Arthur Glen, operator of a recreation parlor. "Last Sunday morning I saw a traffic jam and there was Art. He ignored traffic and just flew up on a nearby awning when a cat or dog got too close or people bothered him. Then he came back."

Mrs. Mae Richards, The World-Herald's area correspondent, mused: "Art's behavior would hardly indicate a normal mind for a wild bird. However, he's a smart bird in anyone's language – keeping an entire town guarding it. It would be just too bad for any car driver unlucky enough to run over him."

I ended the story with "Hayes Center has become Art's private preserve."

Sargent Doc's Chicken Coop Lion's Den

In my Aug. 4, 1971, Byways column I wrote, "Some folks go to a zoo. I just go to Sargent to view exotic animals.

"Dr. Robert Westbrook, and his wife, Gloria, animal lovers supreme, started it all six years ago by moving to the Custer County Sand Hills town of Sargent from Louisiana with six Eskimo Malamute sled dogs, a Great Dane, assorted tropical birds, a bashful African lion cub named Byron – and the doctor's mother-in-law."

The menagerie was an unexpected bonus for Sargent-area residents. The arrival of the country physician not only provided them with much-needed medical service, but allowed the re-opening of the 14-bed community hospital that had been closed for a year. It also meant the opening of a $40,000 medical clinic on Main Street.

It broke the doctor's heart when Byron, the lion cub who was calmed by the hi-fi playing Rachmaninoff's "Concerto No. 2" piped into his former chicken coop den, died of a virus."

When I returned to the backyard zoo in April 1971, the Westbrooks had added two four-month-old lion cubs, a herd of Chinese white deer and assorted tropical birds.

And Mrs. Westbrook had miraculously lost a life-long allergy to animal fur to mother the lion cubs that Dr. Westbrook, a Shreveport, La., native and former new Orleans Tulane University football player, called "our puddy cats."

Mrs. Westbrook was the mother of a baby daughter of her own, Mary Nell, 1, and was pregnant with another child when I was given an unforgettable introduction to the "puddy cats."

They were housed in the reinforced chicken coop and refused to come out. Westbrook squeezed through the small hen door to coax them out while Mrs. Westbrook stood in the chicken pen.

Suddenly there were angry lion roars and physician cussing, and the cub came roaring out the door and made a beeline straight for us.

"Stand still. Don't move!" Mrs. Westbrook ordered as she grabbed my hand.

The cubs suddenly veered, lunged at the top of the fence and catapulted into the adjacent sled dog's pen, launching the biggest of dog and cat fights.

Doc Westbrook emerged from the coop and, roaring like a lion, jumped the fence and threw the dogs over another fence where they started a mad dash for the deer before he headed them off at the pass.

Miraculously, the doctor escaped without a scratch. But I thought he had lost his head when he later introduced me to Jason, another "puddy cat," a mountain lion he was boarding for Sargent crop-dusting pilot Joe Poland. As Dr. Westbrook squatted next to the fence, Jason with a flip of his paw flicked the crimson "Go Big Red" hat from Doc's head.

To Bucktail and Back . . .

Practicing the old adage, "Disgression is the better part of valor," Westbrook waited until Poland entered the cage of his "lovable puddy cat" to get his hat back.

Gravel Gertie, A True Fish Story

Clearwater's Benny Prater told me he'd "swear on a stack of Bibles" the saga of Gravel Gertie was true.

"Honest to gosh," Benny vowed. There is a guy over near Inman who owns and operates a gravel pit lake. He has a pet carp he calls 'Gravel Gertie'." At lunchtime each day he raps on the side of the dredge pontoon. Gertie surfaces and he feeds her part of his sandwich. Then the best part is that Gravel Gertie allows him to lift her clear of the water so he can give her a belly rub. Gertie almost grins in delight."

Since we had imbibed in a couple of tonics at the bar, I agreed to Benny's invitation to "Let's go see," even though it meant crawling across a discharge pipe to get to the dredge anchored at midlake.

Sure enough, Gravel Gertie and her master performed on cue.

And I thanked my lucky stars I had captured the performance on film, especially when Benny's perpetual unlit cigar dropped from his mouth and he gasped, "My God! I wouldn't have believed it if I hadn't seen it with my own eyes."

My Good Deed Made A Sad Ending

It took 20 years for Larry Porter, The World-Herald's outdoor writer, to hunt down my biggest good deed that resulted in the death of two household pets – a tame deer and antelope.

After interviewing Gretchen Hausmann's family and photographing them and their unusual house pets in their farmhouse kitchen, I inadvertently left a pack of flash bulbs.

I didn't know until Porter's story that the pets had eaten them and died. It helped that in stories by Porter and my successor, Paul Hammel, they reported the Hausmanns never told me because "they did not wish to embarrass me and had felt honored that I had driven 260 miles to tell their story."

Hammel, in his June 20, 1999, story marking my retirement as an official employee, softened my chagrin further by quoting Mrs. Hausmann: "There is just one Tom Allan. He reaches out to people and is one of them."

I just wish I had been more careful after a joyous gathering of man and beasts in their kitchen.

Li'l Mutt Steered Me Straight

For 15 years "Li'l Mutt," a tiny mop-headed miniature French poodle and Schnauzer-cross, helped me steer World-Herald Car. No. 18 along the Byways.

She may well be the only dog to have helped irrigate all 93 Nebraska county courthouse lawns. Folks loved her because her usual greeting was sitting up and giving little woofs as if saying, "Ain't I the berries?" Cats loved her because she never growled or chased them. She'd just lay down and let them approach her with their usual inquisitive nature.

Her usual perch in the car was on top of the driver's seat with her paws draped over my shoulder. Leonard McCombe, the famed Life magazine photographer, who I gave a ride to photograph the "Love Life of a Bumble Bee" in a Sand Hills pasture, was so intrigued he shot six rolls of film of her queenly perch. Treasured is a color photo of her on her throne that he sent me.

Bellwood Crows About Joe

In January 1972 I met Bellwood's "Joe the Crow" and we gabbed up a storm in the Butler County town.

Joe is both the town's character and mascot. He plays football and goes skating with the kids. He struts up and down the main street, plays pranks while mooching handouts at homes all over town, goes to church, demands a drink of water at Jerome Didier's Grocery and hobnobs with the likes of R.P. "Pump Handle" Kinnison and the town's old bachelor, Carl Holste.

Joe also talks: "Wow!" "Oh, boy!" "Hello!" "Thank you!" and he even laughs raucously.

"We used to go crow hunting, but we don't anymore," said Didier. "We're scared we might shoot Joe."

It was Pump Handle – a nickname acquired from all the wells he's dug around the country – who helped me find Joe for an interview.

"Hello, oh, boy, oh boy," said Joe when we found him stashing away some goodies under the newly chopped woodpile at Holste's home.

"Joe usually comes over here after he flies the kids to school so we can have an old bull session," Holste said. "Say, you aren't one of those big city reporters who writes all those cock-and-bull stories, are you?"

Joe broke into laughter and I thought it was because Holste had me pegged to a "T." But it was only because he had snatched a tidbit from the paws of Holste's bewildered cat.

"He's got all the dogs in town bamboozled, too," Pump Handle said. "You should see him skating and playing football with the kids. He swoops down and tries to take their hats and then skids down on the ice alongside them. He gets on top of the football and moves it with his wings. He's nuts about kids."

I went over to the playground and watched him perform with the happy kids. A few moments later Joe flew down the street to see if Mrs. C.W. Sorensen was dumping any goodies in her garbage can.

"Oh, boy! Thank you," Joe said when she gave him some meat scraps. Having eaten his fill, he began stuffing the remainder down the air vent under the windshield wiper on Sorensen's car.

"That's his one bad habit," Mrs. Sorensen said. "He usually puts a shiny rock on our porch after we feed him."

The saga of Joe began last summer. The Norman Pillar family found him injured and unable to fly. They took him to their farm home on the edge of town, put him in a pen, mended his wounds and provided tender, loving care and smooth talked him into talking.

Not long afterward, he showed up at the nearby farm home of state Sen. Loran Schmit in the role of a Peeping Tom.

"I didn't know he had learned to talk until one day I was just stepping into the bathtub when I heard someone say, 'Oh, boy! Oh, boy!,' and I almost flipped," the senator's wife, Rene, recalled. "The window was open and Joe had flown up to perch on the sill."

Mrs. Leonard Ronkar said she was hanging up clothes in the back yard when Joe first showed up.

"I told him he was a pretty bird and I darn near dropped the clothes when he replied, 'Oh, boy. Thank you!' "

Didier said Joe showed up at St. Peter Catholic Church, strutting around the front door and greeting folks last Sunday.

"He likes to sit on cars and talk. Just the other night he was crowing away at the store door wanting a drink of water. I got him a glassful, but he prefers to dump it over to drink his way. He's a scroungy-looking old fellow, but he's the town mascot."

Before leaving town I told Joe he was going to be famous statewide after his story appeared in The World-Herald.

Joe, the crow, flapped his wings and let out a raucous cry of "Oh, boy! Oh, boy! Thanks!"

Wheat harvest near Lewellen,
Neb., in full swing.

CHAPTER TWENTY-EIGHT

TRANQUILLITY AND INSPIRATION

Nebraska is blessed with countless spots of tranquil beauty.

Two of my favorites are so misnamed I wonder if their names were given by someone who wished to hide their beauty and keep them for their own.

They are the Dismal River in the heart of the Sand Hills and Sow Belly Canyon of the Pine Ridge country in the far northeastern corner of the state. With their breathtaking panoramas, they deserve more magnificent titles.

Other favorite views are the scenic panorama from the hills just north of Decatur in the northeast corner, and Brownville in the southeast corner with wide-lens views of the Missouri River Valley. Then there are vistas in the ever-changing Sand Hills' "Sea of Grass" ranges beneath a big sky, providing dramatic sunrises and sunsets. They are too numerous to count.

Mother nature also provides a few unforgettable, if momentary, glimpses that are heart-stopping in their grandeur.

Such was the majestic scene on an early October evening on the Frenchman River just upstream from the old mill pond at Champion Mill State Historical Park at Champion in Chase County.

I was lucky to capture the magic instant on film and its story ran on Oct. 13, 1988, beneath a full-color photo.

Champion, Neb. – It was a moment to remember, to relish until life's final sunset.

"There are so very few times when it's perfect," said Celia Cady, a lucky witness. "The clouds come, the wind blows and all of a sudden the golden leaves are gone."

But for a few short moments it was a perfect Monday evening down on the old mill stream. It had suddenly become a perfect mirror, reflecting the old mill and its crescent of golden cottonwood trees.

"Hurry or you'll miss it – it's just too beautiful to miss!" Mrs. Cady shouted as she rushed into Nebraska's last functional water-powered mill to interrupt my conversation with Park Superintendent Tim Hajek.

The high winds, which had prompted warnings on Nebraska's lakes earlier in the day, had died for an evening requiem.

A five-below-zero trail ride near Valentine, Neb.

Dark storm clouds hung in the western horizon, but the setting sun had elbowed through them to add a master's touch to nature's golden October array.

Nary a ripple marred the mirror of Champion Lake. The tall crescent of brilliant yellow cottonwood trees was reflected in golden reverse on the lake's surface. The historic white mill gleamed upside down in still waters.

Awed, we snapped photos.

Then, to get a more perfect angle, Hajek, Mrs. Cady's husband, Dennis, and I carefully launched a rowboat, keeping a wary eye on the threatening clouds approaching.

The sun, as if wanting the moment to be shared, kept the clouds at bay until our wake and ripples had subsided.

Only our camera clicks disturbed the golden benediction.

Too soon it was over. Thunder crashed, jealous lightning filled the dark sky and leaves fell with the rain in gusty winds. Next morning the golden double crescent was gone and snow flurries heralded winter.

But we had a golden moment to remember as well as a poetic nature sermon by poet Humbert Wolfe:

Listen, the wind is rising and the air is full of leaves. We've had our summer evenings, now for October eves.

Sermons Without Words

Favorite spots along the Byways have been country church yards. They provide much more than a tranquil spot to break a long summer day's drive.

They are nature's tabernacles and in them I always feel closer to God than I ever have in big city churches or cathedrals.

I began an April 19, 1958, story with lines from poet Arthur Cox:

I never see the old churchyard but I breathe to God a prayer.
That sleep as I may in this fevered life, may I rest when I slumber here.

A country church has a sermon that needs no spoken words.

It can be felt instead of heard in the quiet solitude of the deserted churchyard. Usually located on bypaths, they are some of the remaining islands on tranquillity in a troubled world.

There, removed from the traffic and other manufactured noises of hectic modern life, one can feel the awesome presence of nature and God.

There are many that are typical. In the yard sleep former members of the congregation. The quiet sermon's prelude is the soft anthem of twittering birds and the muted organ sigh of the spring wind rustling through stately evergreen trees.

A small, weather-aged marker for a child may spark a memory of an all-but-forgotten literature class and Thomas Gray's Elegy:

> *Here rests his head upon the lap of earth.*
> *A youth to fortune and fame unknown.*
> *Fair science frowned no on his humble birth.*
> *And melancholy marked him for her own.*

And for those who treasure worldly goods there may echo another verse from the same poem:

> *The boast of heraldry, the pomp of pow'r.*
> *And all that beauty, all that e're gave.*
> *Await alike the inevitable hour:*
> *The paths of glory lead but to the grave.*

Then again, for some there may be only the physical respite of a refreshing pause by the side of the road at a spot of solemn beauty.

But whatever the reflection or response, the pause there by a weary traveler has made him a better man.

For a few moments, he was alone with God.

Cowboy Dawn at 5-Below

Another spectacular Nebraska scene frozen in memory is one that occurred in a 5-below-zero spectacular dawn in late January 1963 on the range north of the Niobrara River near Valentine.

Indian ranchers and cowboys, aided by area volunteers, had returned to their old school, the St. Francis Mission just across the border in South Dakota, to lend a hand in a sad farewell.

They and the mission were saying good-bye to the mission's 70 years of Hereford cattle operations that had helped finance the school and their education. They were trail-herding several hundred head of Herefords to the Valentine Livestock Commission pens for a dispersal sale.

It was the reason for the frozen tears lingering on the cheeks of Brother Ulrich Rosman, the longtime mission's keeper of the herd.

"We feel bad and sad," said the Rev. Richard Pates, S.J., the mission superior, in announcing earlier in the week the sale of the mission's 10,000-acre ranch to William Adams II of Odebolt, Iowa. "But we do not like to be a commercial enterprise. It is tough to run a business and religion on the same spot. We had to make a decision on our priorities."

Money from the sale of the ranch and the cattle will be invested for the continued operation of the mission and its school, Father Pates said.

Hardly had Father Pates announced his decision to sell the herd when offers of aid poured in.

Ira "Ike" Dotson, Valentine auction company operator, and his son, Larry, offered to sell the cattle without cost to the mission. They also got together with Joe "Bad Land" Waln and Oliver "Ollie" Wright, two respected Indian ranchers and mission alumni.

"We offered to deliver the herd to Valentine for nothing by making a trail drive," Ike said.

Larry, Joe and Ollie were joined by volunteers Mathew Boneshirt and George Haukaas, both of St. Francis; the fun-loving, hard-riding Cornish boys, Claude, Wayne and Max of Valentine; and Joe's son, Carl, all hell-for-leather cowboys. Brother Rosman, making his last roundup, made up the "Lucky 13" trail crew for the two-day, 30-mile drive.

I joined them at their halfway point near Kilgore before dawn on the second day. I wrote in my Jan. 31, 1963, story:

"Their horses balked at the frosty saddles as the boys saddled up at 5:30 a.m. Monday in 5-below-zero weather.

"There was good-natured joshing, then a moment of silence as Father Pates blessed the herd for the last time.

"The cowboys mounted and drifted into the darkness, quietly rousing the reluctant herd, and the day's sub-zero drive began."

I remember the cold that soon numbed my feet and rancher Waln idling up to ask, "Want to know a good Indian secret on how to keep your feet warm?" To my mumbled, teeth-chattering, "Yes," he said, "Get off and walk a ways."

I did and found it was worse trying to walk in the five inches of crusted snow. After struggling back in the saddle, Waln rode up again, grinning this time, to ask, "Now, do you really want to know the good Indian secret of getting warm fast?"

Before my frozen lips could reply, he handed me a bottle of peppermint schnapps, which I eagerly guzzled. The gulp immediately warmed my innards and I no longer felt cold.

But I was warmed more and remember best the spectacular dawn a few moments later. In the panorama of the big sky it ranged from inky black and purple to yellow and an almost blinding crimson.

And it provided dramatic backlighting for the breathtaking scene of the herd and cowboys strung out across the range beneath the big sky's colorful palate.

This time I wasn't lucky. I had erred in having my color film camera hanging outside my parka. It was frozen and refused to operate.

Frantically, I dug out my alternate camera from inside my parka in time to capture a moment of ultimate beauty to remember – in black and white!

The photo was good enough to win first place nationally in the January 1963 National Press Photographers Association's contest.

And it remains my all-time favorite photo.

CHAPTER TWENTY-NINE

STORMY DAYS

During my love affair with my mistress, Nebraska, she enraptured me with her beauty. Then she often shook me from my reverie with savage belts of her capricious weather.

I survived many of her floods, tornadoes, blizzards and forest fires after she indoctrinated me in covering natural disasters in neighboring Kansas.

Kansas, Here I Come

It all began in the summer of 1951 when I strayed from Nebraska's border to cover the devastating Kansas River flood in Kansas City, literally on a shoestring.

Editor Fred Ware dispatched me on a "bargain" assignment to get stories and photos of the devastation in Kansas City with the admonition, "Be back in time for the bulldog (early morning) edition."

He set me up with the owner of an airplane who offered to fly a reporter to Kansas City and back. All I had to do was take aerial photos of his floodwater-encircled grain elevators en route.

"Here's 10 dollars. It should be enough for your lunch," Ware said.

The meagerness of my expense money hit home when, of necessity, we had to land at Independence, Mo. The Kansas City airport was under floodwaters.

When I asked the pilot when were we flying back, he replied: "Didn't they tell you? We're not flying back. I live here."

Cowed, but undaunted, I hitchhiked to Kansas City and its American Red Cross emergency headquarters where I met "Strawberry Hill Joe," an independent cab driver who had volunteered for flood duty. His goal in life, he said, was to be a journalist. He was intrigued by my offer to tag along while I got my stories and pictures.

Joe was a savior. He didn't tag along. He led me to heartbeat stories and photos. He even "borrowed" a rowboat to get to otherwise inaccessible places. Then he took me back to the Independence airport, which was off-limits except for airline passengers with reservations.

Joe was particularly delighted when we were waved through to the terminal by National Guard sentries – after I conned them by showing my National Guard captain's I.D. card and telling them I was reporting for duty.

Joe was so delighted he refused pay or even a tip for his service claiming, "It's been the best day of my life."

My day still had a way to go to be memorable, especially since there were block-long lines at the Braniff counter.

Then luck and perfect timing paid off when I spotted the captain of a Braniff flight about to take off for Omaha.

When I introduced myself and asked him if there was any way he could take a satchel of my Speed Graphic photo plates back to Omaha, he surprised me with: "I live in Omaha. The World-Herald is my paper and I've read some of your stuff. If you don't mind sitting on a stewardess' jump seat, why don't you come along? I'll go around back and get your ticket."

Luckily, K.C.-to-Omaha tickets were cheap in those days. But, unluckily, it took Ware's ten bucks plus the $5.40 I had in my pocket to buy one.

When I got to Omaha I was flat broke! But again luck came to the fore when I bumped into Hollis Limprecht, editor of the Herald's Magazine of the Midlands, who was waiting to board an outgoing flight. The dime I borrowed from him was enough to telephone The World-Herald to send out a copy boy to drive me to the newspaper.

Ware greeted me gleefully, chuckling, "WE did it!"

I was never sure whether his joy was because of my bargain expense account or that I had made it in time for the morning deadline.

Two days later he sent me back to Kansas City with a company car and an ample supply of expense account cash for more stories and photos because The World-Herald was launching a disaster relief fund to help neighbors in need.

It helped that Strawberry Hill Joe was there to greet me. He again chauffeured me and knew all the shortcuts to out-of-the-way places.

Well remembered is the day we waded through the muck of the inundated Argentine district. After I dispatched my story and film, I bought us each a pair of jeans and T-shirt to replace our mud-slimed clothes that reeked from the stench of rotting animal carcasses in the flooded Kansas City stockyards.

After bathing under a hand pump in a park and donning our new attire, we celebrated by going to dinner at a swank steak house. We were amazed when the maitre d' escorted us to red velvet seats at a prime table.

We were even more amazed to learn our meals were on the house until the manager explained, "We are grateful for all you are doing for our city." We forgot we were wearing Red Cross arm bands that Joe had supplied.

In all, I spent two weeks in the muck and the stench, working upstream to cover flood-devastated Perry, North Topeka and Manhattan. I still remember the odor of rotten food in flooded grocery stores on Manhattan's main street. It was so breath-stifling I left my downtown hotel, which had eight feet of water in its lobby, to drive to a hill overlooking the town to get some sleep.

It was all worth it. My initial 10 bucks in expenses paid off more than 11,000-to-one. World-Herald readers donated more than $111,000 to help their flood-stricken neighbors.

South Sioux City Flood and 'Wild Willie'

Little did I know, the Kansas flood just got my feet wet to help cover the devastating Missouri River floods the next April and March of 1952 at South Sioux City and Omaha-Council Bluffs.

When I arrived at South Sioux City, Bill Lee, the colorful editor of the South Sioux City Star who I later called "Wild Willie" for good reason, greeted me with: "You just think you're working for The World-Herald. You are really working for me. I want you to write your stories long and I want copies of them and every photo you take. In return, I'll drive you where you need to go, supply you with grub and booze, and provide you with a cot to sleep on. And I hope to hell you don't snore."

I discovered an old Army blanket hung on a clothesline divided my sleeping quarters from those of Bill and his wife, Marcella.

I also learned later he used my stories and photos to fill out a special flood edition. He drafted fellow editors from throughout northeastern Nebraska to help him print it.

Five minutes after my arrival and getting his orders, we took off to cover the flood in his roadster, with its top down despite the cold weather, and with his foot to the floorboard.

That was the way life was with Wild Willie, a kid who began life in a Catholic orphanage, as we covered the flood at top speed. Our lifelong friendship almost floundered when he discovered I was then a captain in the Iowa National Guard.

His wife told me he hated officers with a passion. During World War II infantry combat he had spent a couple of hitches in the guard house for decking them. But when a raid was scheduled, he always was pardoned so he could lead them.

After his untimely death in 1965, his wife showed me a package he'd never opened. It contained one of Great Britain's highest medals, second only to the Victoria Cross, for the valor he had displayed in a joint British-American assault in France.

He was given a furlough to Paris so the British could officially present the medal to him, but he went AWOL. Being an art lover, he visited the Louvre instead.

When his unit returned to Fort Dix at the war's end, he was given another furlough to go to Washington, D.C., to receive the medal from Lord Halifax, the British ambassador. He went AWOL again, this time to apply at The New York Times for a job as a reporter. The frustrated British finally mailed him the medal – the package he never opened.

He was thwarted but undaunted when New York Times editors, although intrigued at the zeal of the kid with only an eighth-grade education, told him to come back when he gained more education and experience.

But it didn't stop him when he was turned down by the publisher of the South Sioux City Star who told him he needed someone to sell advertising more than a reporter.

Wild Willie hit South Sioux businessmen telling them, "Instead of buying me a drink as a returning war hero, buy an ad in the Star." He got the job when he handed the publisher a full two-page spread of ads. Later, he became the paper's editor as well as receiving national attention for his whimsical columns.

While covering the South Sioux City floods, Willie ordered me to climb atop his shoulders when we got trapped by floodwaters when a dike broke.

"I don't give a damn about you," he told me as we waded chest deep to safety. "I'm doing it to keep our camera and film dry."

I shouldn't have sent The World-Herald a jug of floodwater with a note reading: "A sample of what's headed your way." It reminded editors of where I was and in a few days I was replaced by Bill Billotte, the Herald's South Pacific war correspondent and ace crime reporter.

I was summoned home because my Iowa National Guard unit had been mobilized for flood duty. Since Wild Willie and I had established a fond friendship, he tried to talk me into going AWOL to continue to help him with his flood special issue. But he relented when he discovered I had a more personal and pressing reason to head home.

My family, as well as the rest of the residents of the low-lying west end of Council Bluffs, were ordered evacuated as the Mighty Mo's rampaging floodwaters rolled closer.

Saving Kids Instead of Pigs

Maxine Moul, former director of the Nebraska Department of Economic Development and lieutenant governor, never lets me forget how I scooped her when she was a young reporter for the Sioux City Journal.

She had stood stranded on the shore while I helped pull two children and their grandparents from a nearly submerged pickup that had been swept off the highway by floodwaters at Pender.

Moul credits a "sixth sense" for my being at the right place at the right time to get the dramatic pictures and story. I call it plain luck.

This is the story I wrote for The World-Herald on Feb. 26, 1971.

Pender, Neb. – Pigs are beautiful, but kids are priceless.

That was the byword Friday during a dramatic rescue of two children and their grandparents from the cab of their nearly submerged pickup truck that had been swept off Highway 16 west of town by Logan Creek floodwaters.

Pulled to safety in a boat through a window of the pickup were Mr. and Mrs. Harvey Heineman, who farm west of town, and their grandchildren, Christine, 2, and

Farmer Bill McQuiston rescues Christine Jepsen from a pickup truck swept off the highway by floodwaters.

Kevin Jepsen, 1. They are the children of Mr. and Mrs. Dennis Jepsen of Wahoo.

Except for the scare, the tots are in good condition.

Rescuers were Capt. Merle Renander of the Pender Rescue Squad; Bill McQuiston, a farmer who had brought his boat into this Thurston County seat "to lend a hand"; hog-raiser Dale Legband, and this writer.

We'd set out to save Legband's pigs, but saved kids instead. Fate dealt a lucky hand. Embarking on the hog mission gave us a head start on being at the right place at the right time.

When we got to Legband's flooded hog house after the kid rescue, six of his 200-pound market hogs and a sow with a litter had drowned in the icy water, which swept across nearly half of Pender's residential area and the surrounding farmlands.

An estimated 300 of the town's 1,250 residents had been evacuated to the Thurston County Courthouse, St. John's Catholic Church and the homes of friends during the night. Old-timers said it was the worst flood since 1940.

An initial alert on the snow-melt and rain-gorged flooding creek came about 10 p.m. Thursday. By morning the town was cut off on three sides by water over Highway 9 to the north and south and Highway 16 to the west. Highway 94 from the east was still open, although traffic had to splash through water on the east end of Main Street.

"We should have stayed home, but we were concerned about my parents in town," Grandma Heineman said. "We had gotten through the water going over the highway (16) all right getting into town. Then we discovered my parents were safe at the hotel."

Her husband interjected, "It was just a few minutes later when we started back, but the water had come up and we were swept off the road."

"We sat in ice water up over our hips and held the children above our heads until the boat came by and got us," she added.

It was just seconds before they were swept off the highway and we had embarked on our hog-saving mission, when the town siren blew.

"What's that about?" shouted Capt. Renander above the roar of the motor and the wind.

"Must be the noon whistle," shouted McQuiston from the helm.

But Renander, who had lost his home in a fire less than two weeks ago, wasn't satisfied.

"What are they all hollering about back there?" he asked while pointing at a group frantically waving and shouting, some even wading into the water. "Maybe that wall of water they were talking about is coming. Let's check."

As we swung about and neared the shore, we finally heard the shouts: "A pickup was just swept off the highway over there and people are still in it. Get there fast!"

McQuiston turned the boat on a dime.

"Give her all she's got," shouted Renander above the roar. "Hey! Watch out for the sign!"

We swerved just in time to miss a "Dead End" street sign sticking up from the water and gunned across a flooded cornfield.

Our hearts sank. Through the fog and mist we could only see the top of the pickup cab above the wind-whipped water. On the highway right-of-way we could see Sheriff Clyde Storie's cruiser, its lights blinking in symphony with the frantic gesturing of the sheriff and others to hurry.

The sight of heads through the pickup's rear window as we neared was an additional spur and we wrestled frantically with an anchor when we realized two of them were children.

We didn't need the anchor. McQuiston skidded the bow over the submerged bed of the pickup, holding the boat as it swung alongside the window. In a flash, Capt. Renander plucked one of the children through the window and tossed the tot to me.

Somehow McQuiston got past me in the bouncing boat and grabbed the other child. We relayed them to Legband, who bundled them in his jacket. The man who went for pigs and ended up with kids cuddled the frightened children and stilled their screams while McQuiston and Renander helped their grandparents through the window.

We backed off fast and churned for the nearest land where they were rushed to the warmth of a waiting car.

Only then we remembered the hogs. At the hog barn McQuiston and Renander, equipped with chest waders, plunged in to push some bales of hay from a loft to the survivors. An effort was to be made later to get the survivors out using a snorkel-equipped truck.

Then we headed back to land wet, cold – but happy.

The rescuers were presented "Hero Awards" at the Nebraska Funeral Director Association's annual banquet. My rescue boat buddies deserved it. I didn't.

All I did was go along for the ride, and I was so busy shooting photos I almost dropped the tiny tot Renander tossed to me.

Tornadoes

I spit in the eye of a freak tornado on Highway 92 east of Shelby and

*Storm-spawning tornado
near Shelby, Neb.*

then lived to write about it on May 5, 1964.

Shelby, Neb. – I outran a tornado during the night.

It wasn't fun. Lady Luck was riding with me in World-Herald Car No. 25 as I headed west on Highway 92 about 6:30 p.m. to cover a tornado which earlier had devastated Wolbach.

But this one I almost got in my lap. At Rising City I noticed a storm front ahead. I fastened my seat belt and drove on. It appeared to be clearing to the south and most of the storm clouds were moving to the north.

Two miles east of Shelby I saw a strange cloud on my left. It looked like a huge downpour of rain or hail about a half-mile wide. I pulled into a farm driveway to face the cloud for a better look.

The tornado pulled a dirty trick. It didn't look like one. It was just a half-mile mass of blue clouds touching the ground. Tornadoes are supposed to have a funnel, I thought.

I later learned the low-hanging cloud actually was a wall of mud thrown up by a tornado behind it that had fooled radar by hugging the ground for 75 miles. It had rumbled across farm fields while miraculously sidestepping towns such as Stromsburg.

Suddenly, I saw a barn and debris billowing from the bottom a section line away. I raised my camera to take a picture but everything suddenly went black – and still.

Knowing the storm seemed to be veering northeast, I figured my best chance was to head west and I made a fast Highway Patrol turn backing from the driveway.

Then I gunned Car No. 25. In the rearview mirror I saw the approaching lights of two trucks, suddenly rolling, before disappearing. My ears rang from a horrible screech. Most of it came from the car radio, but there was an overpowering rumble.

There was a deluge of rain. I had no idea how fast I was traveling, but I had the gas pedal to the floorboard as I hightailed it west. Suddenly the "lights" came on. The sky had cleared.

And I realized I had sped through Shelby two miles down the road plus another two miles farther west!

I turned and headed back, picking up two truck drivers, Leonard Portis of Omaha and Lamar Keene of Bellevue, who had run out from a Shelby truck stop in the storm's wake. We headed east to the two trucks whose lights I had seen spinning from the highway.

We found the first truck resting on its side in a ditch with Harold Ecker of Ogallala trapped inside. His companion, Homer Ligett, also of Ogallala, said the tornado had flicked them off the road.

Suddenly someone said, "My God! Look!

The farmhouse and barn in whose lane I had turned to watch the mysterious cloud were flattened. Farmer Robert Rafert, 32, his wife and three children suffered minor injuries although the basement had caved in on them.

Later we learned several other farms were flattened by the cloud that didn't look like a tornado.

Grand Island's Multi-Tornadoes

I considered myself to be an unlucky near Johnny-on-the-spot when a series of tornadoes killed five, sent 266 to hospitals and devastated 150 square miles of Grand Island and its surrounding area on the night of June 3, 1980.

Somehow Carl Keith, longtime World-Herald night editor, learned I was emcee at the evening banquet of the Nebraska Petroleum Marketers annual golf outing at the York Country Club. I never told an editor I was goofing off to play golf.

"Get to Grand Island as fast as you can," Keith ordered. "All hell has broken loose from several tornadoes and we have a news bulletin that several people are trapped in a collapsed cafe on South Locust Street."

I wished I hadn't driven the 44 miles to Nebraska's Third City so fast when I discovered the tornado onslaught wasn't over.

Approaching the eastern edge of the city I joined several cars and trucks attempting to jam under an I-80 overpass when the ferocious wind began to howl again. I watched as a parked station wagon bearing New York license plates was slowly blown sideways against a semi-trailer.

And then over my CB radio came the terrified voice of the woman driver, "My God! What's happening?" The trucker replied: "It's the tail end of a tornado, lady. Hold on to your hat. They don't last long."

The transmission ended in ear-splitting static, but not before I heard loud and clear the woman's anguished voice beg: "But, please. How long is long?"

Presidential Visits

Having witnessed cursory visits by Presidents Harry Truman on April 16, 1952, at the height of the Omaha-Council Bluffs Missouri River flood crisis, and Jimmy Carter in the midst of recovery efforts a week after Grand Island's devastating rash of tornadoes, a lingering question remains: Were the trips really necessary?

True, an angry Truman raised his customary hell, railing at Congress for lack of action in Missouri River flood control. It worked. A few years later completion of major dams erased the threat of Missouri Valley flooding.

Carter's one-and-a-half-hour visit – delayed while he held a press conference on worldwide issues for the national press corps at the airport – delighted residents of the city's Grand Generation Center during a stop. He made another quick pause at the storm-destroyed home of a staunch Democrat. It also provided a diversion for recovery-weary citizens.

But both Presidential visits caused serious disruptions of recovery efforts.

Carter's quick visit was billed as non-political, but was arranged by his Nebraska campaign manager. Remembered is the anger of Grand Island's exhausted Mayor Bob Kriz who was awakened in the middle of the night from his first good sleep in days by a telephone call from a White House staffer.

Kriz, a World-War II Marine colonel, told me the unidentified caller wanted to know his political party affiliation. Kriz, a Republican, exploded with, "What difference does that make in a time of crisis?" The caller said, "We have to know so we can arrange who'll ride with the president during his visit."

The visit meant the emotionally and physically spent Grand Island firemen, policemen and volunteers, who'd been busy burying the five victims and caring for the 266 injured, had to take time out from their recovery efforts for additional traffic and security tasks.

The 'Dirty Dozen'

World-Herald staffers and I were lucky in covering the Grand Island disaster. Getting there in time to be buffeted by one of the last cyclones, I was amazed at the destruction on South Locust Street. While getting stories of some survivors, I detoured to Huston Street to check on my in-laws, Jim and Connie Stroman.

Except for a dented fender on Connie's car and a flooded basement bathroom, they'd safely ridden out the storm. Jim guided me the rest of the night, getting stories of residents at the city's hospitals.

Shortly after dawn the Stromans were hit by the first wave of World-Herald reporters and photographers who were flown in by chartered plane. The Stromans couldn't have stemmed the tide, even if they wanted to. They were powerless in more ways than one.

Like most residents, they had no electricity. By official edict water was cut off for normal usage. Their bathrooms and toilets were showerless and flushless, providing ammunition for such signs as "Blush, But Don't Flush!"

Their greatest misfortune was being my in-laws. They were available and vulnerable because hotels and motels were in much worse shape than their home. They had two working telephones, two cars, extra beds, sofas and carpeted floors, lots of food, drinks, aspirin for deadline tensions and a lot of sympathy.

Thus they became hosts for The World-Herald's Grand Island Tornado Bureau, including reporters John Taylor, Mike Kelly, David Thompson, Frank Partsch, Jim Denney, Al Frisbie, A.J. McClanahan, David Kotok and Tom Ash as well as photographers Jim Burnett, Phil Johnson and Bob Taylor, who at various times during the week joined residents of the "city of the unbathed, unshaved and unflushed."

Connie, a former big band soloist and executive director of the Grand Island United Way, who was secretary to the director of the Platte River Whooping Crane Trust, became the "Mother Superior" of the mangy flock. It was she who dubbed us "The Dirty Dozen."

Jim, a former Navy chief petty officer, was a master of all trades. He sewed or knit all of his wife's stylish dresses and had even spent a week as the only man in a Norfolk cloistered nunnery teaching nuns how to use a knitting machine. He was a master gardener who canned produce, made wine and stocked a supermarket of assorted foods in his basement. He taught Nebraska Extension Service classes on canning. He also was a candy maker and a chef.

He became our "magician," preparing connoisseur candlelight and steak dinners, luncheon stews and bacon-and-egg breakfasts on his patio grill. He drained his garden hose to provide around-the-clock "Navy style" coffee until an hour-long reprieve on the water ban allowed him to fill buckets, pans and his canning jars.

The couple provided us full use of their cars and Jim even borrowed one from his neighbor to make a fast trip to Omaha to deliver our photo film.

Kelly, now a columnist, remembers them for supplying him a lantern so he could finish a story in the middle of the night and later when he went to bed "a hand reaching in from the darkness with a cold 7-Up without my asking." He also boasted that Ba-Ba, the Stroman's black poodle, liked him best.

He claimed he got a wet-nose kiss from her every morning after she had slept on his chest while he slept on a basement floor. "I was the only one who had brought a change of clean underwear, so she ignored the others after a quick sniff," Kelly recalled.

The Stromans refused payment for their extraordinary care. The scruffy crew remembered Connie's kisses and good-bye speech when they left: "Listen, you guys. What you got, you earned. You let me talk a leg off you."

She later added, "Our Dirty Dozen were beautiful. There isn't one of them I won't want to hug when I meet them on the street. Besides, we were the first in Grand Island to get all the news of what was happening before it appeared in the newspapers."

Jim summed it up with, "Hosting you guys was a helluva nice way to spend what would have been a long, dark week."

Magnet's 'Forgotten' Tornado

Luckily, I left Omaha just minutes before the devastating tornado hit in May 1975 and was halfway to Lincoln when I heard the news.

Later that night I was on my way to Magnet, a Cedar County village that was almost totally devastated and became known as the "Forgotten Town."

Tornado experts said Magnet was struck by a twister of greater ferocity than the one that cut a swath through Ralston and Omaha the same day.

Miraculously, there were no deaths and only minor injuries although Magnet's main street was devastated, every public service was disrupted and every one of the village's 90 inhabitants was affected.

On a per-capita basis, Magnet was hit harder than Omaha. Yet in national publicity Magnet was all but forgotten in the shadow of Omaha's plight.

"The funnel was hidden by a sheet of fog and rain, but the unforgettable roar gave it away," said Mabel Yunkers who, with two customers, barely had time to dive into the back room before the twister demolished Yunkers Tavern.

A year later the town that boasted of being "A Town Too Tough To Die" celebrated its centennial on the storm's anniversary with a big thank-you barbecue for the nearly 1,000 volunteers who had given a helping hand.

Flying high over the festivities was the tattered American flag that postmaster Wayne Rohde had saved from the steel flagpole that had been bent double in front of the totally smashed post office.

Birds No Longer Sang at Primrose

The 100 residents of the Boone County town of Primrose felt sympathy for the Omaha victims 10 years after a Mother's Day eve tornado left four dead and all but wiped out Primrose's business district and over half its homes.

"They'll miss the birds," Mrs. T.G. McBride told me in an anniversary visit in 1975. "They came back, but they didn't sing all summer and fall."

"When the tornado hit Omaha last week I cried for the people because we know what they went through," added Mrs. Dorothea Carraher.

But Mrs. Carraher could still laugh recalling the miraculous escape by she and 12 customers of her Dot's Tavern, which was located in an old bank building.

"Just before the roof was torn off, all of us somehow squeezed into the old bank vault that was already loaded with cases of beer," she recalled. "In later anniversaries we tried, but more than half of us couldn't squeeze in no matter how hard we tried."

CHAPTER THIRTY

THE DIKES HELD – BARELY

For sheer drama, it would be hard to beat the epic two-week struggle in April 1952 to curb the rampaging Mighty Mo at its narrow bottleneck of Omaha and Council Bluffs.

I'd been covering the fury of record Missouri River run-off flows at South Sioux City and Sioux City, and was recalled to Omaha for two big reasons.

My home, as well as the rest of the west end of Council Bluffs, was evacuated as the record flood crests approached the twin cities, and I was called to duty with the 168th Infantry Regiment with the mobilization of the Iowa National Guard as well as the 134th Infantry Regiment of the Nebraska National Guard, both of the 34th Red Bull division.

I arrived to find my home empty. In-laws in Omaha had moved my family and furnishings to their homes. In their zeal, I discovered they had even gutted my basement furnace.

I was the regiment's transportation officer, but managed to combine reporting for The World-Herald during off-duty time.

Well remembered are:

■ Using amphibious Duck trucks to help Iowa Power and Light technicians secure high-voltage transformers in the flooded lowlands north of Council Bluffs.

■ The anxiety as the crest roared downstream, and the awesome quiet of the Bluffs' west end, which was all but devoid of pedestrian and vehicular traffic except on Broadway, the main east-west artery.

■ Talking both Omaha and Council Bluffs officials out of using our recoilless anti-tank guns and heavy machine guns to sink a large gas tank floating toward the Ak-Sar-Ben Bridge. We finally convinced them that ricocheting bullets off the tank and surrounding water would endanger life and limb on both sides of the river. The crisis ended when the tank floated majestically under the bridge and on downstream.

■ The gigantic presidential traffic snafu. It occurred on the Ak-Sar-Ben Bridge on April 16, 1952, when President Harry Truman arrived to

A Million Miles of Memories

A high-school track team turned into sandbaggers to save the Missouri River dike.

witness the flood and confer with Lt. Gen. Lewis Pick, chief of the Army Corps of Engineers.

Civil Defense leaders of both cities somehow got the erroneous idea the president and the general were going to inspect the arrival of the river's crest from the middle of the bridge. We got our orders, "Close the bridge to all traffic!"

The president and the general never arrived at the bridge, instead getting a better view in an airplane from Offutt Air Force Base.

But orders were orders, and all hell broke loose with traffic – including hundreds of dump trucks used by 6,000 regular Army engineers hauling dirt and sandbags to build an emergency secondary dike on the Bluffs' side of the river – jammed helplessly back up Broadway for miles.

I drove a Jeep to the center of the bridge to view the supposed flood viewing by the president, and met Capt. Jean Whinnery, the Omaha Police Department's traffic inspector, arriving on the same mission from the west on a three-wheeled motorcycle.

We gaped in astonishment. The bridge was empty except for an Omaha television crew interviewing an Omaha Civil Defense official.

To Bucktail and Back . . .

Cursing, we staged the fastest Jeep-motorcycle race in the bridge's history to the Guard's security headquarters on the east end of the bridge, telling them, "Cut the traffic loose!"

But the commanding colonel, going by the book, refused until official orders arrived from higher authority. We spent several anxious moments locating Omaha and Council Bluffs officials to get the bridge closing order countermanded.

Whinnery and I have often wondered what happened to the television crew when the flood of traffic suddenly roared across the bridge.

The engineers, aided by 25,000 volunteer sandbaggers, completed the emergency dike in the nick of time before the flood crest of 30.24 feet – more than 11 feet above flood stage – arrived on April 17 and lapped just 6 inches from the top of flashboards on top of the emergency dike.

During the eight hours it took for the crest to pass, other engineers and volunteers rushed to plug a storm sewer blowout near Eleven and Grace streets that flooded 1,000 industrial acres north of downtown Omaha and worse, threatened to undermine the levees.

Finally, on April 22, the two cities were declared safe from flood threat. Residents and volunteers gave a collective sigh of relief.

President Truman lived up to his fiery best, lambasting Congress for dragging its heels on flood protection. The result was the construction by the Army Corps of Engineers and the Bureau of Reclamation of major dams at Gavins Point, near Yankton, S.D.; Fort Randall, near Pickstown, S.D.; Oahe, near Pierre, S.D., and Garrison, near Bismarck, N.D.

Along with the pre-flood Fort Peck Dam in Montana, they tamed the Mighty Mo and assured flood protection for Missouri Basin cities.

Drifts stranded northeastern Nebraska residents in February 1960.

CHAPTER THIRTY-ONE

BLIZZARDS AND THE ICE AGE RETURNED

I was too busy on the Omaha police beat to get caught in Nebraska's Great Blizzard of 1949. But my luck ran out in the midst of one of several others through the years and, luckily, I survived.

Blizzards, I think, are relative depending on how cold you get, how hopelessly blind you are in whiteouts, how stuck you are in drifts and how close you come to not surviving.

I covered what I called the "Return of the Ice Age" in late January 1969.

An ice storm riding in howling 60-mph, pole-shattering and power line-snapping winds ripped through 10 Sand Hills counties and parts of five others the night of Jan. 21, 1969.

More than 7,000 customers of the Custer Public Power District in a wide expanse of snow and ice-covered Sand Hills were left in below-freezing, powerless darkness, cut off from the world for eight long days.

Up to 1,300 power poles were toppled. Most nearly disintegrated as the wind-whipped lines, crusted with ice up to three inches in diameter, exerted over two tons of pull on the 235-foot spans between poles.

"It was unbelievable," said Jim Groghan, manager of the district's Stapleton outpost which covers McPherson and Logan counties as well as parts of Custer, Lincoln, Thomas, Hooker and Keith counties. "It was the worse we have ever experienced."

I caught up with Groghan at Tryon two days before his exhausted district crew (aided by equally weary crews from other Nebraska and Kansas power companies) had battled around the clock to restore power to the 4,320-square-mile, windswept icy expanse.

Except for radio communications, Tryon, the McPherson County seat, was cut off from the outside world when the ice-laden winds wiped out the Tryon Telephone Co., one of the state's most unusual telephone operations.

It served 150 area ranches from the kitchen of O.E. Black. His family took turns operating the antique switchboard and making long-distance calls audible by placing one end of a receiver in a cup of wet cotton.

Luckily, when I got there the unique long distance service had been restored. More importantly, two days later the district and volunteer linemen battled through drifts, zero-degree weather and another snowfall to restore power to 55 ranch and farm homes in northern and western McPherson County.

I tailed along to report on the inconvenience, hardships and the sub-zero cold endured by Sand Hillers with their typical stamina and good humor.

Mr. and Mrs. Hank Halsted and their son Keith, 12, greeted the crew of Bob Anderson of Broken Bow and me warmly when we reached their isolated ranch, 19 miles northeast of Tryon.

"Sure glad to see you," said Hank. "The kids ain't had school for eight days now. Aw, we were OK. Hell, we got along before the Rural Electrical Administration ever got here. I just didn't hanker the idea of having to haul water from the horse tank to flush our toilet and it did get a little cool when it dropped to 20 below at night."

There was tentative good news from McPherson County Sheriff Gordon Bassett that there were no reports of major casualties, before he added: "Of course, we haven't been in contact with some folks in the hills. Many of the folks got to town some way and out here neighbors always look out for the other guy."

Dick Wilkerson of Broken Bow, the power district's manager, worried about fatigue as his crews worked in incredible conditions. And he worried that the hard-won victory of his crews would be only temporary.

"My main concern is that January is still not the ice storm season," he said. "We usually don't get icing until late February and March. Of necessity, our repairs had to be temporary. Speed was of prime importance and we had to take a lot of shortcuts."

Luckily, Old Man Winter behaved and the temporary lines held until permanent repairs were made in the spring.

The Great Calving Blizzard

I wrote on April 4, 1975, from Arthur:

A pink-nosed, white face of a tiny dead calf protruded from a huge snowbank along the road leading to the Haythorn Land and Cattle Co. south of town.

The face, framed by a barbed-wire fence, was testimony to the ravages of the "Great Calving-Time Blizzard of '75" in Nebraska's Sand Hills.

At the ranch headquarters, rancher Waldo Haythorn, his face raw from the wind and his eyes weary from lack of sleep, put it into words.

"It was a bitch. Now there is only one thing to do. That's to count the live ones, skin the dead ones, cry a little, cuss a little, pray a little and keep on ranching."

He was expressing the feelings of ranchers who doggedly battled adversity even though the blizzard was the worst they could remember.

The storm, packing gale winds and striking at the height of calving season, drove cows and calves until they bunched up when caught at barbed-wire fences. Many suffocated under deep snowdrifts.

The toll in the 13-county disaster area has yet to be fully tallied, but initial loss estimates range from 20 to 35 percent of new calves.

"I estimate a loss of 35,000 calves in the surrounding hills," Haythorn said, "but I may be underestimating it quite a bit. I think you can safely say we lost 400 calves on our four ranches, but there could be quite an aftermath with additional losses to pneumonia. There ain't a damn thing you can do about it when they get it. When they start to rattle, they're gone within 24 hours.

"We've got a lot of cows with frozen teats and there is no way they'll let their calves suck. This is by far the worst blizzard of them all because it hit at the peak of calving time in the hills. It's worse than the calving-time blizzard of 1931.

"A big one in 1939 killed more big stock, but it happened early, before the calves came. There was little loss to big stock this time."

Hampering efforts to get an accurate toll is up to 17 inches of new snow that fell Monday night and Tuesday across the area. Arthur County Clerk Wilton Dorris said an accurate count of county losses may have to wait until the drifts melt.

"A lot of guys figure they lost half of what they had in calves when the storm hit," Dorris said. "The little guys didn't lose too many because their livestock was close in and they could get their calves into the barn or garages and other kinds of shelter they could find. The big ranches got hit the worst.

"Another problem on some ranches is getting hay and feed to surviving cattle. Many feed grounds are snowed under," he said.

Back at the home ranch, Haythorn went into a bunkhouse and carried out a calf in his arms. When it bawled loudly, Haythorn grinned and said: "He's in good voice. This one will make it."

He said there had been more than nine calves sharing bunks with the cowhands, and added that a neighbor had used a horse trailer to pick up 60 calves and carry them to a garage.

At the company's Ackley Valley Ranch, south across the Keith County line, Haythorn's son Craig was checking his herd on horseback.

He grinned when a hired hand, Jess Armos, drove up with a stray calf he had rescued.

Craig said the sun and rising temperatures were a blessing, but said ranchers were fearful of another storm forecast for the weekend.

His dad, Waldo, rued there was some consolation this year.

"If you want to look at it one way, there is a bright side," he said. "A year ago young calves were bringing $125 apiece. Just a few days ago baby calves were worth about $30 to $35. So, it could have been a worse loss. But it's still a son-of-a gun."

It's a reason the elder Haythorn didn't wish to be photographed with any of his dead calves. "It makes me cry and the tears freeze on my cheeks," he said.

Old Cowhand in 1979 'Siege of White Hell'

I was recruited for three endless days as a tenderfoot cowhand at the 7-reverse 7 brand Paxton Ranch Inc., 35 miles southwest of Thedford during the January 1979 "Siege of White Hell."

Relentless snows and ice storms for almost two months had turned a wide stretch of the Nebraska Sand Hills into what ranchers wryly called "The Siberia of America." Ice and snow-caked ranches were all but isolated for dreary days on end and fatigued, foot-sore cattle were becoming weaker by the day due to lack of feed.

I talked my favorite cowboy, Chet Paxton, former state senator, ex-president of the Nebraska Stockgrower's Association, an executive of the National Cattlemen's Association and Nebraska's representative of the National Cowboy Hall of Fame, into letting me get the feel of the siege for a story.

Chet, who is "chairman of the board" of the ranch via two-way radio, gave his approval in the cozy confines of his home in Thedford and arranged for me to reach the ranch by a plow-equipped four-wheel-drive pickup truck.

His daughter, Jessica, her new husband John Warren, the operators of the ranch, and John's younger brother, Jerry, warily greeted me and then put me to work scattering the dwindling supply of high-protein cake feed for their herd and chopping foot-thick ice from windmill water tanks.

Although my hands, back and legs ached, I was one happy cowhand. My exertions kept me from freezing and made Jessica's home-cooked meals taste all the better.

Jessica, John and Jerry were special delights, personifying the "can do and never give up" philosophies of the Sand Hills.

Chet had warned me: "In '49 we had a spectacular blizzard. But a couple of days after it ended, snow began melting and we had grazing chances. But this is an unrelenting siege of white hell. It is by far the worst in my lifetime and I'm no kid. "This is the first time I can remember there is absolutely no range to feed."

We bounced across and through snowdrifts to get to the cattle, but they were too weak and lethargic to come running when John and Jerry sounded a siren on their pickups or cut loose with their ear-splitting bellowing calls. Often they had to chase the sore-footed critters, who refused to cross drifts to get to bulldozed feeding paths.

The young couple willingly gave up plans to celebrate their first wedding anniversary in mid-January, but incredibly had plowed out to the highway to make a fast trip to North Platte to file their federal income tax estimates.

Thus, their wry humor at hearing a radio report saying the U.S. Department of Agriculture had deemed the "siege of white hell" not critical enough to provide emergency aid.

But Gov. Charles Thone and the state of Nebraska did provide a helping hand. The Nebraska National Guard was mobilized. On the third day of my stay, Chet relayed the good news by his two-way radio.

Guardsmen manning Army trucks were ordered to help get feed to the isolated ranches. "The Guard is on its way behind a bulldozer bringing seven tons of cake, and I'm coming behind them in my pickup," Chet radioed.

After helping stash the feed in the barn, Sgt. Joe McComber and Spec. 4 Pete Wiley of North Platte and Staff Sgt. Charles Gehl of Gering joined in a special "New-Year-a-month-late" celebration dinner prepared by Jessica.

Late that night while riding with Chet in his pickup, we learned the Guardsmen were going above and beyond the call of duty in temperatures ranging from 16 to 30 degrees below zero.

The Army had SNAFUed (Situation Normal All [bleeped] Up) by sending new trucks to frozen Nebraska that had been intended for tropical bases. They did not have heaters.

On the way back, Chet and I alternated with the Guardsmen, giving them reprieves in the warm pickup. And when we got back to the bar at the Cowpoke Inn in Thedford, Chet treated us to traditional end-of-the-trail drinks that warmed the cockles of our hearts.

Close, Cold Call
My coldest, closest call came on Friday, Jan. 11, 1963, alongside U.S.

Highway 30 east of Central City in a howling windswept snowstorm that dropped visibility to near zero.

Suddenly, in a lull in the wind I spotted one of the old Burma Shave sequence signs reading, "Let Folks See." Under the conditions, it was a plea by the few motorists on the road and a heckuva good prop for a photo.

I parked my World-Herald car in the entrance to a farm lane and ran back to take a photo of the ghost-like image of a passing truck behind the sign. Then I started back, taking a shortcut across the right-of-way. Buffeted by the wind and blinded by the snow as I plowed through a snowdrift, I suddenly plummeted 12 feet, deep into the snow-clogged roadside ditch. I was up to my armpits in snow and couldn't move.

I churned like a beaver going after a rabbit. No go! I paused to gasp for breath. A few cars and trucks roared past, but drivers couldn't see me.

Thoughts like, "Well, it'll make a good story when they find me next spring," and "Where's the legendary St. Bernard with a cask of brandy attached to its collar?" flitted through my mind. The last got me laughing and relaxed me.

Methodically leaning back and forward to make footholds, I managed to make it out and started back to the car a little more than a block away. A block? It seemed like 10 miles.

I was tottering from the wind and teetering from exhaustion when I finally reached the car and sagged gasping in its warmth. I laughed when a radio announcer chirped, "The Highway Patrol urges extreme caution ... "

But I wasn't laughing a few miles farther down the road. Despite the warmth of the car's heater turned on full blast, I was getting colder and shivering more. It took only a few more agonizing moments to discover why.

In my exertions to get out of the hole, snow had been forced down the front of my pants and was packed solidly around my crotch, and had begun to melt.

A couple of years later I survived another snowstorm much more comfortably.

When my car became hopelessly mired in a deep drift – again on U.S. Highway 30 – just west of Aurora, I mushed through the deep snow to the nearest home.

How lucky could I get? It was the home of Aurora banker Ed Koblenz and his wife, Nan, who were supreme hosts for a night and a day. Even their phone being knocked out by the storm proved to be a mixed blessing. I couldn't inform The World-Herald of my plight, but neither could they get hold of me to tell me to head elsewhere for blizzard coverage.

CHAPTER THIRTY-TWO

NEBRASKA FOREST FIRE

Rosebud Sioux Chief George Kills in Sight was flown in from South Dakota by the late Broken Bow banker Thomas Tiffany Varney on May 5, 1965, to perform a rain dance in a desperate move to ease the drought in Nebraska's parched Sand Hills.

The chief was too late. Hardly had his incantation to the Great Spirit to bring rain ended when the fire whistles blew. A bolt of lightning struck a soapweed in the tinder-dry range, igniting one of the biggest fires in history at the Nebraska National Forest near Halsey, 54 miles northwest of Broken Bow.

Within minutes, fire-generated howling winds began ripping through the world's largest man-made forest, and eventually destroyed several 4-H cabins and blackened 20,000 acres containing a million and a half trees. Heroic efforts saved the 4-H Lodge.

An even greater disaster was prevented by around-the-clock efforts by volunteer firemen from surrounding communities, 325 veteran Forest Service firefighters flown in from four states, plus 135 of the famed "Black Hats" forest firefighting Indians who came from South Dakota.

Their fight, backed by some 2,000 volunteers from ranchers to 4-Hers and Boy Scouts, was described as "unbelievable" by David Nordwall, forester for the five-state Forest Service Rocky Mountain Region.

"I have seen lots of fires, but I've never seen one in which such a heroic fight was won in saving the Forest Service buildings, the Bessey Nursery and the 4-H Lodge," he said.

I was lucky again, being on hand to cover the rain dance at Broken Bow and then chasing the city's volunteer fire department to the scene. I gave a ride to an Omaha TV crew that had flown in for the rain dance, provided they took my photo film back to Omaha. All we had to do was zero in on a towering black cloud that could be seen for miles.

When we arrived, I hitched us a ride with a warden in his Forest Service truck to the burning 4-H camp high in the smoke- and blaze-filled hills.

I made a mistake, standing with one foot inside the truck and another on the ground to snap photos of stately pine trees exploding like Roman candles. Suddenly, one of the gusts of fire-whipped winds ripped the truck door from my hand, slamming it against my knee. In the excitement, I didn't feel a thing.

Noting the wall of flames rapidly approaching, the warden shouted, "Let's get the hell outta here!"

As we wound down the forest road we were suddenly engulfed by utter darkness. With a hissing, flames rolled over the crest of the hill and all we could see for a time were fiery embers raining down on the truck. Our headlights were of no help.

The heat was intense and we were tense until the warden joked, "We don't have to worry about a thing. If it gets too hot, all I have to do is turn this baby hard left into the South Loup River."

Minutes seemed like an eternity as we drove behind another truck, crawling to daylight at the end of the tunnel of blackness and soot.

I drove the Omaha TV crew to the Broken Bow airport so they could fly back in time for my deadline. They barely became airborne when a thunderstorm and rain hit Broken Bow.

After driving back to the fire area I discovered nary a drop had fallen on the stricken forest.

I was shooting photos on the fire line after midnight when suddenly one of the rancher volunteers threw down his shovel and rolled on the ground laughing uproariously.

We rushed to his side thinking he had become overcome with fatigue, heat and smoke. But he brushed us aside with: "I'm OK. But I just got to thinking, this is the first time in my almost 50 years of marriage I have a good excuse to be out late with the boys. And look where the hell I am!"

An hour later one of the wardens sought me out saying I had a "dire emergency" call at the forest headquarters.

It was Broken Bow banker Thomas Varney. "Chief Kills in Sight's rain dance and incantation to the Great Spirit worked like a charm," Varney chortled. "We're sitting under the awning of my backyard patio having a few snorts and I just thought you'd like to know it's raining like a cow pissing on a flat rock."

I was so pooped I was speechless. And I was so tired I didn't feel any pain in my banged-up knee until driving back to Omaha five days later, although I had noticed it was black-and-blue. It turned out to be a minor injury.

Luckily, I was the only "casualty" of the fire, and Forest Service officials arranged a special ceremony in The World-Herald office of Editor Fred Ware.

While Ware chuckled with delight, I was presented a large plaque with a Purple Heart cushion and the citation: "For outstanding valor in the Great Fire at the Nebraska National Forest May 5-7, 1965."

I asked the officials: "What valor? I was ducking and running. Give real medals to all the firefighters and volunteers who valiantly fought the fire."

Another epic effort by the Forest Service and volunteers from throughout the state helped replant and restore the forest glory in the following months and years.

Della's Lifetime Among Trees

A special sweetheart was Della Mooney of Dunning, and her love was the Nebraska National Forest. As a young girl she helped her father plant by hand what was to become the world's largest man-made forest.

And she dedicated most of her life to serving it – either working in the Bessey Nursery or climbing high in the fire tower as a spotter.

I remember interviewing her at age 83 as she sorted seedlings at the annual tree harvest in March 1994. "I love the forest. It has been my life and I wouldn't want to be anywhere else," she said.

Later that year she even blushed when Forest Service officials praised her for more than 50 years of devoted service at a special retirement party.

"I don't deserve all this," she said. "I was just doing a job I love."

Della died two years later. The forest hasn't been quite the same since.

CHAPTER THIRTY-THREE

STATE FAIR TRAGEDY

L uck has always been a factor in finding stories around the next bend of the road.

But one of my closest calls was the Sept. 5, 1965, midway carnival tragedy at the Nebraska State Fair when the Skylift, circling 40 feet in the air, suddenly collapsed, killing four and injuring 44 others.

I was walking across the crowded midway shortly after 11 a.m. on Sunday, the biggest day of the fair, when the story nearly landed on my head!

The screams of the injured, shouts of rescuers, the wail of ambulance sirens and the calliope tune of the merry-go-round combined in a macabre symphony. It and other nearby rides never stopped.

I rushed to aid and comfort a family that landed almost at my feet. Speaking in shocked tones, her face ashen and her legs bloody, Mrs. Joseph Hoer of Crescent, Iowa, told me: "It was funny. I had just said to my husband, 'What if it breaks down?' Then it did. At first we thought it was just part of the ride. Then we hit hard!"

Mrs. Hoer sat cradling her husband's head as he lay on the midway asphalt. With her other arm she was attempting to comfort her son, Larry, 12, seated beside her, hurt and crying. "We just saw the post tip over ahead of us and down we came," said her husband, grimacing in pain.

Kneeling nearby, trying

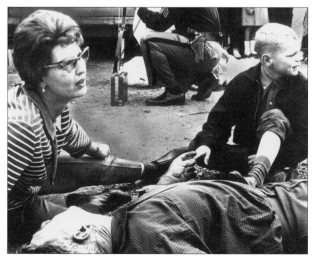

Mrs. Joseph Hoer of Crescent, Iowa. cradles her husband's head while comforting her injured son, Larry, after the Skylift ride collapsed at the 1965 Nebraska State Fair.

to comfort his motionless wife, Carol, and calmly asking for help was Bert Wells of Greenwood.

"I just don't know what happened," he said. "We were standing below it when it dropped and hit."

An emergency crew rushed up and swiftly carried his wife to an ambulance. Wells walked alongside the stretcher, holding her hand.

The two families were just part of the scene of the tragedy on the midway of the William T. Collins Carnival after two pylons on the block-long Skylift ride toppled. Gondolas and passengers plummeted to the ground. Many struck pedestrians who were walking below. A gondola smashed a ticket booth. Another crushed an empty baby stroller.

As ambulances continued to screech in and rescuers quickly carried the injured to them, a man screamed from a gondola still dangling overhead.

"Get me down! Get me down!" he screamed. "That's my wife you're carrying and I want to go with her!" A fireman shouted at the man attempting to climb from the gondola: "Get back! We're coming with a ladder."

Fair Manager Henry Brandt rushed to the scene with more than one reason to be shaken. It was his first year as manager and he had just learned his daughter, Connie, 20, a University of Nebraska-Lincoln student, was on the ride when it fell. She had walked to his office with a broken wrist and strained back.

Despite his concerns, Brandt calmly took over helping direct the rescue efforts and policing the large crowd that had rushed to the scene.

Survivors who could talk spoke in jerky sentences, their faces still reflecting the shock of high-flying joy suddenly ending in terror.

Terry Rush, 15, a member of the Lincoln High School band that had just paraded around the fairgrounds, was panting from exertion after running to the Administration building for help.

"I was riding with Connie Pettigrew (14, also of Lincoln) and we were just about to finish the ride when everything started shaking. I saw a few people fall. Then I saw LeRoy Leland – he's my best friend – hanging from a car upside down.

"We were right at the platform at the end of the ride and jumped out. I saw Pam Koranda on the ground. She's in the band. I stopped to see what I could do. Then I jumped up. I asked a guy where a phone was, and then I ran as fast as I could to the (Administration) building."

Tears streaked the face of husky Carl Powers of Lincoln and his son, Curtis, 7, but they were happy tears as they hugged Vicky Volguardsen, 17, who lived with them.

Vicky had just been lifted safely from one of the gondolas where she had been trapped in midair.

"The boy and I were just getting off the ride and at first didn't hear a thing," Powers said. "Then I saw people and baskets bouncing around like all hell. That's when we got scared and began looking for Vicky, who was riding behind us."

Among those who managed to remain in their gondola seats were Dick Stoddard of Seward and his two children, Dean, 7, and Debbie, 13.

"I had Dean around the neck and was holding on for all I was worth," Stoddard said. Dean admitted, "I was a little bit scared." Debbie, with tear-stained cheeks, couldn't say anything.

Mrs. Stoddard was on the ground waiting for the ride to end and saw what was happening to her family.

"I never prayed so hard in all my life," she said while enveloping her husband and children in a big hug.

There was consolation in the tragedy's aftermath. Better and safer rides were developed and state engineering specialists check their installation before the fair begins and daily during the fair's run.

Give Me a Freckle-Faced Kid

In my 40 years of covering the Nebraska State Fair, my biggest thrill was watching the faces of young 4-H exhibitors of grand champion livestock.

I always felt there was as much suspense and drama in the moment of truth at the 4-H beef market show as in a winning Husker touchdown in Memorial Stadium.

The look of exultation on young owners' faces when the judge gave their entry the traditional thump on the rump signifying it was the grand champion was memorable.

Through the years I always had a two-bit bet with Harold Stevens of Lexington, the longtime Dawson County Extension agent and coach of 4-H national champions in beef and livestock judging. We'd bet on which of the five division and reserve champions would get the highest honor.

Harold always won because of his expertise. I discovered it also helped when he took the judge to lunch before the parade of champions.

I always lost because I based my selection on the young exhibitor, not the animal, for good photo reasons. I always picked a young, freckle-faced boy or a cutie-pie blonde girl in pigtails.

Launching of the Crossbred Reign

For years the grand champion beef was selected from the winners in the British breeds – Angus, Herefords and Shorthorns.

In more recent years, crossbreds made their way into the winner's circle.

Eched forever in memory is the first year a crossbred was chosen grand champion at the fair, in keeping with similar selections at major livestock exhibitions throughout the nation.

The overflow crowd in the Youth Complex Arena roared. But above the deafening noise came an anguished, "Hell no!" from a former secretary of the National Shorthorn Association.

No Champion Corn in the Cornhusker State

A time-honored tradition of selecting a grand champion bushel of corn befitting the Cornhusker State ended more than 20 years ago in a comedy of errors.

Jim "Rags" Raglin of the Lincoln Journal and I were chuckling observers of the demise of the once-royal ceremony that included Nebraska's governor and dean of the University of Nebraska College of Agriculture.

The proud exhibitor of the grand champion bushel arrived in bib overalls, gingham shirt and traditional farmer straw hat – not a modern-day farmer baseball cap.

Except it was not a farmer who clutched the coveted grand champion's purple rosette while Rags and I interviewed him.

"Where's your farm?" we asked.

"Ain't got none. I'm a railroader," he replied.

"Raise the corn in your garden?" we asked.

"Nope," he said.

The Ag dean almost choked at the winner's reply when we asked incredulously, "Well, where in the hell did you get the corn?"

"Just walked down the railroad tracks and whenever I saw good ear in a field, I picked it," he said.

It was too late to change the judge's decision. But the best was yet to come when I said, "Well, let's get a photo of you and your champion bushel of corn."

It had disappeared from its throne just inside the open door of the old Agricultural Hall.

The biggest corn hunt in Nebraska's history was launched by a posse that included the State Highway Patrol, Lancaster County Sheriff deputies,

Lincoln police, fair officials, the distraught railroader, and Rags and me in hot pursuit.

We found the near-empty bushel basket and splattered champion corn kernels on the stage of the Game and Parks Commission minipark a block down the street. A whip-cracking artist was busy popping the ears with a blacksnake whip as they were tossed in the air by an assistant.

While both the handcuffed artist and helper were being led to the Administration building for questioning, the railroading would-be-farmer was tearfully down on his hands and knees harvesting the kernels muttering, "My poor grand champion corn!"

The suspects were released after explaining they were running out of corn ears when a teen-age boy approached the stage, telling them he knew where they could get a bushel and would fetch it for 50 cents. They agreed. The kid disappeared for a couple of minutes and then showed up with the grand champion bushel he'd swiped.

Thus ended the crowning of the State Fair's Grand Champion Bushel of Corn for evermore.

To Bucktail and Back . . .

CHAPTER THIRTY-FOUR

BY THE WAY, YOU MISSED IT!

Some of Nebraska's most intriguing and beautiful spots are so off the beaten track most visitors as well as Nebraskans miss them.

Dr. Robert Manley, Nebraska historian and troubadour, once suggested a rating system much like Hollywood's Jimmy Fidler's bell ratings for movies. Manley's is a barbed wire and obstacle rating and is based on how many you have to cross or overcome to get there.

The Iona 'Volcano'

The once hot and burning geological freak lay cold and dead when I first found it in early June 1972 high on a bluff overlooking the Missouri River, 4-1/2 miles northeast of Newcastle in Dixon County.

Indians didn't miss it. It was the site of an early fire-worshipping tribe.

And Lewis and Clark didn't miss it during their epic 1804 voyage of discovery up the Missouri River. Neither did other famed explorers such as artist George Catlin, Prince Maximillian and his artist companion, Karl Bodner. The Iona "volcano" was smoking hot and very much alive when they recorded its sighting in their journals.

Here's hoping it is not overlooked by the Nebraska Lewis and Clark Bicentennial Commission in its plans to observe in 2004 the epic journey that opened the West after the Louisiana Purchase.

Lewis and Clark, according to their journals, first saw the "volcano" – a bluff 150-feet high – on Aug. 24, 1804.

A historical marker on Highway 12 in Newcastle explains: "Clark wrote that it appeared to be on fire and was still very hot. He also detected signs of coal and what looked like cobalt. Later, fur traders frequently noted dense smoke and fire in the region.

"In 1839 J.N. Nicolett attempted to prove the phenomena were not of volcanic origin. Nicolett theorized the decomposition of iron pyrites in contact with water resulted in heat capable of igniting other combustible materials.

"Unaware of the explanation, early settlers continued to fear the Iona volcano. An earthquake in 1877 aroused new fears of an impending volcanic eruption."

Most of the volcano disappeared after the flooding Missouri River caused it to topple in 1878. The high water also started the demise of Iona.

The fears and stories died with the village after its post office was closed in 1907. Only its cemetery remains.

But the legend of "tears of a beautiful Indian Princess" remained in the mind of Patty Curry, the 12-year-old daughter of Mr. and Mrs. Darrel Curry on whose farmland the volcano was located, when I first met her.

Dixon County Clerk Irma Foulks, who saved the legend from old records, passed it on to Patty's family. The legend also was recorded by Newcastle postmaster Mrs. Adeline Breslin, past president of the Dixon County Historical Society.

Indians told the legend to Lewis and Clark and showed them excavations and mounds of a large capital city of ancient Arapaho Indians two miles south of the volcano.

According to the legend, Wachepa and his brother and sister were captured by the fire worshippers, who sacrificed victims in the burning volcano. The chief offered to save the life of Wachepa's brother if Wachepa tortured his sister in sacrificial rites.

But at the last moment, Wachepa and other captives turned on their captors.

"But the great spirit became angry," the recorded legend says." A roar like the concentrated thunder of a thousand years filled the temple. The ground shook. Rocks overhead trembled. With a crash, the earth opened to make a grave for both the living and the dead."

Those were the ruins shown to Lewis and Clark by the Indians, the Currys said.

Such was the story that led Patty to gather "tears" at the site. She often wandered into the volcano's remains, the slag-encrusted slope beneath the site to dig in the black and rust-colored soil, to find clear crystals formed by once-intense heat in mineral deposits.

To her, they are the tears of Wachepa's beautiful Indian maiden sister. They are the most prized among her collection of arrowheads and tomahawks found on her father's farmland.

At the time of my visit, her father said there had been no chemical reaction at the site in the 19 years they had farmed there.

But the spectacular view of parts of Iowa, South Dakota and

Nebraska as well as the picturesque Missouri Valley from the bluff makes the trek on winding gravel roads more than worthwhile.

Devil's Cattle Trap

In June 1962 I had a hard time convincing a county surveyor in Scottsbluff County there was such a thing as the Devil's Cattle Trap.

But a young University of Nebraska-Lincoln engineering student working in his office for the summer came to my rescue. He showed me the way by digging an ancient pioneer map from the office files.

"Could this be it?" he asked, showing me the map bearing a skull and crossbones at the site seven miles south of Lyman and a half-mile from the Wyoming border.

"Yep. This is the place of the Devil's Cattle Trap," said Bob Brammeier, owner of the farm with a boiling quagmire of chalky alkaline mud that regurgitates bones of long-dead livestock. It was so feared by early settlers that they marked it with the skull and crossbones warning.

"They didn't have to remind me how dangerous it is," Brammeier said. "Two years ago we had a tough time pulling my son Jonnie, then 3, to safety when he got caught by one of the sucking boils. He was up to his armpits when my Mom got to him."

He then led me on marked paths between the still-bubbling and heaving boils to show me the whitened bones of cattle they had spewed out.

"I've had some steers get in, but I never lost any, although an old cow later died from injuries received when we had to use a log chain to pull her out by tractor," Brammeier said. "The near tragedy of Jonnie and the close livestock misses I've had is the reason I've got the area fenced in with three rows of barbed wire. It is always changing in the spring and summer. A boil will form, go down and come up in another place. The sun will bake a gray crust on top but underneath it's a white mud that's hard to wash off."

When I returned 26 years later in April 1988, the Devil's Cattle Trap had become almost angelic. The boils were gone, but horses and cattle still gave the spongy spot a wide berth.

Mrs. Tim Blevins, wife of the new owner after Brammeier and Jonnie moved to Oregon in 1976, was unaware of the once-feared 66-foot trap in their spongy pasture. "We like history, but we didn't know we were sitting on it," she said.

But in Lyman, Jonnie's grandparents, Mr. and Mrs. Donald Brammeier, knew its history well. "It seems like only yesterday when I had to pull Jonnie out," Mrs. Brammeier said.

Her husband said he didn't need to be reminded, and had a collection of histories and Western adventure magazines with stories of the Devil's Trap.

A favorite, written by Harry E. Chrisman in a July 1967 edition of "The West – True Stories of the Old West" magazine, details Jonnie's dramatic escape and gives a history of the trap.

"It was nature in a cantankerous mood, not rustlers, that caused the mysterious losses to Nebraska ranchers a century ago, and still claims victims today," Chrisman wrote.

Brammeier's collection also includes a small handwritten book by George Fairfield, a pioneer U.S. deputy surveyor, that was found in the vault of the State Board of Educational Lands and Funds office.

In it, Fairfield wrote of finding the triangular valley "nearly destitute of vegetation except some sagebrush" and described the trap as "a wonderfully deceptive quagmire called Greasewood Springs which is about 10 chains – 660 feet – square.

"Any beast that walks on top of the mounds is doomed and will speedily sink out of sight. Ranchers say there are hundreds of cattle lost there every year. I submit this place should be called the Devil's Cattle Trap."

Grand Duke Alexis Buffalo Hunt

I've always been amazed that the site of one of the first major acts of détente between Russia and the United States is almost ignored and forgotten.

It's some 11 miles northeast of Hayes Center and is the site of the famed buffalo hunt for Grand Duke Alexis of Russia staged with pomp and ceremony by the U.S. State Department and conducted by William "Buffalo Bill" Cody in 1872.

Cody enlisted the aid of Indian chief Spotted Tail and a band of his warriors. And the State Department and the U.S. Army built a royal purple-lined tent city to house the Russian royal court. When I first found the campsite in 1960, you could dig a heel in the sandy soil and unearth stems of glasses used for post-hunt champagne toasts.

I can understand why it is overlooked by visitors. It's tough to get to. I gave it a four-barbed-wire-fence rating when I got there because I had to straddle that many, plus cross Red Willow Creek on a toppled log to get there.

On Oct. 12, 1988, the state historical society finally got around to replacing a 1931 crumbling sandstone marker with a larger granite one.

Hayes County road maintenance crews had to blaze a winding, rough trail through timber and underbrush along Red Willow Creek to allow 125 members of the United South Platte Chambers of Commerce, state Game and Parks Commission and the state historical society to get to the rededication ceremonies.

Nellie Snyder Yost Lidic of North Platte, author and former longtime state historical society board member, was instrumental in getting the new marker. "I thought this place should not be forgotten because the hunt was an international event that happened in Nebraska and we haven't had too many," she said. "The two leading powers in the world today are Russia and the United States, and both were represented in a spirit of friendship on the hunt."

Still today, all efforts to get an access road to the site on the Clifford ranch have failed. But it's still worth the torturous trek to get there.

Close your eyes in the picturesque valley and you can hear the joyous whoops of Spotted Tail and his braves, and even hear the boast of the grand duke when he bagged a giant buffalo "he thought he'd shot."

An historian wrote that Buffalo Bill fired over the grand duke's shoulder "just to make sure the grand duke had a grand trophy."

Fort McPherson's Ghost Bridge

Nellie Snyder Yost Lidic, author of "Pinnacle Jake," the story of her Texas trail-driving cowboy father, as well as other books of Western lore, got me intrigued with old frontier Fort McPherson's legendary ghost bridge in the early 1960s.

It was built across the Platte River south of Maxwell by running old Army caissons and wagons into the river and then laying logs across them. Legend fodder was a report of an Indian attack just as an Army detachment, bringing the monthly payroll to the fort, was crossing the bridge. The soldiers stuffed the gold down the mouth of a canon and rolled it into the river when they escaped.

Truer than legend was the fact the running trees of the old wagons often appeared and disappeared ghostlike with the rise and fall of the river's flow.

So Nellie goaded me into a combined ghost and gold hunt. I was still busy removing my shoes and socks to go wading when Nellie, a tiny woman, stood with skirts akimbo in the middle of the river channel, hollering: "We haven't got all day. Let's get the lead out!"

Together we splashed and waded up and down the river in vain for three hours under a broiling sun. We searched everywhere except the other side of an island that was rife with poison ivy.

After my story, a Mississippi State University history professor who was spending the summer in his native Maxwell and serving as its Boy Scout leader, wrote a week later he and his troop found one of the running trees of the ghost bridge "on the other side of the island you wrote you bypassed."

Then North Platte Judge Sam Diedrick, son of the legendary frontier pioneer "Barefoot Bill" Diedrick and a leader in the Lincoln County Historical Society, chuckled while informing me another week later how he had gone out and recovered the running tree. It rests high and dry and poison ivy-proof in the society's historical museum.

Before she got married, sweet Nellie and I always vowed we were going to set a date to find the gold "come hell, high water or poison ivy."

CHAPTER THIRTY-FIVE

CHARACTERS I HAVE KNOWN – AND LOVED

Ole Herstedt was one of Nebraska's best known big game hunters who bagged world-class trophies on safaris throughout the world.

Then he gained fame in establishing Ole's Big Game Lounge, "Nebraska's best known watering hole" in his hometown of Paxton. Decorated with his collection of big game trophies, it draws hunters and tourists from throughout the world.

It's the only tavern-cafe I know that draws buses of school children studying natural history on field trips. And it's my favorite spot to cut the dust along the Byways.

Ole for years used one of his trophies, the stuffed head of a baboon, as my on-the-road mailbox. He reasoned, "The baboon looks just like you."

Burly and tough, Ole cussed like a cavalry trooper. But he is the only man I ever knew who made cussing sound like poetry. He had a soft heart. I've seen him cry at the death of one of his favorite hunting dogs.

And he was a one-of-a-kind hunter. He refused to hunt the fiercest of animals from an elephant's back, Jeep or tree.

"The beast has his fangs, claws and cunning. I have a rifle to even the odds. So on all my safaris I have insisted on standing on the ground, face-to-face," he reasoned.

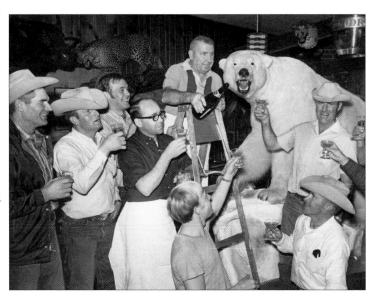

Paxton's Ole Herstedt dedicates his polar bear by pouring champagne over its nose.

Because of his stubborn stand, he narrowly escaped death several times, including the time in Portuguese East Africa an enraged cape buffalo, he claimed is the world's most dangerous animal, charged and slid nose first to a halt at Ole's feet despite being hit by several high-powered bullets.

My favorite Ole hunting story is how he bagged the giant polar bear that stands in a glass cage just inside the lounge's door and is the logo used in its advertisements. He first related it to me in a call from northern Alaska.

He had hired a bush pilot of a ski-equipped airplane to take him hunting over ice floes.

"I'll deny it," he said, "but if the truth were known, we were way out in the Bering Strait in Russian territory when we spotted the big (bleep bleep)."

In my story I told how Ole had to argue with the pilot to set the plane down on the ice so he could stand face-to-face with the bear. For family newspaper consumption I changed the pilot's reply to, "OK, buster. Hang on to your HAT!"

In the only letter Ole ever wrote to me, he angrily scribbled, "You are a lousy reporter. You known damned well the pilot didn't tell me to hang on to my hat!"

The pilot was barely able to take off in a ground blizzard after they had skinned the bear and lugged its head and hide to the plane.

Ole anguished for weeks in calls telling me the progress of a taxidermist and later, when its shipment was delayed, lamenting, "My poor bear is freezing his butt in some damned truck stop."

We held a memorable polar bear dedication when it finally arrived. The attendees included a bunch of cowboys – a Keystone-area rancher was observing the old range tradition of cutting the dust after trail-herding his cattle into the Paxton rail yard. The cowpokes were already in a mellow mood when Ole brought out a case of special imported champagne for the ceremony.

When I suggested he dedicate the bear in the time-honored manner of launching ships, Ole shouted from atop a step ladder: "Like hell we will. Nobody is gonna bust a bottle of booze over my bear's nose!" My framed photo of Ole pouring the champagne over the bear's nose is on the wall next to the bear.

But the best action was yet to come after a round of drinks on the house. Ole, the rancher and I were seated at the bar when one of the inebriated young cowboys approached and challenged his boss to arm wrestle.

The rancher, who looked like John Wayne, told the bartender to give the cowboy a drink and then turned to him and said: "Son, don't interrupt.

Mind your manners. We're having a conversation."

The angry cowboy drew back his fist. That's as far as he got before the rancher threw a punch that sent the cowpoke sailing across the floor, crashing into a pinball machine that the other cowhands were playing. The best of John Wayne movies couldn't have duplicated the ensuing free-for-all.

I remember the Paxton town marshal jumping up and ordering a group of startled Tennessee pheasant hunters to "stand back! You don't understand folks out here."

Ole, who had climbed atop the bar and was waving a baseball bat shouted: "You know we don't allow fights in here. Everybody get out back."

En route to record the outcome for posterity, I got slammed into a wall and instinctively swung my fist and cold cocked the biggest, meanest looking cowboy I ever saw. I was anxiously bent over him ready to supply first aid, when he came to.

To his "Who did it?" I hurriedly told him: "He went that-a-way. Let's go get him."

We did, to discover a melee in which everybody was falling down after missed swings. Ole surveyed the scene for a moment before bellowing: "That's enough. A drink is on the house." Everybody picked everybody else up, dusted each other off and joyful peace reigned.

Early the next morning I received phone calls from both Editor Fred Ware and my wife wanting to know what I did to cause an angry ranch wife to call and threaten to "snatch you bald," if the newspaper ran a photo of her husband.

Later I learned she was the wife of the cowboy who had started it all and ended up with a beauty of a black eye. He couldn't remember a thing when he got home except, "Honey, Tom Allan took my picture and it's gonna appear in The World-Herald."

Ole, before his passing, refused lucrative offers from buyers as far away as Louisiana and Texas for one of Nebraska's oasis treasures, fearing they would move his prized polar bear and some 200 other trophies out of the state.

Instead, he sold it to a hometown man, Tim Holzfaster, son of a prominent ranching and farming family. Tim changed the name to Ole's Steakhouse and Big Game Lounge, expanded its cramped space and made it into a full-menu facility. He built Ole's Lodge, a plush 34-unit motel, service station and campground at the Interstate 80 entry intersection to Paxton, and established Ole's Prairie Ridge, a combination retreat for corporate meetings and hunter's paradise.

More importantly, Holtzfaster is dedicated to keeping the legend of Ole alive.

Dr. "Big Mike" Chaloupka of Callaway and Broken Bow is my all-time favorite Doc who was the epitome of Nebraska country doctoring.

The South Omaha-born and University of Nebraska-educated Big Mike was a gregarious, lovable hulk of a man.

He was a Strategic Air Command flight surgeon with dreams of becoming a big city specialist. But before opening a practice in Omaha, he went to Callaway to give "The Heart of Seven Hills" community's longtime country doctor, R.D. Bryson, his first vacation in years.

"Shortly after I arrived Dr. Bryson took me out to the banks of the South Loup River and pointed to an abandoned ranch house on the other side," Big Mike recalled.

"Dr. Bryson said to me, 'Kid, you think you have the makings of a great physician? I am here to tell you that you can't claim the title of a real doctor until you are willing to swim across this river full of ice floes at flood tide to save a mother and her baby with a breach delivery on the kitchen table.' Then Dr. Bryson punched my shoulder and added, 'I did. That's why I can rightfully call myself a doctor.' "

Chaloupka added, "His words challenged me and at that moment I decided to give up dreams of big city doctoring and become a country doctor in Callaway."

Big Mike stayed, fell in love with the country and Rhoda, the daughter of an area rancher, married her, and became a legendary doctor in his own right.

He convinced the old doctor he had the makings of a real doctor by beginning his country doctoring career with an emergency delivery during the Great Blizzard of 1949 at the farm home of Glenn and Dorothy Adams, 10 miles northwest of town.

Big Mike enlisted the aid of Bert Tubbs, a state highway roads worker, to get him most of the way through blinding snow and deep drifts in a road maintainer before it became stuck in a giant drift.

Pulling two large medical bags, Big Mike crawled the final 2-1/2 miles, pulling himself along barbed-wire fences to reach the ranch and, like Dr. Bryson, made a breach delivery on the kitchen table. He didn't make it back to Callaway for three days.

He nicknamed the Adams' new baby son, Roger, "Blizzard." Not so incidentally, Blizzard had Doc deliver his own two children 20 and 23 years later – in better weather and medical conditions.

My story on how he had angrily balked at "asinine red tape" of

Medicare and Medicaid bookkeeping requirements and told officials: "Go to hell. I'm too busy savings lives to put up with your bull," gained him national television acclaim.

He also gained a reputation as a doctor who flew back from a well-earned vacation in Mexico after a patient insisted he was the only surgeon she'd allow to perform an emergency operation on her at Kearney. Then he flew back to complete his vacation.

He was known to stay up all night with his patients, once driving through the night to rush a blue baby to Omaha's Children's Memorial Hospital and then driving back in time to see patients in his Seven Valley Clinic the next morning.

His status as an official-baiter with his loud voice at high school basketball games grew so intense, officials refused to start games until he left the gym.

He insisted I come out and do a story on the first of the Seven Valleys Rodeo he'd help found.

Big Mike bellowed his disgust at a cowboy who lost his grip on the horns in steer-wrestling competition. The cowboy walked over to the fence and angrily shouted, "Well, Fatso, can you do any better?"

Big Mike let out a roar, jumped the fence and threw a block, cartwheeling the steer. He walked gingerly back through the gate before gasping as he sat down next to me. "We can't leave now, it wouldn't look good," he said. "But pretty soon we're going to sneak out and you're going with me to my clinic to tape up my ribs. I think I busted some."

His nurse was there, thank God, and she did the taping. And Doc, despite two broken ribs, won the jigging contest that night at the barbecue.

He was country medicine and Callaway's chief supporter. He presided at the rebirth of the Callaway Courier and installed his wife, Rhoda, as its prize-winning editor-publisher for several years.

Only when he had to slow down for health reasons did he move to nearby Broken Bow where he could share his medical service load with other doctors. But he refused to let heart attacks diminish his concern for his patients.

His passing ended a legacy of country doctoring at its best.

Rhoda lives on in retirement at Callaway.

Seraphine Willard was a saint, content to sit by the side of the road and be a friend to all.

She was 98 when I found her in October 1983 at her old-fashioned "forgits" combination store and one-pump gas station alongside U.S. 183, eight miles north of Miller and just a squeal of brakes south of the Custer County line.

The operator of the store more formally known as "Milton's" in honor of her late husband, lured customers with warm hospitality, a cozy rocking chair atmosphere, folksy conversation and shelves full of what she called "forgits."

Thus the name, "Forgits Store." Seraphine explained, "I carry things people forgits on shopping trips to Kearney and Broken Bow.

Bankers are usually conservative and laid back. But not Thomas Tiffany Varney Jr., president of the Broken Bow State Bank whom I first discovered during the Custer County seat's annual Hay Days in September 1959.

He was a lovable prankster inflicted with a severe case of "telephone-itus."

It made no difference that it was cold and raining when I found him attired in a frontier cutaway coat and Western hat and seated at a rolltop desk on the sidewalk in front of the bank. He had a bucket of gold-painted pebbles he was handing out for free goodies at neighboring stores.

When I started to take his photo, he said: "Wait! A better shot is coming. I've been tipped off that some of my businessman friends are going to hold me up and steal my gold. Do I have a surprise for them. I borrowed some blank, race-starting ammunition from the high school track coach and I'm gonna blast them with my trusty .22."

Wow! Did B.V. Holmes, Bob Dickinson, Charles Huff and Bill Pokorney, posing as masked bandits, ever get blasted when they showed up shouting, "Stick-em up, Tom!" They took full flight, dashing across the street and then, not around, but through the bandstand in the center of the town square.

While Hary Purcell, publisher of the Custer County Chief, rounded them up for photo identification, I asked Varney, "Are you sure you had blanks in that gun?"

"Yep," he answered, pulling a drawer out from the desk and firing his last shot into it. The bottom of the drawer disintegrated!

The four "bandits," limped back picking bird shot from the south ends of their northbound anatomies. Otherwise unhurt, they vowed, "Crime doesn't pay."

Varney was abashed and apologized. Then saying, "We need a drink!"

drove me in an open Model T Ford to his home, pausing along the way long enough to give a rush order to a seamstress to create Purple Heart pillows he presented to his victims that night at the barbecue.

After pouring our drinks, he picked up the phone and told me he was calling Colonel Figby, saying he would love to hear of his marksmanship.

That's how I learned Figby was a "figment of his imagination" and Varney was indeed inflicted with telephone-itus. He caused consternation at Miami's plush Fontenbleu Hotel when, after being informed they had no Colonel Figby registered, he demanded: "What do you mean? He just called from his yacht that's docking in your marina and told me he has your presidential suite."

My wife well remembered the call she received a few days later from "Colonel Figby" telling her that I had graciously invited him to dinner that night at eight and asked, "Would it be all right if I bring two of my distinguished friends?"

Of course my wife, always a perfect host, agreed. But she wasn't in an agreeable mood when I arrived home and she asked, "Just who and where is Colonel Figby?" She fumed when I told her, especially when I added that the special candlelit dinner she had prepared was one of the best we'd ever eaten.

Varney knew better than to call and apologize the next day. Instead my wife received two dozen red roses bearing a card reading, "Oops sorry! Got my dates mixed up," and signed, "With love, Colonel Figby."

Later that first night at Broken Bow, I discovered Varney had checked me out of my room at the Arrow Hotel and delivered my luggage to a guest room at his home. Before we retired he said, "Let's call Bob Hope!" A moment later he shouted from the kitchen: "Get on the extension phone. Bob Hope wants to meet you!"

It was the famed movie and USO entertainer on the phone! He told me: "It's nice to know you, Tom. But would you mind finding out from Varney how he got my unlisted number this time?"

Hope told me he and Bing Crosby had become friends of Varney when they competed in the annual One Shot Antelope Hunt at Lander, Wyo. Varney later used the idea to launch the annual One Box Pheasant Hunt at Broken Bow.

But Varney's best phone call was yet to come. In the middle of the night after the lights came on in my bedroom, I found him standing at the foot of my bed. "Would you mind if I used your shower?" he asked as he began stripping off his pajamas. "I always get up early. I'm a gourmet cook and I'm going to prepare you the best breakfast you ever had."

When I answered groggily, "Please, be my guest," he paused before he got to the bathroom door, snapped both his fingers and me awake by shouting, "Let's call the governor's mansion in Lincoln!"

It didn't deter him when I told him, "It's 3:30 a.m. and Governor (Ralph) Brooks will kill you." He strode to the phone and called the governor's mansion. Mrs. Brooks answered.

"Mrs. Brooks," Varney said sweetly. "Sorry to awaken you, but this is Washington calling and we have a national emergency. Please get Governor Brooks on the phone and tell him to hold the line while we set up a conference call with other distinguished governors."

Assured by Mrs. Brooks she would get her husband on the phone immediately, Varney laid the phone on the pillow next to me. Then humming a happy tune, he headed for the shower.

Varney may have taken five minutes to shower, but it seemed like an hour as I warily looked at the phone as if it was a rattlesnake and listened to Gov. Brooks ranting and raving on the other end of the line.

Finally, Varney, toweling his back and humming an even happier tune, came back, picked up the phone and said, "Governor Brooks, were you waiting to talk to Washington?" Varney had to remove the phone from his ear at the explosion of Brooks' verbosity, then asked: "Sincerely governor, isn't that rather foolish? Washington has been dead for over 200 years!" Then he quickly hung up.

Several years later after Brooks had passed on, I bumped into Mrs. Brooks at McCook's Modrell's Bakery and we shared cups of coffee and old times. She gasped when I asked if she remembered the "Washington-calling" phone call.

"Did you make that call?" she further gasped. I quickly assured her I was an innocent bystander and told her who the culprit was since he, too, had passed on.

"Oh, my poor dear R.G. (Brooks' initials). He knew Tom Varney well and should have known. But I remember well my dear R.G. came close to complete apoplexy that night."

Irma Ourecky, national Czech capital queen, is "Mrs. Wilber." She personifies the can-do spirit of the Saline County seat that created one of the state's most colorful annual ethnic festivals.

She wasn't satisfied that her town became Nebraska's Czech Capital. With the help of the late U.S. Sen. Ed Zorinsky, she got it named the National Czech Capital by Congressional resolution in 1987.

And at an age when most women have long retired to a rocking chair, she keeps busy administering Wilber's Czech Museum and making rugs on the museum's ancient loom.

Scribner's longtime hardware merchant, "Uncle John" Lamberty, used to delight in getting medical exams so he could astound doctors. They'd do double-takes at finding an 8-penny nail imbedded in his heart.

At age 100 he astounded me in October 1996, exercising by bending over to touch his toes and then demanding and getting "heart palpitating" hugs from the nurses at Scribner's senior citizen home.

Lamberty, affectionately known as "Uncle John," survived one of the most tragic fires and explosions in Nebraska's history the night of March 7, 1929. He was one of the volunteer firemen who answered an alarm in a shed in which county-owned dynamite and kegs of nails were stored.

Six of his fellow firemen were killed in the blast. Thirty persons, including firemen and bystanders, were severely injured by the shrapnel-like flying nails.

Uncle John was blown several yards over a ditch and one of the nails penetrated his back. With other wounded, he was rushed to an Omaha hospital where surgeons deemed an operation to remove the nail from his heart was too risky.

Uncle John not only survived, but thrived. And until his death in May 1998 at age 102, he loved to wiggle his fingers through the gaping hole the nail made in his treasured jacket that he kept through the years.

In the May 18, 1975, Byways I wrote:

She's as tiny as a primrose in the wide expanse of Sand Hills near her Lakeside, Neb., home.

Her soft voice echoes the poetry she writes.

Her eyes, gleaming with mischievous good humor, reflect thousands of sunrises and sunsets spanning the history of the Sand Hills from sod houses to scientific farming.

But there is a dynamo of energy in Mrs. Hilda Black, matriarch of the Black Lakeside Ranches, one of the largest and most successful of Nebraska's cattle operations.

Mrs. Black, described by author Nellie Yost in her "Call of the Range," as a "cattle queen in her own right," is the dainty but determined woman who is perhaps known best as the one who lit up the Sand Hills by bringing rural electric power and all its blessings to them.

Hilda Black

She used her cowhand know-how, learned from driving mavericks, to ramrod skeptical Washington bureaucrats into accepting the feasibility of providing Rural Electrification Administration power to ranches in the vast expanse of the Sand Hills.

When the bureaucrats balked, asking who would underwrite the initial cost, she whipped out her checkbook and offered, "Whatever you think you need."

She modestly explained her leadership role with, "I just did what needed to be done," before revealing the secret of her success was in a poem she'd written years before.

Titled "Ambition's Small Flame," it reads:
"Gently seek your goal. Stride not with giant step. Walk softly, go far."

Col. Barney Oldfield is the retired Air Force colonel who ranks as "Nebraska's Santa Claus of Beverly Hills, California."

The Johnson County, Neb., native, headed up Gen. Dwight Eisenhower's press corps during World War II, but gained equal fame as "King of Hollywood Press Agents" and later head of public relations for worldwide Litton Industries.

But he and his late wife, Vada, never forgot Nebraska. They have provided millions in scholarships honoring Nebraska D-Day veterans who died on Omaha Beach, the state's Navy vets who lay in final rest in the hulk of the battleship Arizona at Pearl Harbor, as well as Nebraska youth in a unique Dollars For Scholars program, plus George Foreman Scholarships for minority students in communications at the University of Nebraska-Lincoln, and other endowments to the UNL Alumni Foundation.

When his wife died from Alzheimer's disease, Barney launched a major foundation in her name for education and research for a cure of the disease at the University of Nebraska Medical Center.

The colonel, who I affectionately call an "Old Coot" became angered at the action of a State Historical Society Foundation official over the awarding of his veteran scholarships, and swore he'd never return to Nebraska.

I told him, "Oh, yes you will!" Vada is buried close to my wife, Marilyn, at Fort McPherson National Cemetery at Maxwell.

"Barney," I told him, "every time I pause for a visit, our wives are talking about us. You gotta come back to help protect our reputations."

CHAPTER THIRTY-SIX

CHIMNEY ROCK TRAILS AND TALES

The arrival of the wagon train to celebrate the 150th anniversary of the Oregon Trail in 1993.

Perhaps no landmark is more synonymous with pioneer trails across Nebraska than Chimney Rock near Bayard.

The spire-shaped tower is a guidepost most often mentioned in journals of Westward Ho!-ers of the Oregon, Overland and Mormon trails and the Pony Express.

It has been a spectacular backdrop for numerous Trails West re-enactments.

Among the best-remembered is the covered wagon train commemorating the Oregon state centennial in 1959 in which several Oregon cities sponsored wagons. Bayard and area ranchers made their stopover at Chimney Rock extra special with an Indian raid.

Enlisted were a "war party" of Ogalala Sioux from the Pine Ridge Reservation. In a rehearsal for the wagon train's arrival, a rancher told the Indians to select their horses from a band he'd rounded up.

The Ogalalas, once the world's greatest light horse cavalry, looked aghast. Only eight volunteered to try riding. The rest became foot soldier infantrymen.

The attacking force was hidden behind a knoll and told to come out charging with war whoops and firing blank ammunition upon hearing a gunshot signal. The signal shots were to no avail. The Indians were taking a nap.

The rancher had one of his cowhands, stripped to a loin cloth and feathered headdress, join the band to lead them.

One thing was forgotten in the attack when the wagons arrived – the promoters forgot to tell the Indians the modern-day pioneers would be firing blanks back at them.

The result provided spectacular photo footage when the horses of the Indian cavalry spooked and Indians toppled to the ground. One horse galloped wildly through the crowd of spectators. It balked at a fence. The Indian rider was hurled through barbed wire, severely gashing an arm.

But overall, the raid was hailed as both a resounding and astounding success.

Quieter, but equally spectacular, was the arrival of the wagon train on June 25,1993, commemorating the 150th anniversary of the Oregon Trail.

Cheryl Burkhart-Kriesel of Gurley and her friend, Mary Dwyer of Fort Collins, Colo., survived the 13-mile leg of the ride from Bridgeport to "the rock" much more comfortably than their trail-bouncing ancestors.

"I made our matching gingham dresses, but I also added matching pillows for us to sit on after remembering accounts of the jarring wagon ride," Burkhart-Kriesel said.

The wagon getting the most attention from the crowd, attending both the train's arrival and Bayard's three-day Chimney Rock Pioneer Days, was one from Aurora, Ore., bearing a large sign reading "Bringing Willie Home."

It contained a rough-hewn, tin-lined casket containing a mannequin representing Willie Kiel.

Laura Cookman, chairman of Aurora's centennial committee and one of the wagon's riders, explained, "Willie was the 18-year-old son of William Kiel, the leader of a wagon train who founded Aurora.

"Willie caught a fever just before the wagon train set out from the East," Mrs. Cookman said. "Before Willie died, he got a promise from his father he would not be left behind. So his father had the special tin-lined casket made and added three barrels of alcohol to Willie's remains to preserve him during the long trek. We'll have a ceremonial burial for Willie during Aurora's centennial when we get him back home."

Lanky Joe Vogel of Red Cloud, the wagonmaster of several re-enactments and the driver of the official Nebraska wagon, said, "Just like it was for those early pioneers, it's always a special thrill to reach Chimney Rock and be close enough to touch it. It makes history come alive."

Although another monument, Smokestack Rock, gained national publicity in the syndicated "Strange As It May Seem" cartoon series, I discovered few Nebraskans have ever seen or heard of it.

Smokestack Rock, so named because it's shaped like an ancient steam locomotive, is in an isolated spot west of Chimney Rock and southwest of McGrew. The cartoon said it was a popular place where pioneers used to hold picnics on its flat top.

No one had heard of it when I first stopped at the McGrew pool hall in August 1959 on a trek to find it. But just when I was leaving, an old-timer said: "Whoa! Seems to me there is such a place south of here." He gave me the phone number of rancher Rolland Roberts of Bayard, who might know.

Mrs. Roberts answered my call with: "It's certainly here! I'm looking at it right now through my kitchen window."

Later, when I was taking a photo of her holding an armload of wildflowers with the towering rock in the background, she said quietly: "Tom, stand still. Don't move."

A couple of agonizing moments later, she said: "OK, you can breathe now. The big, old rattlesnake is gone!"

I warily looked and discovered he'd left a slithering trail in the dust just behind my heels.

Memories of the 150th anniversary re-enactment of the Mormon Trail, from Florence in North Omaha to Salt Lake City in 1997, include a poignant one on May 6, 1997.

Members of the Church of Jesus Christ of Latter-day Saints from around the world relived history step-by-agonizing-step pushing or pulling handcarts. And there were sad tears in their eyes during a seven-mile trek between Wood River and Shelton on a county road that was part of the original trail.

The faithful paused en route to pray and place 600 cross-armed stakes decorated with 6,000 multicolored ribbons. Each ribbon represented a Mormon who died from the ardor of the trail.

"We didn't want anyone to forget, especially since most of the casualties were children and the very old and weak," said Ronnie O'Brien of Shelton, coordinator of Shelton's special welcome to the trekkers.

Making a trip from Salt Lake City for the event was LaPriel Herrick, 85, and her daughter, Jean Ostler.

"I am the great-granddaughter and my daughter is the great-great granddaughter of Joseph Johnson, who was ordered by Mormon leader Brigham Young to establish a freight and supply station at Shelton," Mrs. Herrick said.

The two women were delightfully surprised to meet a great-grandson of Johnson for the first time who was traveling with the handcart train.

"We did not know him before today because our great-grandfather had three wives," Mrs. Herrick said.

The day also was special for Larry and Jodie Crowder of Sandy, Utah, and their children Heather, 12, Jeff, 10, and Kim, 4.

"We are part of a group of 250 volunteers from Utah who are taking turns spending a week on the trail our ancestors forged," Mrs. Crowder said. "My great-great grandmother, Phoebe Lee Drowne, made one of the first Mormon migrations across Nebraska to Utah."

CHAPTER THIRTY-SEVEN

I Got a Bee in My Bonnet

During my travels of the Byways I became a man of many hats, ranging from Alpine styles and western Stetsons to golf caps and Scottish tams.

My original chapeaus eventually became a problem. So many towns and organizations insisted on pinning their logo badges on them, I was getting round shouldered under their weight.

I finally decided to put the first one out to pasture literally after Charlie War Bonnet, an Ogalala Sioux Indian friend, asked me, "Where did you get that crazy hat?" When I asked what was wrong with it, he replied "It's got no feather!"

Afraid the addition of a feather would be the straw that broke my back, I mistakenly offered in my Byways column to donate it to a worthy cause. I received so many demands from bar owners and curators that it be hung in their taverns or museums, I decided the easy way out would be to hang it on a fence post at an undisclosed spot in the Sand Hills.

I made an error in taking my wife to the spot, which we found was guarded by an angry rattlesnake. Unbeknownst to me, she contacted the ranch owner, an old friend, and retrieved the hat.

Then she made it rattlesnake proof by getting it bronzed before returning it to me as a surprise birthday present along with a new hat that also became laden with logo souvenirs.

I discovered again how difficult it is to get rid of an old hat with so many memories when I donated the third edition to the Omaha Press Club's annual scholarship auction.

World-Herald Executive Editor Larry King returned it to me "to have and to hold" after making the highest bid on the newspaper's behalf at the auction.

After I started wearing golf-style hats, I paused one day at the Bowring Ranch near Merriman to visit ranch matriarch and U.S. Sen. Eva Bowring. The spread became the Arthur Bowring Sand Hills Historical State Park after Eva's passing.

I was wearing a black golf hat bearing the logo of an Angus equipment company when I knocked on the door.

"How dare you wear a black Angus hat on a white-faced Hereford ranch!" shouted Eva in mock rage when she greeted me. "Where is your regular hat?"

When I explained it was in the backseat of my car, she bid me, "Go get it and get rid of that Angus hat right now!"

When I got back she had rummaged in her jewelry box and presented me with a gold bee which she ceremoniously pinned on the old chapeau.

"There," she said. "Everybody should have a bee in his bonnet and now you also have something to remember me by."

I always remember the gracious lady fondly, anyway. But now I treasure both her friendship and the gold bee in my bonnet.

Allan in his various hats.

Other Unforgettables

The late Joe DeFilipps was best known to his friends in Lexington as "Chicago Joe" because he was a native of the Windy City. He was known more for his statewide lectures on mailboxes and old barns, and conducting tours to China than for heading Lexington's Holiday Travel and Cruises agency. I knew him best as my "international and central Nebraska stringer" for his numerous story tips. He's the one who tipped me on doing a story on Nebraska Street in London.

The block-long street got its name because it leads from the dock on which buffalo hides from Nebraska's frontier were unloaded.

Les Fitch is the only mayor anywhere to have his town moved from under his feet. The late Fitch, a banker, was the mayor of Niobrara when the Army Corps of Engineers condemned and rebuilt it on a hill to the south because of high groundwater caused by the Gavins Point Dam.

He was one of the chief promoters in the construction of the Missouri River Chief Standing Bear Bridge between Niobrara and Running Water, S.D., and saw his dream come true before his death in 1999.

Marilyn Johnson is known in her hometown as "Dannebrog's Dynamo," and is the power behind the throne that made the town the Danish Capital of Nebraska. She also spearheaded numerous community development projects.

She was a most deserving winner of the state tourism division's 2001 top honor, the Henry Fonda Award, for promoting tourism and pride in ethnic heritage in Nebraska.

Phil Pagel, the retired longtime public relation's ace and later vice president for college relations of Blair's Dana College, became known as "Mr. Dana."

I consider Phil the one most responsible for forging the college's rich heritage ties with Denmark. He promoted tours by Dana's choir and students to the old country, was mainly responsible for luring Denmark's Queen Margarethe II to the campus for an honorary doctorate, and helped establish friendships and honorary doctorate visits by such Danish stars as pianist-comic Victor Borge and international opera and Hollywood star Lawrence "The Great Dane" Lauritz Melchior.

Pagel also originated the "Sights and Sounds of Christmas," Dana's annual festive Yuletide gift to the public.

And he did it all with grace and infectious good humor despite a spinal infliction that confined him to a wheelchair.

Anne Christopherson's husband, Myrvin, is president of Dana College. She is the college's director of special campus activities, and makes the hilltop campus tick, heading such events as the "Sights and Sounds of Christmas."

And the vivacious lady is proof that something is rotten in Denmark. When her husband was made a Knight of Dannebrog by the Danish ambassador to America in a special campus ceremony, the ambassador, citing Danish protocol, announced that unlike the British royal court, the wives of Danish Knights do not gain the rank of Lady.

The slight to womanhood is the only thing I have against the Danes. Anne is a Lady in every sense of the word. It's the reason I ignore Sir Myrvin, and bow and kiss the hand of Lady Anne every time we meet.

Nebraska's Chambers of Commerce can't seem to make up their mind on what title to give to their office executives. Titles range from executive vice president to manager and secretary.

But personifying all of them plus being the "mother hen" of the community and being the most versatile of women was Aurora's Donna Rasmussen. Donna served the chamber as its office executive for more than 35 years, until her retirement in 2001. That's longer than any other chamber manager in the state. She also was the first woman to serve as president of the Nebraska Chamber of Commerce Council.

When she retired and moved to her hometown of Norfolk, Ron "Butch" Furse, retired publisher of the Aurora News-Register wrote in a special column, "Thanks, Donna, for taking the community under your wing." He praised her seven-days-a week, behind-the-scenes work as Aurora's "economic developer, community guide and goodwill ambassador whose friendship and smile went beyond the boundaries of this community."

She was the voice of Aurora, broadcasting Aurora news daily on York radio station KAWL, and was the heart of the Bremer Community Center, home of the chamber's headquarters. She baked cakes for the center's card players on their birthdays and cookies for office visitors.

I missed her when she retired. She made Aurora more than a convenient rest stop heading west out of Lincoln. Her cookies, ever-ready cup of coffee and her sunny friendship always made it a pause that refreshed.

Pat Fritz is another of Nebraska's top Chamber of Commerce managers and a community "mother hen" for O'Neill. She uses her perpetual smile and engaging personality to promote her community as the official Irish Capital of Nebraska as well as help ramrod its economic development.

The late Mary Ellenwood was a rancher's widow who helped start Atkinson's Hay Days before moving to O'Neill where she restored the historic Golden Hotel and really put the Irish Capital on the international map.

Best remembered is when she asked me how to make an international phone call to invite the Lord Mayor of Dublin to the community's centennial featuring the annual St. Patrick's Day Festival.

After following my instructions, she frantically bid me get on an extension phone because she was having difficulty understanding the thick-as-Irish-stew brogue of the "mayor's" secretary.

The secretary was delightful. I explained that the festival salutes the Irish settlers of the town with the "world's largest shamrock" painted on its main intersection, and residents would like a congratulatory telegram from the Lord Mayor to be read at the banquet.

The secretary interrupted me with laughter and then explained we had reached much higher than the Lord Mayor's office. We were talking to a secretary of the Prime Minister of Ireland.

Mary interrupted with: "Well, he'll do. Nothing is too good for O'Neill!"

The delighted secretary not only delivered the Prime Minister's blessings, but arranged for another congratulatory telegram from Dublin's Lord Mayor.

Another Mary gem resulted from her difficulty in remembering names. She couldn't remember the name of Republican gubernatorial candidate, Clifton Batchelder, who was guest of honor at a tea in the Golden Hotel's foyer.

I told her to practice word association to help her memory. If you can't remember Batchelder, I said, think of a batch of cookies. She dutifully practiced, and when the candidate arrived she greeted him warmly with: "Hey, Cookie! How you doing?"

Ed Nelson, the late longtime president of Chadron State College, wasn't content with a president emeritus status when he retired.

He traveled statewide and gained the title of "Nebraska's Small Town Cheerleader" while conducting community improvement and development seminars in which better school and community relations were a major factor.

My wife affectionately called Nelson her "Doll Baby," not only for his ever-ready smile beneath his bald pate. She discovered he and his wife had such a large doll collection, they purchased a house next door to their home to display their surplus.

Good Gray Buffalo was an oil painter and tribal historian of the Oglala Sioux Indians at Pine Ridge, S.D., and claimed his English name, Jake Herman, "Is proof the Sioux are descendants of the long-lost ancient tribes of Israel."

Once he offered to show me sacred teepee circles. He said the stones, once used to weight down the sides of teepees, had been hidden for years in a remote spot in the nearby Badlands.

We had long left a road and then a trail on the long trek. But I had no worries because I knew the Sioux were supposed to know the land like the back of their hand and, luckily, I had filled the gas tank before we started.

After driving aimlessly for three hours, I stopped and asked Jake if he was sure he knew where we were. He got out of the car and gazed stoically in all directions before muttering, "Damn, we're lost!"

But in wending our way back, we actually came upon the circles. After inspecting them, Jake placed his hands on my shoulders and solemnly said: "Friend Tom. You have a great honor. You are the first paleface to ever set foot in this sacred place!"

Looking over his shoulder, I noted a U.S. Bureau of Reclamation crew had arrived a short distance away and were setting up surveying instruments.

"Good Gray Buffalo," I said, "you have given me a great honor. But what's that crew doing here?"

Startled, Jake turned and watched them in silence for a few moments before turning back to me. His face was impassive as he said, "Friend Tom, the trouble with big government is it always louses up a good Indian story."

Robert Burns, former president of Peru State College, more than lived up to his namesake, Scotland's famed national poet. He had Scottish bagpipers lead commencement processions and featured the choir of

Omaha's Salem Baptist Church at graduation programs.

He also was a conniver, joining my wife, Marilyn, Deanna Sands, Joanne Stewart, The World-Herald's managing and assistant managing editors, respectively, and Kent Propst, his vice president for campus advancement, in surprising the daylights out of me.

"Give me your camera and notebook. You won't need them," he said when I arrived to cover the PSC commencement on May 11, 1996. "Give me your jacket. Here, put this on."

Then he handed me an academic robe that I first thought was a nightshirt, and a commencement program revealing I was being given an honorary Doctor of Letters degree.

Peru State College President Robert Burns pulls a surprise.

Ben Johnson, Peru State College president, also bears the name of a British literary giant. The enthusiastic Johnson not only spearheaded campus and academic program expansion, but also preserved a landmark monument to Nebraska's one-room schoolhouses.

After leading 50 volunteers in a "Pick-Me-Up Greenhouse" project to hand carry the college's old greenhouse nine blocks to the other end of Peru's main street to provide a new florist business for the town, he launched another brick-by-brick endeavor.

Johnson led volunteers in saving Nemaha County's historic little red brick schoolhouse from destruction in the modernization of U.S. Highway 75, nine miles east of the campus.

This time, thankfully, they dismantled it, moved it by truck and restored it at the college's entrance. It is a monument to the value of one-room schoolhouse education, is a research lab on the history of such schools and is a Welcome Center to the college.

Belvidere's women provided delightful proof of "The Power of Women." In 1971, housewives led their Thayer County village to one of the first No. 1 Small Town ratings in the Nebraska Community Improvement Program contest with, "We won't take no for an answer," determination.

One of their main projects was the restoration of a park that had become an eyesore.

When their husbands scoffed and refused to help, they had effective answers. Arriving home for lunch, the men found notes pinned on refrigerator doors reading: "Hungry? You know where the bread and lunchmeat are. Help yourself."

The notes changed at dinner time, reading: "Still hungry? We're busy. You know where the can opener is and you know where we are."

Facing starvation, the men capitulated and pitched in to help clean up the park with their tractors and pickup trucks.

But the women's best coup was rousing the Thayer County Board of Supervisors headquartered at Hebron to frantic action.

Belvidere is located on a spur county road leading from U.S. Highway 81 that included an ancient, accident-battered bridge long rusted with age.

The women had appeared before the supervisors asking the bridge be painted before visiting NCIP judges arrived on a seeing-is-believing inspection tour.

"Yes, we'll get to it," the supervisors promised. But they didn't. Three days before the judges' arrival, the women launched a "We'll paint it ourselves" project.

The supervisors, meeting as a board of equalization, were jarred to action by the arrival of Jim Johnson, the late longtime county sheriff, who was in cahoots with the women.

"I just wanted to know how much liability insurance the county has," said the sheriff as he interrupted the meeting. "I've just been to Belvidere and there's a bunch of angry and determined women hanging from the girders painting the bridge you promised them you would paint but haven't."

The meeting was immediately adjourned and Sheriff Johnson led a fast convoy of worried supervisors followed by a county road maintenance paint crew to the site.

To pleas of, "Ladies, please get down. We are here to do the job," the paint-stained women replied, "We'll get down just as soon as your crew starts painting."

Three days later the NCIP judges were pleased by the shiny bridge and, of course, they were clued in on how "Women Power" got quick action on two projects.

And Belvidere won first prize!

CHAPTER THIRTY-EIGHT

SURPRISE HOMECOMING

I had the best of homecomings on June 24, 2001, the sunset year of my journalistic career, when I arrived in New York City after a 21-day cruise of the Mediterranean and the Atlantic.

My son, Tam, a Lincoln developer, developed a major surprise by greeting me at the pier when the Queen Elizabeth II pulled into the harbor.

"I wanted to rewrite a bittersweet chapter in family history," he explained. Tam did much more with a big grin and bear hug!

He had flown to New York to surprise me with a more heartwarming homecoming than I experienced when I first arrived from Scotland, my native land, on a frigid Jan. 27, 1927, morning.

The dockside welcome to America 74 years earlier was marked with tears and sadness.

I could see my father, the Rev. William Allan, waving joyously on the dock as I stood on the stern deck of the H.M.S. Cameronia.

But it would be 10 long, dreary days before two scared "wee Scots – me, 9, and my brother, William Patterson MacKenzie Allan, 7, – would be clasped in our father's embrace.

Brother Bill had come down with chicken pox midvoyage, and we were moved to an isolated cabin on the stern of the ship. Upon arrival at Ellis Island, we were immediately quarantined with no chance of being greeted or visited by our father.

My defiant screams that "I already had the pox!" and didn't need to be imprisoned in a 24-bed hospital ward that was empty but for us, were in vain. So were my anguished yells for help from my cowboy heroes, Tom Mix and Hoot Gibson. America and my two cowboy heroes, who had never before failed to come galloping to a rescue, had let me down.

I escaped the ward once, only to be captured in the immigration center's Great Hall by a burly guard who threw me over his shoulder and whupped my fanny all the way back to confinement.

Five years earlier, my Baptist pastor father, heartbroken over the death of my mother in childbirth, had migrated to America, leaving us with our granny and three teen-age aunts. He sent for us after gaining U.S. citizenship, remarrying and settling at Oxford, Neb. With tags around our necks and in the care of a couple too seasick to tend to us, we had the joyous run of the ship – until chicken pox struck!

My daughter, Mary, and Tam had heard the story many times. But this time Tam wanted my welcome to be warm and become alive. Not only did he surprise me with his dockside greeting, but he accompanied me back through Ellis Island. I had made four previous trips there with my late wife, Marilyn, during its development as the American Family Immigration History Center as well as a national monument.

I was eager to plug in the center's new computers. With a click of a button, an immigrant's "Voyage of Discovery" spews forth, including date of arrival in America, photos of the ship, its passenger manifest, his age, possessions, baggage carried, how much money he had and his final destination.

I was disappointed when Jeffrey S. Dosick, ranger-librarian, explained that my 1927 arrival was three years too late. Federal privacy safeguards limit access only to records from 1892 to 1924. I'd have to wait a few years until later arrivals are included.

But Tam was undaunted. He remembered that I had given a personal interview about my experiences during a 1984 visit.

Dosick brightened and immediately led us into the computer-filled library of the monument's Oral History Project. A push of a button and my story unfolded.

It got even better with the arrival of Janet Levine, the museum's oral historian. Saying she was "particularly delighted to meet one of the dwindling number of immigrants who passed through Ellis Island," she talked me into an hour-long interview updating my coming-to-America adventure.

I told her any bad feelings I had about America caused by the tribulations of my first arrival had changed dramatically.

"Unlike native-born Americans, who never had the option, Ellis Island gave me a chance to start a new life," I told her. "I have been blessed, and have never regretted my choice because here I was born again in a new and exciting land that I love."

Tam was touched and silent when I led him to the stainless steel-paneled Wall of Honor facing the towering skyline of Manhattan and showed him my name, along with my brother's and our father's, among the multitude of others who passed through the gateway to freedom.

I'll always remember how he put an arm around my shoulder and said simply, "Dad, I'm proud of you!"

It was the best of awards or accolades, and a homecoming to remember always.

In July 2002, while en route to Europe, I stopped at Ellis Island to tape an interview at the invitation of Lori Conway, a filmmaker who is making a documentary on the old hospital.

My brother, William, now a retired Stanford University librarian in Palo Alto, Calif., and I are two of the fast-dwindling number of immigrants who were patients at the hospital.

"You are but the sixth former hospitalized immigrant I have found," said Conway of Brookline, Mass.

Workers have just started to stabilize the hospital's red brick building, which stands deserted and in decayed disarray on the other side of a short quay.

The film will be used in a private industry and public fund-raising campaign much like the one used to renovate both the Statue of Liberty and the Immigration Center, Conway said. The goal is to resurrect the old hospital for use as the World Immigration Center's Oral History Department.

Conway said she found me through a taped interview I made last year at the island. "I was intrigued by your story of how your son Tam surprised you at the dock to rewrite a chapter in your family's history," she said.

Thus, Tam also was included in the invitation for the filming of our visit to the old hospital.

Don Siorino, park service architect, guided us through the dark, debris-laden halls. But he didn't have to tell me when we reached the well-remembered isolation ward, despite its dusty, run-down condition. Memories floated back and I was moved almost to tears as I gazed out the window at the Statue of Liberty across the bay.

It had signified a warm welcome to a new life in America after all.

The next day Tam bid me a temporary farewell as I left via the Concorde to go "hame" to Scotland for a visit.

Allan revisits Ellis Island's old hospital ward in 2002.

A Tilden, Neb., old-timer.

CHAPTER THIRTY-NINE

MILEPOSTS

L ike signs and mileposts, there always were little stories of people and events along the way that were head-turning, drudgery-breakers that brought a smile and warmed the heart. Here's some:

Plow Deep and Straight

May 2, 1963: Tilden, Neb. – Both the soil and the years were turned back on the rolling hills beneath a cloud-splotched sky a few miles south of town.

Providing a picture to rekindle memories and quicken the heartbeat were six stalwart Belgian horses – heads bobbing in rhythm, muscles straining, tails whisking in the breeze – pulling an old two-bottom riding plow.

In was spring again both on the rolling farm and within the heart of Herman Lind, 65.

"I started working this field when I was a boy of 9 with three horses and a single plow," he said. "I've always had horses."

His horses are here to stay. So are his old-fashioned ways of plowing.

"Some say you can't plow deep enough or straight enough with horses," he said, gazing back down the arrow-straight, deep rows. "Yes, sir. Something was lost in farming when they forgot the horse."

Who could argue, seeing those proud Belgians and the old farmer atop a plow silhouetted against the sky?

Oops!

Jan. 18, 1966: Near misses in World-Herald cars I have driven included:

■ Screeching to a halt to miss a flying saucer. A nightmare but no dream. A new circular horse tank on the back of a pickup rounding a curve near Sutton was caught by a gust of wind. The tank sailed high in the air, spiraling, to crash on the shoulder of U.S. Highway 6, some 50 yards in front of me.

■ Tried to miss but didn't quite get the job done on a skunk near Ord. World-Herald garage employees still haven't forgiven me.

■ Almost snagged a teal flying across Highway 2 from a low slough near Hyannis. Almost bent the radio aerial double.

■ Skidded when I ducked as a cock pheasant almost flew in an open side window near Emerson.

■ Gave a ride to a hitchhiking sparrow that flew in a window at a McCook stoplight and left only when I parked in front of the Keystone Hotel several blocks away.

■ Halted numerous times to let trail-herded Angus, Shorthorns, Herefords and crossbreeds have the highway right-of-way near Dunning and Arabia and assorted other Sand Hills communities.

■ Ruffled the tails of a few pheasants, grouse, coons, chickens, cats and almost two coyotes, surprisingly wanting to play tag down the road near Gandy.

■ Cussing and with tires screeching, barely missed the dumbest creatures, Homo sapiens, attempting to pass on a brow of a hill or pull out from a side road.

■ Surviving driving on the Byways by considering every other driver a maniac and not being sure of my own sanity behind a steering wheel.

Whittling Artist

March 3, 1967: Farmer Hugo Wuebben feeds cattle and hogs and raises corn and oats.

Otherwise, he just whittles away his time.

The big ham-like, work-callused hands of the 56-year-old bachelor are busy evenings, creating whittled masterpieces in miniature from the ends of old peach crates and other scraps of wood.

Hugo has a one-man show on display at the Pleasant Valley store. It halts traffic and gets rave notices from motorists on Highways 81 and 84, eight miles west of town.

Neighbors claim he can whittle just about anything with his two old pocketknives and a sharp-pointed tool made from a hacksaw blade.

They tell of the time he proudly showed off a tiny chain with movable links carved from a single match stick.

"I jokingly told him that was nothing much and that some other guy was going to bring in a chain he'd carved from a toothpick," storekeeper Francis Anderson said.

"The next day Hugo came in with a big grin and a chain whittled from a single toothpick."

GIs' Pen Pal

Jan. 6, 1991: Kearney, Neb. – Suzanne Morrissey, Kearney's Good Samaritan, is at it again.

Mrs. Morrissey is heading a "Love and Support – The Pen Is Mightier Than the Sword" project for service personnel in Operation Desert Shield.

She is promoting a letter-writing campaign and a drive to supply troops with personal items. Her kitchen table and basement office desk have been turned into a postal clearinghouse. She collects names and addresses of service personnel and gives them to letter writers, whom she recruits.

She later was commended for her efforts in a personal letter from Chief of Staff Colin Powell and Gen. Norman Schwartzkopf.

Nebraska's Aardvark?

Aug. 4, 1991: Arnold, Neb. – It's open season on an aardvark in and around Arnold.

An aardvark? The posting of bounties for the ant-eating nocturnal animal in Nebraska may come as a surprise to the Nebraska Game and Parks Commission.

But not to Kip Varney, undertaker in this western Custer County town, who instigated the idea to promote its annual Fall Festival Aug. 14-18.

And it's not a surprise to folks caught up in the hunt, even though "Antsy" is a figment of Varney's imagination.

"It's kind of hard for a funeral home to come up with something exciting to promote a festival," Varney said, "so I thought, well, why not sponsor a mystery hunt for some kind of exotic animal. An aardvark is my favorite. I even have the outline of one on my cowboy boots. And I didn't have to hunt far to learn how to spell it. Aardvark is one of the very first words in the dictionary."

Hunters are having a harder time tracking "Antsy" – a stuffed replica made by an area taxidermist and hidden about town – even though Varney furnishes clues in the weekly Arnold Sentinel newspaper. He also furnishes the bounties, which began at $20 and will peak at $50 the week of the festival.

Sentinel employee Janet Larreau said, "We didn't think it would turn out so good when the hunt started, but we've had tremendous response and inquiries from all over."

Added Varney, "Just what I'd hoped for."

Harold Lloyd's Hometown

April 26, 1993: Burchard, Neb. – Movie and television stars came to this Pawnee County village of 122 people Sunday to help celebrate the 100th anniversary of the birth of Harold Lloyd, one of Hollywood's legendary comics of the silent screen.

But while Patrick Duffy of "Dallas" and "Step By Step" fame, former Lincolnite Julie Uribe of "General Hospital" and Hollywood director Richard Correll were engulfed by fans wearing Lloyd's trademark-horned-rimmed glasses and flat straw sailor hats, a star in his own right stood beaming in the background.

"I like being the forgotten man. I'm too busy trying to pay something back to Nebraska for a wonderful boyhood on a farm north of town," said Don McCormick of Lake Geneva, Wis.

The publicity about the stars attending the benefit, being held mainly in Lincoln, made no mention of McCormick. But McCormick, a semi-retired car dealer, is president of the Harold Lloyd Foundation of Burchard. He and the Pawnee County Promotional Network were behind the fund-raiser to restore Lloyd's Burchard home and to build a silent movie theater and museum.

Mighty Mitey Cody

Nov. 7, 1993: Cody, Neb. – Cody, whose slogan is "A Town Too Tough To Die," probably was the happiest village in the Sand Hills this week.

The Cherry County village of 177 people was named Nebraska's No. 1 Small Town and one of seven "Best Small Towns in America."

Cody took first place in the Nebraska Community Improvement Program in the under-300 population class. The Jack Daniels Distillery of Lynchburg, Tenn., conducted the best-in-the-nation contest among towns with 1,000 or fewer residents.

Marguerite Wobig, Cody's historian, didn't waste words in her essay netting the national award. She wrote: "Just south of the South Dakota line on the rolling Nebraska Sand Hills, Cody is a little town with grit, billed at the city limits as 'A Town Too Tough To Die.' Though long ago abandoned by the railroad, Cody's 177 citizens refuse to leave, as do the wild turkey and deer that wander the peaceful region. In fact, Cody is attracting newcomers and its population is on the rise."

Wobig added a clincher, "Enough said."

Senior Prom Dates

May 6, 1996: Verdigre, Neb. – Pat Cassidy, 91, a retired Lynch-area farmer, Alice, his wife of 61 years, and 69 other young-in-heart residents of a nursing home can't wait for their big date with Verdigre High School teenagers on May 16.

For the fifth year in a row the Alpine Village Nursing Home residents and the youngsters plan to bridge the generation gap at a joint prom, "cocktail reception" and dinner dance staged to the beat of polka music.

The prom has become a tradition in this Knox County village. It's believed to be one-of-a-kind in Nebraska.

The tradition was started by Nicki Sonder, now a Chadron State College student, five years ago when she worked as an aide at the home.

"She figured it would be neat if the kids save their long dresses and tuxes from the regular high school junior-senior prom and share a second prom with residents of the home," said Diane Sukup, the home's activities director.

Sara Jane Sukup, one of the student organizers but no relation to Mrs. Sukup, described the annual gala as "an opportunity to learn of the residents' lives and to bridge the generation gap.

"It's neat for them to see us all dressed up," she said. "It gives some of the ladies a chance to get dressed in long gowns. And we have so much fun dancing with the residents. We even dance with some of them in wheelchairs who are still eager to try."

Historic Bridge Completes Move

Oct. 25, 1996: Valentine, Neb. – A former bridge at Verdigre found a new role in history Thursday. It was resurrected at Smith Falls State Park.

In a dramatic, two-hour, 20-minute engineering feat that ended at high noon, the 30-ton span was waded across the Niobrara River and gently nestled into place.

It became the first public access – other than by canoe – across the river to Smith Falls, Nebraska's highest and one of its most scenic waterfalls.

The bridge, a pin-constructed truss span, for years provided highway access to the north end of Verdigre in Knox County. But six years ago when Nebraska Highway 14 was modernized and a new bridge was erected on the south side of the community, the old bridge was removed.

Verdigre historians engaged a medicine man from the nearby Santee Sioux Reservation to say a prayer for the bridge, but it couldn't be saved. It was dismantled and kept in a heap because of its historic designation. Four years ago, the Nebraska Game and Parks Commission stepped in and bought it. It was moved to the Niobrara site and plans were drawn to make it a foot-bridge across the river.

A six-member crew from Milford began fitting the pieces together after Labor Day. Thursday they were ready, and with the help of cranes and bulldozers they pushed the entire framework of the 160-foot span across the 157.5 foot-wide Niobrara River.

CHAPTER FORTY

LOVE SONG TO NEBRASKA

A Nebraska dawn from Lincoln's Capital Beach.

Aye! You're a Bonnie Lassie.

One of the welcoming group at Oxford's Burlington Station let out a blood-curdling Indian war whoop as the train squealed to a halt late one cold January night in 1927.

Another gave a cowboy yell as he grabbed a sleepy 9-year-old boy in a bear hug, flipped him in the air and caught him on his shoulder.

I was that lad. And from that precarious perch I got my first look at a strange and beautiful land called Nebraska.

I was both petrified and delighted that the cowboys and Indians I'd dreamed so much about in my native Scotland had finally captured me.

I fell in love – hopelessly – with Nebraska that night.

Despite the passing of 72 years, the cynicism of manhood has not dimmed that love. During my years with The World-Herald as its roving reporter-photographer, I traveled the width and breadth of the state, driving up to 50,000 miles a year and wracking up more than one million miles "to Bucktail and back."

Covering the Byways I figure I wore out 20 company cars and about as many editors.

But the thrill, excitement and zest for what was just around the next bend of the road never waned!

Although I have been in every corner of the state and, I think, every one of its communities, I always felt more of the best in Nebraska has yet to be discovered.

I am still that wee Scot laddie at heart, and even more in love with a wonderful state.

Aye! She's a real beauty, this Nebraska. But I know from experience she can be a temperamental and cantankerous old biddy at times. Just when I languished in her tranquil beauty, she has belted me with her tornadoes, the icy glare of her blizzards and the stifling heat of her searing summers.

But her unpredictable weather enhances her charm.

I often witness proof of the old saying, "If you don't like the weather in Nebraska, hold your breath or drive down the road apiece." Once I photographed Osceola grade schoolers frolicking in eight inches of snow. An hour later and 50 miles down the road I shot another photo of Wahoo school children, jacketless in the warm sun, playing hopscotch and softball on their snowless playground.

One Mother's Day weekend I didn't make it home from blizzard-bound Cheyenne, Wyo., where I had gone to cover a story on the antiballistic missile build-up in far western Nebraska. A wire photo, showing travelers finding a haven in the Cheyenne National Guard Armory, saved me from the wrath of my unbelieving editors. I crawled back to Nebraska behind a snow plow a day later only to discover at snowless Kimball, 75 miles east, bright sunshine and balmy 70-degree temperatures.

Variety is the spice of life with this not-so-old gal whose topographical garments range from the forested hills in the east, the ever-rising plains of the fabled Sand Hills, "God's Own Cow Country," to the buttes, high plains and the striking beauty of the Pine Ridge country. Missing is the monotony of many other states I have traveled.

Here the industrialized East meets the lingering frontier of the West. Here North meets South.

A university professor once told me Nebraska is the "lousiest" state in the nation, entomologically speaking. The great number of varieties of bird and animal lice are found here because it is the crossroads of their annual migrations. The variety of plants and trees also proves Nebraska is a national meeting spot.

The state entertains the past, present and future. The most modern industrial plants in Omaha and Lincoln and the electronic industries in Columbus and Ogallala, are but a hop-step-and-a-jump from the frontier lore of cattle roundups and branding.

Pioneer history can still be seen, lived and felt, from the red-bricked mansions of historic Brownville to the still-lived-in soddies in the Sand Hills. And it takes little imagination to hear the ghostly echoes of bugles and the war whoops of the Sioux and Cheyenne at Fort Robinson State Historical Park.

The road to tomorrow is being outlined on drawing boards and legislative tables. The road to yesterday is still outlined in ruts of the Oregon Trail.

Nebraska's main motorway, Interstate 80, closely follows the Oregon Trail as well as the routes of the Pony Express, Overland and Mormon trails and the Union Pacific, the first transcontinental railroad.

But, sad to say, how many of our visitors know it? It's a disappointment – and a challenge being met by the state's tourism division – that too many out-of-staters think Nebraska is part of Major Long's "Great American Desert."

Tourists praise our rest stops as "the best in the west by test." But, astonishingly, some still write chambers of commerce asking about travel safety and Indian attack danger. One New England couple asked a Kearney motel operator if the water was plentiful and safe to drink farther west in Nebraska.

A journalist from the London Daily Telegraph was intrigued by a Sand Hills cattle roundup staged for one of Gov. Morrison's "Know Nebraska" tours on the O'Kief ranch near Valentine.

The Englishman interviewed one of the cowpokes, Jerry O'Kief, son of the ranch owner, perhaps because he looked the raunchiest. Jerry, an attorney, had come out from town to help in the roundup in dirty jeans, a shirt with the sleeves ripped off and a grubby, battered cowboy hat.

Winking at me and with tongue in cheek, Jerry told the English scribe about the hardships of cowboy life, from sleeping in the barn to bathing in the horse tank before getting to town once a month for a Saturday night dance.

But Jerry was speechless after the scribe dutifully wrote down his actual educational experience without question and walked off saying: "Most interesting. Thanks, Old Top."

Jerry couldn't wait for me to get him a copy of the paper's story, and he still hasn't lived it down.

The Englishman wrote in detail about Jerry's cowboying "hardships" and dutifully ended his story with: "By the way, cowpoke O'Kief has a law degree from Omaha's Creighton University and a master's degree in law from Harvard. He is a typical Nebraska Sand Hills cowboy."

Industrialists well know the facts about Nebraska. They have been lured by its abundant water supply in the "desert," transportation facilities, and perhaps most important of all, its work ethic where men and women still believe in the joy of craftsmanship and in giving a good day's work for a good day's pay.

William McIntyre, head of Monroe Co., told me at the dedication of the company's Cozad plant that Nebraska workers during their training period out-produced veteran company workers at a similar plant in Georgia almost two-to-one.

Thanks to the Nebraska Centennial in 1967, many communities discovered pride in their heritage and began promoting area attractions that have lured international tourists.

Yet, I find Nebraskans overlook the three most evident assets appealing to visitors – the big sky land, clean air and Nebraskans themselves.

I once guided two young New York City women to their heart's desire, a genuine ranch. I led them to the ranch of the late author Nellie Yost, up Hackberry Canyon near Maxwell. Both Nellie and I gaped in disbelief when the women, on their way to new nursing jobs in San Francisco, jumped from their car and began running across the range with their arms akimbo and shouting with joy.

Breathless, they apologized when they came back with: "You don't realize that we have lived all our lives in the concrete jungle of Manhattan. Because of the tall buildings, we get to see only a piece of the sky and the sun part of each day. To walk on grass, we have to go to Central Park. We just couldn't get over the wonderful feeling of freedom in the horizon-to-horizon open spaces you have."

Visitors from smog and industrial-polluted air on both coasts marvel at Nebraska's clean, fresh air. Rancher Harold Fenwick from near Ogallala told me his answer to a group of Eastern goose hunters when they marveled at the champagne-like sparkling air at Lake McConaughy.

"That's because it don't get smelled much out here," he said.

Nebraskans are the greatest, I'm sure a breed apart. Pioneering on the frontier has left its mark in hospitable neighborliness in much of the state, with an unlatched door still a way of life. A man's word is still accepted for what he's worth. In the rangelands, a man's word and handshake are still as good as a contract.

V.O. Roty, from the Malaysian Embassy, who had taken time to tour the state while en route to Kearney State College's World Affairs seminars, found Nebraskans to be: "Not as sophisticated as those on the East and West coasts of America. But they are delightfully friendly, frank and honest, sometimes brutally so. But this is good. With you, we know where we stand. The hand that pats the back does not conceal a dagger. The world needs more of this."

Visitors often express concern over the loneliness of Sand Hills ranch life. Yet ranch wives often have more social life than their city cousins. A 100-mile trip to a dance or show is common. On some of the big spreads, a ranch airplane has made shopping in Denver, Chicago and Dallas as easy as Omaha and Lincoln.

Perhaps, because of the geographic distances involved, there is a division, mostly figurative, between western and eastern Nebraska.

There still is an occasional cry in the Panhandle for secession to Wyoming. The lament, "Omaha and Lincoln will never understand or care about our problems," sometimes flares. Too often, eastern Nebraskans lump everything west as "outstate."

People of both areas forget their economic interdependence. Often forgotten is that Omaha and Lincoln are peopled by those from Arapahoe, Grand Island, North Platte, Scottsbluff and Bucktail. They, in turn, forget "outstate" is home.

The secession threats usually end with: "Fine. Go ahead. But first sell us your Nebraska season football tickets. The Huskers often are described as the "single most solidifying force in the state."

Yet, I know, there are those both east and west who'd fight at the drop of a hat should an outsider slight one or the other.

Unlike many other states, glutted with population and affiliated problems, there is still room to breathe, to expand and develop. Beautiful and provocative Nebraska still has to be discovered by most of the people in the nation. I'm glad I got to know her first.

Nebraskan-ese

Nebraska has a language of its own besides "Go Big Red!"

You Bet! Las Vegas and Reno casino pit bosses have often mentioned that Nebraska must be a gambling state.

They explained, "We know a person is from Nebraska when we ask them a question and they answer in the affirmative with a 'You Bet!' "

Hi Guys! It's the usual greeting of waitresses to customers regardless of whether there are ladies in the party. I've had women write me that they resented their omission in the greeting. When I've asked an offending waitress if my female companion looks like a guy to her, she apologizes. But next time around asks, "Will that be all for you guys?"

Two-Fingered Greeting. Visitors to the state have often expressed delight at the friendly silent greeting given them as they pass cars on Nebraska's highways.

It originated in the Sand Hills, and is the raising of two wagging fingers from the steering wheel accompanied by a big smile.

Folksy Philosophy. Once, when I asked an old Swede in a senior center if he had any message for the world as he celebrated his 100th birthday, he replied, "You may tell the world it takes one helluva long time to get as old as I am." Then after a pause, he added with his still-bright blue eyes twinkling, "But every damn minute has been worth it."

The best example of this folksy philosophy was given by a matronly waitress at a Big Springs truck stop. It was during a sugar shortage some years back and customers were being given a single pack for their coffee. When a burly trucker complained and demanded more, the waitress answered, "Buster, use what you got and stir like hell!"

When you think about it, it's better than a sermon.

It may well be what Nebraska and Nebraskans are all about.

"Using what we got and stirring like hell" may well be the state's secret of success.

CHAPTER FORTY-ONE

'30' – THE END

My 54-year career at The Omaha World-Herald officially ended with my Nebraska Byways column on Sunday, Jan. 13, 2002.

The last item in that column read:

"Sad to say, but this column marks "30," the old reporter's and Linotype printer's code for "end of the story."

"It's the finale of a 62-year career in journalism, with five years' time out for World War II Army service. It means fond adieu to The World-Herald after 52 years as a regular staff member plus 2-1/2 years as a contract employee writing this column."

My next paragraph was edited out of the story. It read: "I haven't run out of gas after a million miles roving the Nebraska Byways to Bucktail and back. But The World-Herald editors think it is time. Perhaps they are right."

Printed was my ending: "But it is not good-bye. I still plan to wander at times the Byways of the greatest of states.

"And I'll have the consolation that without the press of deadlines, I'll be able to sit and visit longer with the greatest people on earth.

"So this is not really good-bye – just '30'."

Since I had a business appointment in Omaha the next day, I turned in my computer at The World-Herald's main office. I got a hug from Deanna Sands and Joanne Stewart, the managing and assistant managing editor, respectively.

I have additional consolation. The end of active duty allowed me to compile this book, which my family and readers had long insisted I write.

I used my scrapbooks of clippings as well as copies of the Dec. 24, 1978, "Tom Allan Along the Byways – A Christmas Album" by The World-Herald's former Magazine of the Midlands, as well as another "Holiday Special" compilation of my stories and photos printed by The World-Herald on Dec. 27, 1997, marking my 50 years with the newspaper.

The World-Herald has graciously allowed me use of their library files of stories and photographs. Librarians Michelle Gullett and Sheritha Jones and Photo Chief Jim Burnett labored above the call of duty to lend a helping hand. I also am indebted to Paul and Nancy Hammel for long hours editing the manuscript and providing advice.

I also used my memory's ken to add personal observations to stories and how I found them. All are written from the heart. If there are errors, they are mine and are unintentional.

I rue the omission of so many good stories of great people and places in Nebraska due to space limitations.

Regrets? I have but one.

Having been a city editor on the Topeka Daily Capital, I'm well versed in space and time limitations for so many stories in a daily newspaper.

But I regret I was never able to explain to a mother or father in Greater Nebraska when they asked me why a story I wrote about them or their town either was condensed or worse, wasn't printed in the Omaha edition of The World-Herald for their sons and daughters, who live in Omaha, to read.

Too often editors, having to make room for pressing Omaha news, forget Omaha is made up of kids from Arapahoe, Cambridge, Mitchell, Rulo and Bucktail who are eager to read about their hometown.

I once wrote a story about a Gothenburg high school French teacher who begged the school board to be allowed to teach an hour of French to a class of kindergartners. Within six weeks the tiny tots had far surpassed the high schoolers in conversational French.

I began my story with, "Parle vous Francais?" asked the teacher. 'Oui' enthusiastically shouted Gothenburg kindergartners in reply."

That was the only sentence that made the city edition.

Another time I thought I had a cinch to break the sanctity of the Omaha home edition. But my story of an old Nemeha County bachelor farmer who left his entire estate to Omaha's Children's Memorial Hospital, the "baby" of the late World-Herald publisher, Henry Doorly, never made it.

I waited a day before approaching Editor Lou Gerdes with an "I surrender!" He couldn't believe it had happened. As a result, it may be the only time in the newspaper's history the same story appeared on the front page of the Midland's section on successive days.

But otherwise, I had the best job in the world working for the greatest of employee-owned newspapers, one that really cares about its readers and their welfare as seen in the annual Good Fellows fund drive, sponsoring other charitable drives and providing scholarships for youth.

For me, my World-Herald career wasn't work. It was fun.

There always was a touch of embarrassment receiving such awards as three Honorary Doctorates of Humane Letters from Dana and Peru State Colleges and the University of Nebraska-Kearney, induction into the Nebraska Journalism Hall of Fame, the Distinguished Nebraskalander Award, the John G. Neihardt Foundation's "Word Sender Award" and the Nebraska Tourism division's Henry Fonda Award as well as enough other plaques and citations covering the walls of my Lincoln apartment.

One of the best and most truthful awards is the embroidered pillow I received from the South Platte United Chambers of Commerce on my 50th anniversary with The World-Herald. Stitched in bright red letters above an outline of Nebraska is the message: "Tom. Happiness Is 50 Years on a Job That Isn't Work."

In the words of John Neihardt, the awards made me "humbler beyond tears and more joyous than laughter." I always felt I didn't deserve them because I was just doing my job, which was reward enough.

I feel some jobs are duties that must be performed. Some are arduous tasks that must be endured. But my job was a privilege to be thoroughly enjoyed.

To Bucktail was a great ride, truly providing a million miles of memories. And I am beholden.

"30"

To Bucktail and Back . . .